D1599354

REFLECTIONS ON THE JUST

Reflections on

THE JUST

Paul Ricoeur

Translated by

DAVID PELLAUER

The University of Chicago Press
Chicago and London

The late PAUL RICOEUR was the John Nuveen Professor Emeritus in the Divinity School and a member of the Department of Philosophy and the Committee on Social Thought at the University of Chicago. In 2004 he was awarded the Library of Congress's John W. Kluge Prize for Lifetime Achievement in the Human Sciences. Ricoeur wrote many books, including the three-volume *Time and Narrative* (1984–88), *Oneself as Another* (1992), *The Just* (2000), and *Memory, History, Forgetting* (2004), all published by the University of Chicago Press. David Pellauer has translated several of Ricoeur's books, including *The Just*.

The University of Chicago Press, Chicago 60637
The University of Chicago Press, Ltd., London
© 2007 by The University of Chicago
All rights reserved. Published 2007
Printed in the United States of America
16 15 14 13 12 11 10 09 08 07   1 2 3 4 5
Originally published as *Le Juste 2*, © Éditions Esprit, 2001.

ISBN-13: 978-0-226-71345-8 (cloth)
ISBN-10: 0-226-71345-8 (cloth)

Published with the support of the National Center for the Book—
French Ministry of Culture.

Ouvrage publié avec le soutien du Centre national du livre—
ministère français chargé de la culture.

Library of Congress Cataloging-in-Publication Data

Ricoeur, Paul.
[Juste 2. English]
Reflections on the just / Paul Ricoeur ; translated by David Pellauer.
    p.   cm.
Includes bibliographical references and index.
ISBN-13: 978-0-226-71345-8 (cloth : alk. paper)
ISBN-10: 0-226-71345-8 (cloth : alk. paper)
1. Justice (Philosophy).   2. Law—Philosophy.   I. Title.
B2430.R553J8813   2007
172'.2—dc22

2006030303

Contents

INTRODUCTION

This second volume of essays, *Reflections on the Just,* differs from the first collection, *The Just,* in the way the adjective "just" is employed both in the title and in the body of the book. In *The Just* the principal axis was the relation between the idea of justice as a moral rule and justice as an institution. In the present volume the adjective "just" is traced back to its terminological and conceptual source, as we find it in Plato's Socratic dialogues. This adjective is taken in the sense of the connotation of the Greek neuter: *to dikaion* (which will also be that of the Latin and German neuter), brought to the level of a substantialized adjective. It is as an echo of this emphasis that I say "*the* just."

This return to the properly neutral use of the neuter adjective, turned into a substantive term, authorizes a broader opening to the conceptual field than that explored in *The Just,* as can be seen in part I of this new volume, placed under the heading "Studies." The "Readings" and "Exercises" that follow in parts II and III explore in different styles the space of meaning broadly outlined in this series of studies. Setting aside my "readings" as not requiring any superfluous commentary, in this introduction I shall concentrate on relating the studies and exercises to one another.

I

In the first study, titled "From the Moral to the Ethical and to Ethics," I outline the broader circle of my inquiry, namely, the way in which today I structure the whole of the moral problematic.

I present this systematic attempt as a complement and a corrective to what, out of modesty and irony, I called the "little ethics," placed at the end of my *Oneself as Another,* the work stemming from my Gifford Lectures in Edinburgh in 1986.

The corrective is twofold. First, I did not see at that time the strength of the connection that links this ethics to the main theme of that book, that is, the exploring of the capacities and incapacities that make a human being a capable, acting and suffering, being. The lynchpin is the specific capacity designated by the term "imputability": our ability to recognize ourselves as accountable (*comptable,* from the Latin root *putare*) for our acts in the sense of being their actual author. I can hold myself accountable, imputable, in the same way that I can speak, can act on the course of things, can recount my action through an emplotting of events and characters. This imputability is a capacity homogeneous with the series of capacities and incapacities that define the capable human being. I shall not say more in this introduction about imputability inasmuch as the second essay deepens the analysis in terms of the very concept of justice and the third one sets it against the background of capacities and incapacities having to do with the most fundamental basis of the human condition.

Second, in *Oneself as Another* I adopted the chronological order of the sequence of great moral philosophers: an ethics of the good following Aristotle; a morality of duty coming from Kant; practical wisdom in the face of singular situations marked by incertitude. One result of this categorization modeled on the history of doctrines was the impression of a juxtaposition and of a weakly arbitrated conflict of positions. The first essay in the present volume is meant to thematically reconstruct the whole domain of moral philosophy in taking as its primary axis what is both our most fundamental and our most ordinary moral experience, namely, the conjunction between the positing of a self that is the author of its choices and the recognition of a rule that obligates us—at the intersection of the self that posits itself and the rule that imposes itself stands the autonomy thematized in Kant's practical philosophy. It is in relation to this new median that I see the realm of ethics split between a fundamental ethics that we can speak of as anterior and a cluster of regional ethics that we can speak of as posterior. Why this split that still seems to conform to our ordinary use of such terms? It seemed to me, on the one hand, that the rootedness of moral experience in desire, which with Aristotle we can speak of as reasonable or rational, does not exhaust itself in the test of a claim to the universal validity of the maxims of our action. What is it that we fundamentally desire? This seemed to me to be the basic question that Kant undertook to place in parentheses when he attempted a rational purification of moral obligation. This question leads upstream from moral obligation to a fundamental ethic. On the other hand, on the downstream side of morality, I see ethics as being distributed into different domains of application, such as medical ethics, judicial ethics, business ethics, and, today, environmental ethics. Everything suggests that the basis of rational desire, which makes us aspire to happiness and seek to stabilize ourselves in terms of a project of a good life, can only reveal, expose, and unfold itself by passing successively through the filter of moral judgment and the test of practical application in determinate fields of action. From a basic ethic to ethics passing through moral obligation—this seems to me to be the new formula for what I called my "little ethics" in *Oneself as Another*.

But, it may be asked, where is the just in all this? Here is my answer. The just is at work in each of the way stations of ethical and moral inquiry. Better: it designates their circularity. Moral experience, defined by the conjunction of the self and the rule, under the sign of obligation, refers to what is just as soon as others find themselves implied in the formulating of the rule, others to whom harm, a tort, can be done and therefore who can be treated unjustly. In this regard, it is not an accident that in Plato's Socratic dialogues the unjust—*to adikon*—is regularly named before the just. The just person is fundamentally one who does not commit injustice, even the one who thinks it better to submit to injustice than to commit it. In a more formal sense, the unjust and the just are named by Kant at the level of the second formulation of the categorical imperative: do not treat others merely as a means—this is the essence of injustice—but also as an end; what is just is what leads to a respect for the dignity of the other that is equal to the respect one has for oneself. At this level, justice equals equality in the distribution of esteem. The just thus appears everywhere along the path that leads back from moral obligation to rational desire and the wish for a good life. For this very wish asks to be shared, a happy life with and for others in just institutions, as I said in discussing my little ethics. But, even beyond any institution capable of framing interactions in stable, recognized forms, more durable than any of our singular experiences, there is an orientation toward others in all of our virtues. The just—*to dikaion*—says Aristotle in book 5 of the *Nicomachean Ethics,* is "what is lawful and what is fair, the unjust [*to adikon*] the lawless and the unfair" (1129b).[1]

Inequality (unfairness, in effect) takes more than its due and less than its burdens. In this sense, all the other virtues—temperance, magnanimity, courage, and so on—are encompassed by justice, in the complete, integral sense of the word:

> Moreover, justice is complete virtue to the highest degree because it is the complete exercise of complete virtue. And it is the complete exercise because the person who has justice is able to exercise virtue in relation to another, not only in what concerns himself. . . . And for the same reason justice is the only virtue that seems to be another person's good [*allotrios*], because it is related to another.[2]

In this regard, justice and friendship have in common the same concern for the community of interests. Yet, as Aristotle already noted, this complete, integral, undivided virtue can be apprehended in social reality only at the level of particular (*hōs meros*) justice (*kata meros*), whether it be a question of the distribution of honors, wealth, or rectitude in private transactions (1130b). This is also my own thesis concerning the application of the virtue of justice in determinate spheres of action. We then have to do with regional ethics: medical, judicial, and so forth, as will be shown in the third part of this volume. In this dialectic, where moral obligation ensures the transition between a fundamental ethic and regional ethics, the just and the unjust advance in step.

The second study, "Justice and Truth," is inscribed in the following way in the sequence of studies devoted to the great articulations of moral philosophy in *Oneself as Another.* The distribution

1. Aristotle, *Nicomachean Ethics,* 117.
2. Ibid., 119.

into ethics, morality, and practical wisdom is taken up from that work prior to the new order just proposed, where the morality of obligation is taken as the turning point between the side of a fundamental ethic and that of regional ethics. This revision, however important, does not call into question the two major considerations that structure this moral philosophy, namely, the preeminence of the category of the just in each of the compartments of my little ethics and the convertibility that the ideas of the just and the true allow for in speculation at a higher level having to do with transcendental categories.

The first consideration again stems from a rereading of my little ethics, not in order to modify the order of construction, but in order to attach each of the steps in its course to the just and the unjust. In this sense, this rereading ends up by reinscribing the whole dialectic of the little ethics in the field of the just, taken in the sense of the Greek, Latin, and German neuter adjective. The proposed perspective makes the just appear in terms of two different relations: a horizontal relation having to do with the threefold relation of the self, neighbors, and others and a vertical relation having to do with the hierarchical model of the good, the obligatory, and the fitting. The first ternary relation is repeated at each level—teleological, deontological, and prudential—and at each level justice appears in the third position, which is not inferior but truly culminating as a position. The split designated by the encompassing term "alterity" makes its greatest impact at the level of practical philosophy. It adds to the self's movement toward the other the step from the neighbor to the distant other. This step begins at the level of an ethics inspired by the *Nicomachean Ethics* and moves from friendship to justice. The progression is from a private to a public virtue, which is defined by the search for a just distance in every situation of interaction. In the version in *Oneself as Another,* in speaking of the wish for a good life with and for others in just institutions, I immediately referred the vow for justice to institutions. Aristotle does it indirectly by including conformity to the law and respect for equality in his definition of justice. The *isotes,* the fragile equilibrium between the disposition to take more (or greed) and the disposition to take less of one's share of burdens (which today is called a lack of civility), is clearly announced as a civic virtue, where the institution is indicated both as already existing and as a project to be realized, the same word being taken in a substantive sense and in a transitive verbal one.

At this first level the just should be taken, not as an alternative to the good, but as its developed figure in terms of the just distance. Justice appears in the third position again at the second level, that of morality properly speaking. Here the self is the autonomous self, which posits itself in positing the norm. The connection is so strong and so primitive between moral obligation and justice that the revision proposed in the preceding study becomes the term of reference for the whole enterprise of moral philosophy. With the norm come formalization and the test of the possible universalization of the maxims of action. I propose not separating the well-known formula of the categorical imperative from its rewriting in terms of Kant's famous three formulations: taking the moral law as the practical analogue of nature's laws; respecting humanity in my person and in that of others; and taking myself as both the legislator and the subject in a kingdom of ends. This triad of imperatives constitutes the homology of the triad of wishes in my fundamental ethic: a good life, solicitude, justice. I do not spend a lot of time on contemporary analyses meant to give developments and corrections to the Kantian heritage worthy of it. I devote just a few words to John Rawls's *Theory of Justice,* to which I devoted two studies in *The Just* ("Is a Purely Procedural Theory of Justice Possible?" and "After Rawls's *Theory of Justice*"). Following in his wake, I again mention Michael Walzer's project of pluralizing justice in his *Spheres of Justice.* Here, too, I draw from the study already devoted to this work in *The Just* ("The Plurality of Instances of Justice"), paralleling it with Luc Boltanski and Laurent Thévenot's *De la justification: Les économies de la grandeur.* I also mention in passing Jean-Marc Ferry's *Les puissances de l'expérience,* the second volume of which is titled *Les ordres de la reconnaissance,* which I reviewed when it first appeared. This volume could have led us to the work of Jürgen Habermas, of which Ferry is an excellent interpreter, and which directly concerns the other discussion about the place of the just and the unjust in relation to the self.

If a convincing revision of historical Kantianism has ever been proposed on the plane of practical philosophy, it is surely the reformulation of the rule of justice offered by Karl-Otto Apel and

Habermas, which transforms its monological presupposition into a dialogical one. These two founders of a communicational ethics hold that a "rational foundation of ethics in the age of science" can be articulated only in terms of what Apel calls an "ethic of discussion." The foundation that Kant assigned to the *fact* of practical reason—namely, the always-presupposed conjunction between the self and the rule—cannot be separated from the requirements for validity that we assume whenever we produce acts of language presupposing a norm.

Disengaging these validity requirements comes down to a formal pragmatics of discourse. So it is henceforth in the sphere of language already invested by intercommunication rather than in an allegedly solitary conscience that the final ground of morality is to be sought. Argumentation is the site where the bonds between self, neighbor, and others are established. Whereas in Kant, at least before the examination of the three formulations of the categorical imperative, the search for the conditions of coherence of moral systems takes place without regard for the dialogical dimension of the principle of morality, for Apel and Habermas the theory of argumentation unfolds from one end to the other within the framework of communicative action— hence their focus on situations of conflict arising from everyday action. The question of a final formulation, itself communicative, comes down to actual arguments among participants, without, as in Rawls, resorting to the fiction of an original situation and the fable of a hypothetical contract. Whether with Apel we can trace back to an ultimate ground that will once and for all silence the skeptics may be doubted, as Habermas indicates, who limits himself to a corroboration stemming from a therapeutic, or a maieutic, borrowed from psychology and genetic sociology and applied to the development of moral and juridical consciousness.

Whatever may be the case as regards this hesitation concerning the foundation of moral judgment in an ethics of discussion, the enterprise can be considered a reconstruction starting from the last link, namely, justice, of the whole ternary that forms the set of the wish for a good life, for solicitude between neighbors, and for justice among all the members of a historical community, extending virtually to every human being in a situation of communication through language.

This preeminence of the just on the level of practical philosophy is reinforced when situations of conflict and violence, which nourish the tragic dimension of action, give rise to the formulation of maxims of practical wisdom in circumstances marked by uncertainty and urgency. As in the little ethics in *Oneself as Another*, I plead directly for the passage from a strictly deontological conception of justice to its reinterpretation in terms of practical wisdom, "prudence," in the wake of the *phronesis* of Greek tragedy and of Aristotelian ethics. I could have drawn my argument from the difficulties that communicative morals encounter on the way to application, something dear to the advocates of a hermeneutical reason, to use the vocabulary of Jean Greisch. However, the regressive trajectory, which leads from the norm to its foundation, does not dispense with the progressive one, from the norm to its actualization. The cultural and even historical mark that conflicts inherent to concrete situations of transaction exhibit requires taking into account the contextual character of realizations of the ethics of discussion. These conditions of actualization have to affect the very rule of justice. Then the historically and culturally determined character of judgments presiding over distributions of commercial and noncommercial goods imposes itself, along with the positions of power and authority, of charges and honors, which are the theme of Rawls's theory of justice. A universally viable system of distribution (in the broad sense of the word) does not exist. Revocable choices, linked to the struggles that mark the violent history of societies, have to be taken into account from a contextualist point of view. If we do not want to be caught in a sterile quarrel between universalism and contextualism or communitarianism, we must, as I proposed in *The Just*, correctly articulate the argumentation and interpretation at work in the process of making decisions in the course of applying norms. In this regard, argumentation in its codified, stylized form is only one abstract segment in a linguistic process that, in complex cases, brings into play a diversity of language games. It is at this level that the exemplarity of certain narratives exercises its pedagogic and therapeutic action at the intersection point of argumentation and interpretation. Thus, the long path that leads from problems of foundation to those of the application of norms is the same as the one that, beyond the rule of justice, restores to the idea of equity the force that Aristotle himself had recognized in his treatise on the virtue of justice.

In the second essay in this volume, I adopt a more direct, shorter route in the direction of applied ethics. I rapidly evoke typical situations that represent the conflict between apparently equal norms of value, conflicts between respect for the norm and solicitude toward persons, a choice between gray and gray rather than between black and white, and finally—here the boundary narrows—between the bad and the worst. A whole study will be devoted to these exemplary cases in part III, under the rubric "Decision Making in Medical and Judicial Judgments." There I shall verify the assertion that, in the course of a trial, stating the law, speaking the word of justice, brings the rule of justice to the prudential plane of fairness. To judge fairly will be the highest expression of the preeminence of the just at the end of the process during whose course we have seen the good behind the wish for a good life unfold, pluralize, and institute itself in the strongest sense of this verb.

However important may be this peregrination through the compartments of practical philosophy with the idea of underscoring there the preeminence of the idea of justice and of the just, nevertheless it is not the privileged target of the second essay. That essay has no less an ambition than to reinscribe this idea in the table of "Great Kinds" that have been called transcendentals: the good, the true, the beautiful. According to this speculative mode of thinking, these would be three master notions capable of being converted into one another, under the aegis of a notion of being beyond any genus. This speculation, I admit, is not something habitual for me. Yet, when I taught the history of philosophy during the 1950s, I did have to deal with it with regard to such Platonic dialogues as the *Theaetetus, Sophist, Parmenides,* and *Philebus* and also when it came to the well-known text of book 3 of Aristotle's *Metaphysics,* where it is said that being is said in many ways.[3] I was brought back to this sovereign meditation on the occasion of the centennial issue of the *Revue de métaphysique*

---

3. See Ricoeur, *Être, essence et substance chez Platon et Aristote.* This is a reprinting of a course that Ricoeur had originally given at the University of Strasbourg in 1953–54. A mimeographed edition first appeared in 1957.—Tr.

et de morale, which endeavored to renew the proposal connecting metaphysics and morals made by one of the founders of that
journal, Félix Ravaisson.[4] There, encouraged by the powerful reflections of Stanislas Breton, I wished to blow out of proportion,
as did Breton, the prefix "meta-." I saw it burning so brightly
as to bring together the Platonic dialogues just mentioned and
Aristotle's famous text from his *Metaphysics.* May we not say, as I
also suggest in an essay titled "Multiple étrangeté," not included
in this volume, that Aristotelian being taken in terms of actual-
ity and potentiality governs from above and afar the pyramid of
figures of action, from the plane of fundamental anthropology
to that of the modes of capacity and incapacity referred to in my
first essay—while the Platonic Great Kinds govern the major di-
visions, such as being and nonbeing, the same and the other, the
one and the many, rest and movement, as the very title of *Oneself
as Another* presupposes? It seemed to me that it is at this level of
radicality that the well-known speculation of medieval thinkers
on transcendentals and their interconvertibility is to be situated. I
only considered one trajectory from this great tangle in the essay
mentioned, the one that, taking justice as its benchmark, disen-
tangled the true from justice.

What should we say about the truth of the just, once we admit
that the just culminates in a vision of the good? It turns out that
this question, so patiently worked through by medieval thinkers, comes back in force in the setting of analytic philosophy in
English, which is preoccupied by skepticism, and also, as we saw
above, in that of Apel's and Habermas's transcendental pragma-
tism. The concern in both cases, in speaking of moral truth, is
to preserve moral propositions from subjective or collective arbitrariness, as well as from any naturalistic reduction of deontological assertions (what ought to be) to constative ones (what is). In
this regard, it seemed to me that the synthetic a priori structure
constitutive of autonomy, in that it joins a self that posits itself
and a norm that imposes itself, answers the challenge of skepticism and reductionism, at the price of the dialogical rewriting
already spoken of. Like Charles Taylor, whom I discuss at some
length in one of the essays in part II, I see the self and the good

4. See Ricoeur, "From Metaphysics to Moral Philosophy."

as profoundly interconnected on the plane of what Taylor calls strong evaluations.

Therefore, if I have anything to add to this discussion, it is something other than a theory of moral truth, namely, an epistemological reflection that bears on the correlation between moral propositions and the anthropological presuppositions presiding over the entry into morality. These presuppositions have to do with the mode of being of a subject supposedly accessible to a moral, juridical, or political problematic. We rediscover here the idea of imputability, considered this time, not from the point of view of its relation to the other figures of capacity covered in *Oneself as Another*, but from the point of view of its own epistemic content. What is the truth status of a proposition that says that I am accountable for my acts and, in this sense, their actual author, invited to repair any damage they do and to be constrained to accept any penalty imposed for having done them? What is the truth claim of the self-positing of a capable human being? Here I come back to the theme of *attestation* I had elaborated in *Oneself as Another*. I want to reaffirm its character of trustworthiness, not as something irrefutable but as contestable, as submitted not to doubt but to suspicion. What I want to add comes from my recent discovery of the work of Thomas Nagel on partiality and impartiality.[5] The capacity for impartiality is what caught my attention in that Nagel connects this idea with that of equality: "Every life counts and no one is more important than anyone else." "Equality," ever since the Greeks, has been a synonym for "justice." It is the capacity to pronounce this judgment of importance that brings to light the anthropological presuppositions of the entry into ethics. It merits a distinct formulation inasmuch as the capacity for impartiality does not exclude conflicting points of view and therefore the search for arbitration with an eye to establishing a just distance between opposed parties. Is not a more primitive capacity at work here, that of sensing others' suffering, something that leads us back toward the discussion of pity in Rousseau and the English-speaking moralists of the eighteenth century? But it is surely attestation that is at issue at each stage of the exploration of the anthropological presuppositions of the entry into morality.

5. Nagel, *View from Nowhere;* Nagel, *Equality and Partiality.*

As for the kinds of arbitration required by situations of conflict, they come from interpretation as much as from argumentation, as is shown by the search for an appropriate, fitting solution, not only in what Ronald Dworkin calls "hard cases" but in any conflictual situation brought before some tribunal, as will be shown in the essays in part III of this volume. This applies to medical ethics, to historical practice, and to the exercise of political judgment. In all these situations, the judgment of what fits, which indicates what is to be done here and now, is no less attributable to attestation than is the more general capacity put to work by the idea of imputability from which I began. Attested truth thus clothes the form of justice.

At the end of this essay I express regret for not having known how or been able to complete and balance the movement of disentangling the truth starting from the just by a similar movement that would show the just emerging from the sphere of the true, in virtue of the ancient idea of the convertibility of the transcendentals.

I want, therefore, to outline what still needs to be done.

Just as I looked at moral propositions as such, not as having a kind of truth called moral truth, but only for the anthropological presuppositions of the entry into the sphere of morality, similarly I did not look at scientific propositions as having a moral quality that would make them not only true but also just. I look for this instead in the moral dispositions presupposed by the access to the sphere of truth in its full amplitude.

Scientific truth thinks of itself as true without any recourse to a criterion of morality. It is no longer about a controversy having to do with physical nature. Since Galileo and Newton, there is no other form of cognitive thought worthy of acceding to the status of science other than one that passes through the formation of hypotheses, with the aid of imagining quantifiable models, and through the verification (or, at least, falsification) of these models by direct observation or experimentation. The spirit of discovery applies to this interplay of modeling and verifying/falsifying. If this must be the case, it is because the human mind has no access to a principle by which nature is produced from itself or through something other than itself. We can only gather the naturally given data and try, as it is said, to "save the phenomena." This is not nothing, in that the field of observation is unlimited, and our ability to extend the field of scientific imagination and to replace models following the process known as paradigm change so powerful. This is what the spirit of discovery seeks to do.

With phenomena relative to human beings, however, this asceticism of modeling and experimenting is compensated for by the fact that we have a partial access to these phenomena beginning from what we understand as our action. It is possible for us to trace back from the observable effects of our own actions and passions to the intentions that make them meaningful, and sometimes to the creative acts that engender these intentions and their observable results. Thus, actions and their corresponding affections not only are observable to us, like every other natural phenomenon, including action and passion, but also are to be understood starting from those expressions that are both the effects and the signs of the intentions that give them meaning and even the acts that they sometimes produce. As a result, the spirit of discovery does not operate only on a single level, that of the observation and explanation which, as said, undertake to "save the phenomena." It also unfolds at the interface of natural observation and reflexive understanding. Discussions like the one I had with Jean-Pierre Changeux about the relation between neuroscience and reflexive knowledge are situated at this level.[6] But does this then mean that all inquiry into the truth falls under moral obligation and hence that truth falls under the control of the just? No, however irreducible reflexive knowledge may be to scientific knowledge, its claim to truth is as independent of moral criteria as is that of scientific knowledge. For example, in history, there are situations that have to be understood without condemning them, or that need to be both understood and condemned, albeit in terms of two different registers, as one of the protagonists claims in the controversy among historians I discuss in *Memory, History, Forgetting*.

Having said this, the situation at the intersection of reflection aimed at mere understanding and reflection aimed at moral judgment is incredibly complex. Reflection on action and its opposite, passion, cannot fail to involve moral preoccupations once the action of an agent on a victim [*patient*] is an occasion for harm

6. See Changeux and Ricoeur, *What Makes Us Think?*

and a tort, and in this sense has to fall under the vigilance of moral judgment. There is not an identity between the truthful dimension of reflection and this vigilance inspired by respect, but a crisscrossing through a single point. For example, current debates about experimentation on human embryos, even over therapeutic cloning, are situated at the level where the scientific spirit of discovery interacts with questions bearing on the degree of respect owed human life at its beginnings. Touched upon here indirectly are the anthropological presuppositions mentioned above in relation to moral judgment. What is now at issue is their position in relation to the spirit of scientific inquiry, which is impatient when it comes to questions of constraint and censorship. This also applies to the genre of discourse dealt with by ethics committees, especially when concerning life itself but also when charged with judicial and penal policy or the domains of commerce and finance. More and more, it is not just life as a fact of nature and the basis of psychic life but nature as a whole as the human environment that asks to be protected. The whole cosmos falls under human responsibility: where something is possible, there is the possibility of harm and therefore the need for moral vigilance.

If we now consider that, in commissions dealing with ethics and other sites of discussion and controversy, scientists are confronted with representatives of different cultural and spiritual families, and other members of civil society, we must admit that epistemology is not exhausted by reflection on science. The accent has to be on scientific activity as a kind of practice, theoretical practice. From this angle the implication of the just in the true is directly revealed and made manifest. No longer does the question occur only on the level of the human sciences, where the dialectic of explanation and understanding unfolds, but it also occurs on the level where understanding intersects with the anthropological preoccupations of the entry into morality and, through this, with the ethical and moral demands of justice. In the end, the question arises at the level of the episteme taken in the whole breadth of its project, which is that of reason. At this level, it is necessary to speak with Jean Ladrière of a hermeneutic of reason.[7] It is no longer a question of hermeneutics as a method that is supposedly

---

7. Ladrière, "Herméneutique et épistémologie."

antagonistic to scientific observation, hence of a distinct cognitive procedure connected with the comprehensive reconstitution of actions and passions that one uses to evaluate the conjectural, indirect, probabilistic aspect of the reactualization of real processes. At this level, interpretation figures as one variety of explanatory approach, to be placed on the same level as other modes of reconstituting the real starting from a principle that is specifiable in terms of some model. At this higher level, it really is a matter of a hermeneutic of the episteme that is equated with reason. The question is how this affects the rational project, "what it applies to, what it inspires, what it calls for."

As Ladrière comments:

> The path is not laid out in advance. . . . It is proposed in the very act of stating it. [It has to be grasped] starting from the contingency of a historicity made up of surprises and improbabilities. A contingency that leads back to a founding moment. . . . But this founding moment, like an event that is always yet to come, has itself to be questioned regarding its meaning.[8]

It is at this level of radicality that the truth claimed by scientific knowledge has ethical implications that verify the convertibility between the true and the just, taken this time starting from the true and moving in the direct of the just. This convertibility is to be sought nowhere else than in the pair seek-find. This fits together on the practical plane with the pair model-verify/falsify on the epistemological one. Science cannot be defined apart from the scientist, as a human being. Its activity is not solitary. It requires teamwork in centers, laboratories, clinics, and research institutes. The power at stake in it interferes with its research projects. The ethics of discussion is brought into play on the occasion of a very specific kind of communication activity, with its own language games, under the banner of intellectual integrity. Those interpersonal and institutional relations, which give rise to the dynamic shared by the whole scientific community, make scientific research that unpredictable undertaking so magnificently described by Ladrière: immersed in history, bound to key events of intellectual discovery, such as great discoveries, paradigm shifts, innovations, and

8. Ibid., 123–24.

advances, but also polemical and marked by power games. Concerning this quest rightly defined as a quest for truth, and whose norm is grasped as immanent in scientific activity as a theoretical practice, we can say that it does not recognize its goal except by proceeding along the path to it.

The next question is how this practice is inscribed among other, not properly scientific or even theoretical practices (for example, speculation about transcendentals such as I am pursuing here), that is, practices like crafts or moral, juridical, and political activity. From their point of intersection, theoretical and nontheoretical practices project, in a risky, always revisable way, the horizon of meaning in relation to which we define the humanity of human beings.

So the true is not spoken apart from the just or the just apart from the true. What remains to be spoken of is the beauty of the just and the true and their harmonious conjunction in what the Greeks called *to kalonkagathon*, the "beautiful good," the ultimate horizon of the just.

I have placed the essay "Autonomy and Vulnerability" in the third place in this sequence of studies. The notion of autonomy first appeared in the first essay in the section relating to moral obligation (part I), at the junction of a self that posits itself and a rule that imposes itself. But this definition from this angle retains only the active dimension of the amplitude of imputability, that ancestor of our more familiar notion of responsibility. Still to be clarified is the obscurer face of this capacity, that is, the forms of incapacity stemming from the passivity of moral experience. To take both these aspects of the capable human being into account means to link the active and the passive, suffering sides of moral obligation itself. The title of this essay states without beating around the bush the paradoxical character of this ideational pair: paradoxical but not antinomical, like the "antinomies of pure reason" in the theoretical order. But paradoxical in what sense? A threefold one.

In a first sense, activity and passivity work together in the constitution of what is designated by the term the "subject of rights" announced on the poster for the seminar at the Institut des hautes études sur la justice (IHEJ), which this lecture opened. It is no longer a question of the just in the neuter sense of a term qualifying action but of the just human being as the author of actions held to be unjust or just. The pair autonomy-vulnerability constitutes a paradox in that it presupposes autonomy as the condition of possibility of unjust or just action and of a judgment about this in some judicial setting and, at the same time, as a task to be accomplished by subjects on the political plane: to leave behind the state of submission or, as was said during the Enlightenment, the state of "tutelage," of minority. Condition and task—so appears autonomy rendered fragile by a vulnerability constitutive of its human character.

This pair also constitutes a paradox in that autonomy presents features of great stability, stemming from what in phenomenology is called eidetic description, inasmuch as this reveals a conceptual ground characteristic of the most general and most common human condition and the vulnerability of the more flexible aspects that go with the history of any culture or collective or individual education. This is the paradox of the historical and the universal. It seems to me that the most characteristic features of autonomy, taken both as a presupposition and as a task to be accomplished, have to do with the fundamental more than with the marks of vulnerability. But we do not know how finally to weave together the fundamental and the historical when it comes to the structure of moral action. This aspect of the paradox thus seemed so important to me that I devote a whole essay to it in part III of this volume.

To carry through this investigation it was necessary to take things up again at the highest level and to set imputability against the background of the other modes of capacity and incapacity constitutive of acting and suffering in their full breadth. At the same time, this essay contributes directly to redoing the little ethics of *Oneself as Another* by linking imputability more closely to the three themes dealt with there of "I can speak" (chapters 1 and 2), "I can act" (chapters 3 and 4), and "I can narrate" (chapters 5 and 6). Imputability adds a fourth dimension to this phenomenology of the I can: I can take myself to be the true author of acts assigned to my account. At the same time that imputability completes the table of capacities and incapacities, it confirms the epistemological feature assigned to affirmation having to do with capacity and the states of capacity and incapacity. Like every other capacity, imputability can be neither proved nor refuted; it can only be attested to or brought under suspicion. So I speak here of affirmation-attestation. It is this epistemic constitution, itself fragile, which leads to the paradox I have been discussing. The connection between imputability and the other modes of capacity and incapacity is so tight that the first infirmities that sum up the experiences of heteronomy are those that affect the power to speak, to act, and to narrate. It is a question of forms of fragility that are certainly inherent in the human condition, but reinforced, even inaugurated, by life in society and its increasing inequalities—in short, unjust institutions in the first sense of the term, in light of the equation of justice and equality successively affirmed by Aristotle, Rousseau, and Tocqueville. As for the forms of fragility inherent in the quest for personal and collective identity, they are clearly linked to the power to narrate, insofar as identity is a narrative identity, as I suggested in the conclusion to volume 3 of *Time and Narrative*. Narrative identity is said to be a mark of power in that it has as its counterpart the temporal constitution of an identity, along with its dialogical constitution. Here we find the fragility of human affairs submitted to the double test of temporal distension and confrontation with the disturbing alterity of other human beings. Imputability does not come on the scene therefore as something absolutely heterogeneous to the history of customs, as we can see by referring to obligation, the obligation to do what is right, to make up for harm done, to undergo penalties.

What is assuredly new with this constitutive capacity of imputability is the conjunction between the self and the rule wherein Kant rightly saw the synthetic a priori judgment that alone defines the moral level of action. From this follow new forms of vulnerability in relation to those inherent in the three great basic forms of being able to speak, to act, and to narrate, among them being the difficulty of being able to enter some symbolic order and thereby give meaning to the cardinal notion of a norm, of an obligatory rule. In discussing this, I run up against the difficulties attached to the notion of authority in its political dimension, to which the fourth essay is devoted. The legitimation crisis that is discussed at length there is only mentioned in passing in the third essay from the angle of moral authority.

Nevertheless, I do not leave the perplexities relating to the entry into a symbolic world without any answer. I outline prudently and no doubt too briefly a meditation on the symbol as a sign of recognition, in line with my older work on the symbolic function and my more recent work on the social imagination as expressed in the ideas of ideology and utopia.[9]

At the end of this sequence, I ask myself what has become of the idea of the just. In the two preceding essays the idea of the just was taken in a neuter sense: *to dikaion,* just and unjust as applicable to actions. In the third essay, it designates the disposition to just actions that the seminar at the IHEJ indicated by speaking of the subject of rights.

With the fourth essay, "The Paradox of Authority," paradox comes back onstage, that is, a situation for reflection in which two contrary theses equally oppose being refuted and, as a result, require being preserved or abandoned together. In offering this definition at the beginning of the third essay, I distinguished paradox from antinomy by the feature that with an antinomy it is possible to apportion the two theses among two different universes of discourse, as Kant does with the thesis and antithesis on the plane of the confrontation between freedom and determinism. The paradox of autonomy and fragility does not allow for this kind of solution. They confront each other in the same field in such a way that each one becomes the presupposition of the other. The question of authority poses a similar situation.

In truth, the paradox of autonomy contains the seed of that of authority in the guise of the moral authority exercised by a symbolic order as the bearer of norms. It is the normative side of autonomy—its lawlike side—that gives rise to the paradox, namely, whether the authority of a symbolic order is operative only when it has been recognized and acknowledged. What is acknowledged here if not the superiority of the symbolic order? But what ensures that the norm of some symbolic order is truly superior and worthy of allegiance and recognition? Is there not a circle here, concerning which we do not know if it is vicious or virtuous, between the requirement that we should be obedient, declared from on high,

9. Ricoeur, *Lectures on Ideology and Utopia;* Ricoeur, "Ideology and Utopia as Cultural Imagination"; Ricoeur, "Imagination in Discourse and in Action"; Ricoeur, "Ideology and Ideology Critique." See also Ricoeur, *Course of Recognition.*

and the belief on the part of those below in the legitimacy of the claimed authority?

The same difficulty returns with the paradox of political authority, but at the price of a displacement that shifts the axis of discussion from the properly moral problematic to a more precisely civil one. What is at stake is no longer the norm in the broad sense of a source of obligation at the heart of the pair formed by the self and the rule, but the power of an authority charged with governing human beings to make itself obeyed. In a word, the shift is from the authority of obligation to that of being able to command, to give orders. In one sense, it is the same problem at bottom once the question posed is that of the legitimacy authorizing the authority to give orders, power in the political sense of the word. Yet it is not exactly the same inasmuch as the accent is shifted from the force of moral constraint, constitutive of moral obligation, to that of the social, psychological, political constraint that is constitutive of the power to make oneself obeyed. The question of legitimacy is connected here to a power more than to an obligation, the power to give orders and, in so doing, to be obeyed. What accredits, we may ask, such power? The major advantage of shifting the axis from the moral to the political is that it immediately brings to light the embarrassing question of the nature of the authorizing act that, in the order of language, brings to the fore the force of the verb at the source of the substantive sense of "authority." In turn, the verb "to accredit," as a synonym of "to authorize," orients the investigation to the side of belief, credibility—trustworthiness—but also to that of making something believed and its craftiness. The question of legitimacy first posed in terms of prior authorization becomes more precise when it is posed as a question of legitimacy recognized after the fact. It becomes embarrassing as soon as we ask where this authority comes from. What authorizes the authorization? With this, our earlier problem of fragility changes form. It has become that of the crisis of legitimation, at a time when the discrediting of the authority of authorized individuals and institutions seems to be the tone at the level of public discussion.

I thought I would focus my examination on the aspect of the asserting of authority in order to distinguish it from its institutional aspect. In this way, the role of cultural statements, of so-called founding texts, in the genealogy of belief in the legitimacy of authority is emphasized. And we again find the question of the power of persuasion emanating from what in the preceding essay I called a symbolic order bearing norms. Now it is a question of a discourse of legitimation meant to uphold a claim to authority, that is, the right to give orders. In truth, the distinction between asserted authority and institutional authority is only provisory and didactic, insofar as it is actually institutions that are legitimated by such discourse and writings, and where these latter are produced, declared, and published by institutions in need of legitimation.

Turning to the method of ideal types practiced by Max Weber, I examine two ideal types of authority that are largely declarative and that have succeeded one another in our cultural era: that of medieval Christianity, on the basis of scripture and its "authorized" commentaries, and that of the Enlightenment as found in the text of Diderot and d'Alembert's *Encyclopedia*. In the model of medieval Christianity, institutional and declared authority are closely interconnected, the ecclesial *magisterium* basing its authority on scripture, and the interpreters of scripture basing themselves on the ecclesial *magisterium*. I note, however, that the ecclesiastic institution found itself the beneficiary as well of a base coming from a political origin heterogeneous to the Bible, the authority of the Roman *imperium*. Hannah Arendt has argued that the Romans were different from the Greeks in the sense of the sacred foundation attributed solely to Rome, the city par excellence—*Urbs, ab urbe condita*—and that the *religio* succeeded in communicating the energy of this foundation across the era of Roman domination to the Catholic Church rightly called Roman. This Roman origin explains the competition, throughout the Middle Ages, between ecclesiastic authority and monarchical power within a divided political theology.

As for the authority that is attributed to the *Encyclopedia*, it was meant to be fundamentally declarative, in the same way as the scriptural authority claimed by the church. In this sense it was unable by itself to give rise to a revolution—the French Revolution—even if it politically contended with absolute power in a struggle against censorship and the repression of heresies and in favor of its plea for "publicity."

The outcome of the competition between these two ideal types, a competition in which the second emerged victorious thanks to the French Revolution, raises the problem of the nature of authority issuing from the will of a sovereign people. Can this power be held to be the political equivalent of moral authority at the intersection of the self and the norm, as it was defined in the preceding essay? If we consider that this synthesis constituted in Kant's eyes a "fact of reason," in other words, the recognition of the constitutive structural basis of moral experience as in my first essay, what would be the political equivalent of this "fact of reason"? I do not have anything to add to the discussion of the theoretical difficulties attached to contractual theories of the origin of political authority. I do consider briefly the practical difficulties that burden the application of an essentially ahistorical agreement—the social contract—in given historical circumstances. Legitimating a principle is one thing; inscribing this legitimacy as a fact is another. The paradox of authority springs up again in the terms formulated by the Romans: distinguishing the *auctoritas* of the ancients from the mere *potentia* of the people, as though the great age of power by itself constituted a factor of legitimacy.

I admit that today this essay seems insufficiently developed.

Along with the theoretical difficulties that come with the process of legitimizing authority, the reader will find in my essay devoted to the basic categories of Max Weber's sociology a systematic exploration of the dialectic, opened on the plane of the legitimation of authority, between the demand for recognition issuing from existing authority and the capacity for recognition on the part of the subordinate parties. The fundamentally fiduciary character of the relation between above and below then comes to the fore. It is in terms of belief that legitimacy henceforth poses the paradox of authority.

Since having written this essay I have continued to reflect in different ways upon this paradox, which can be sharpened in the following way: how, in a democratic society, can we connect the horizontal axis of wanting to live together and the vertical axis that Weber calls the axis of domination? If the vertical axis turns out to be irreducible to the horizontal one, as it implicitly is in the definition of authority as the power to give orders, to make oneself obeyed—and if this power is taken to be legitimate and is not reducible to violence but is power seeking recognition—then, where does this power come from? It is not easy to shake off this question. I see it returning in new ways in the question of grandeur. Grandeur did not disappear along with absolute power, centered on the figure of the king, the prince; it was multiplied, dispersed among what Luc Boltanski and Laurent Thévenot call "economies" of standing. But why grandeur as a measure of standing?

Here is where on the theoretical plane my current reflection lies in prolonging the examination of the difficulties arising from the contractualist paradigm of authority. What is still poorly understood is the kind of superiority presupposed by the idea of grandeur.

As for the difficulties attached to the historical inscription of authority stemming from the sovereignty of a people, I see this today as centered in representative democracy, following the reflections of Claude Lefort, Marcel Gauchet, and Pierre Rosanvallon. Contemporary democracies have more or less settled the question of elections. They have not resolved that of how those elected represent the people. This difficulty does not come down to a question of delegation but rather culminates in a question having to do with symbolic force. In saying this, the question of the political paradox is brought back to the region of the symbolic order whose authority seemed inherent in the constitution of autonomy, in the full range of its political, juridical, and moral scope.

I hope to persuade readers that my essay on translation belongs in this collection and that it finds its place at the end of part I, "Studies," which forms the base of this book.

This essay is not about translation considered from the point of view of translation studies but rather about the paradigm of translation. What is at stake for philosophy is how to model what is at work in the act of translating.

A first indication of the exemplary character of this operation is given by the very scope of the phenomenon as a twofold problem: translation from one language to another and translation internal to some spoken language. This second consideration greatly enlarges the scope of the phenomenon: everywhere where there is the foreign, there is a place for a struggle against noncommunication.

Having reread this essay, I would like to emphasize two aspects in which translation reveals its paradigmatic character. On the one hand, the difficulty in translating; on the other, its weapons—on the one hand, the presumption of untranslatability; on the other, the very work of translation, in the sense that we speak of a work of memory or of the work of mourning.

As for the dark underside of the problem of translation—the presumption of untranslatability—it is worth noting that entering the problematic of translation from one language to another has the advantage of immediately bringing to the fore the major phenomenon of the diversity of languages, the subtitle Wilhelm von Humboldt used for his book on Kawi studies.[10] The initial threat of incommunicability contained in this first condition can be assigned to the modes of vulnerability already referred to in the preceding essays. This threat is more precisely inscribed among the figures of incapacity that affect our capacity to speak and, step-by-step, to say, to recount, up to and including moral imputability. One form of vulnerability at the root of this incapacity results from the irreducible plurality of languages. This specific vulnerability affects another specific capacity, translating in the sense to be dealt with in the second part of this meditation. This capacity of speaking subjects to translate—whether provisionally or professionally—is one of languages themselves before being one of such speaking subjects. What is at issue here about translatability, about the difficulty in translating, about the untranslatableness of a given language? In what way is their untranslatableness taken for granted? Is it so radical that translation has to be declared impossible in principle? And if translation exists as a fact, as an actually practiced operation, what is it that makes it theoretically possible at the level of the deep structure of language?

I will not dwell on the details of the discussions arising from the alternative: translatability versus untranslatability on the ethnolinguistic plane, of lexicography, comparative grammar, or on the plane of speculations about a universal language, whether this be sought at the origin of language or at the horizon of a systematic reconstruction. I want to confine myself here to what is paradigmatic in the problem before examining what might be paradigmatic in the answer, that is, the indefatigable work of translation.

10. Humboldt, *On Language: On the Diversity of Human Language Construction and Its Influence on the Mental Development of the Human Species.*

The diversity of languages has to do with a major structure of the human condition, its plurality. In turn, this plurality affects identity, as the famous chapter 22 ("Of Identity and Diversity") of Locke's *Essay concerning Human Understanding* recalls. There is no self-identity without diversity in relation to others. The interval of plurality stands open between human beings. *Inter homines esse,* Hannah Arendt liked to repeat. Now this aspect of plurality affects not only languages but also sociability taken in its full amplitude. Humanity exists as fragmented—into populations, ethnicities, cultures, historical communities, belief systems, and religions. We saw above a corollary on the plane of juridical systems, of institutions of justice, of penal practices—and again on the occasion of the division between the universality of principles of morality and the historical character of justifications offered in situations of conflict. Politics more than anything else is affected by this condition of plurality. There are states because first of all there are distinct historical communities upon which their political form confers a capacity for decisions. At this highly conflictual level, the relation friend-enemy tends to transform political diversity into unbending feelings of animosity, owing to claims for sovereignty, a political form of identity. There is no need to turn to religion to underscore the irrevocably pluralistic range of the human condition. Yet perhaps here we touch upon the enigmatic point of the conversion of plurality into hostility. If the sacred as an object beyond appropriation is the object of rivalrous envy and is expressed at first only in the all-against-one ritual of the scapegoat, then we have to place plurality on the plane of basic beliefs affecting the most dreadful occasions of fallibility and fallenness.

This move from plurality to hate was once magnified into the language of origin myths by the famous Hebraic story of the Tower of Babel, magnificently translated into French by André Chouraqui. Two aspects of linguistic plurality are named there: dispersion on the plane of space and confusion on the plane of communicability. That this bifid condition should have been preceded by a state of affairs in which there existed only "one tongue, one language," that it came about in time as a catastrophe, stems from the narrative aspect of myths of origin. What is important on the plane of meaning is the treatment of an advent in the form of an event, an advent in a properly immemorial sense, an advent that is the advent of our linguistic condition. In turn, this mythic fragment was inscribed by the narrator—the J source or another—in a sequence of founding events that together speak on a cosmic scale of the progress of the distinction and separation of chaos and confusion, from the setting apart of light and shadow up to the rupture within the family bond by the fratricide that makes fraternity henceforth a task rather than a given. The dispersion and confusion of languages is inscribed in this sequence of separations. The myth of Babel gives the peopling of the earth—an almost innocent form of plurality—the dramatic turn of dispersion and confusion. Like the whole sequence of narratives that the Tower of Babel story crowns, the myth can be read as the pure and simple advent of our factual linguistic condition: no recrimination, no deploring, no accusation . . . Starting from this reality: "Translate!"

This reversal of adversity into a task to be accomplished is expressed in my essay on the paradigm of translation by the replacement of a speculative alternative (translatability versus untranslatability) by a practical alternative: fidelity versus betrayal. However much the former, in the current state of the discussion, is unsolvable, the second turns out to be negotiable. It's a fact: people have always translated; travelers, merchants, diplomats, and spies have always practiced this negotiation, with the help of bilingual and polyglot people, before the existence of professional translators and interpreters, hence before the establishing of translation studies as a discipline. If they do translate, I ask, how do they do it? It is in the answer to this question that the act of translating reveals itself as exemplary. Following Antoine Berman, in *The Experience of the Foreign,* I draw upon the desire to translate that underlies the effort to do so. What is the obstacle here? Why the dilemma between fidelity and betrayal? The reason is to be sought in the articulating of the theoretical problem of translatability and the practical problem of the activity of translating, the articulating of competence and performance at the level of the speaking subject. Before the practical dilemma—no fidelity without some betrayal—the theoretical paradox: lacking a third text that could demonstrate the identity of meaning, the only recourse is to seek an equivalence of meaning between the message in the source language and that in the target language. It is this presumed equivalence that gives room for the practical dilemma of fidelity/betrayal, a dilemma for which there exist solutions only in the form of paradoxes: bring the reader to the author, the author to the reader. This is not just where the work of the solitary interpreter listening to discourse or faced with a text leads; it also applies to the chain of those who unceasingly take up the task of retranslation. For where else do we better read the desire to translate than in that to retranslate?

Here is where the act of translating, motivated by the desire to translate, reveals its paradigmatic character. What is exemplary is not just the difficulty but also the labor required to overcome it. I risk speaking in this regard of a hospitality of language, in order to speak of the virtue that adds its moral note to the desire and pleasure of translating.

It is this virtue that I want now to spell out further than I did in the essay I am considering. To begin, I would like to restore the full breadth of the work of translation. This is the moment to recall that translation is a problem with two entry points: translation from one language to another but also translation internal to one's own language, one's mother tongue. This second approach is the one George Steiner privileges in his *After Babel*. After Babel, he says, "to understand is to translate." In what way is this use of translation exemplary? In the sense that translation internal to a language brings to light the incredible resources for self-interpretation in natural languages, resources capable of being transposed to translations from other languages and, beyond them, to situations where understanding is confronted with misunderstanding. This is the original situation taken into account by every hermeneutic theory. In order to understand, we unendingly interpret our language by means of another version of that language: what we call "definition" is using one fragment of discourse for another; explanation, and even a whole argument, are other equivalent forms of this same language; all are forms of discussion. And this is done not by one person alone but in situations of dialogue for which ordinary conversation can serve as the prime example. To say the same thing in another way is the secret of how we deal with the ambiguities of a word, the equivocations of a sentence, the misunderstandings of a text. Beyond these discursive strategies, with Steiner we need to advance as far as those uses of language that define translation and point toward the enigma, the artifice, the hermetic, the secret. Here the use of language is confronted, not with the test of the foreign, in Berman's phrase, but with a kind of untranslatability that can not only be suffered as an infirmity but also be cultivated as a higher form of mastery, the untranslatability of the secret. The test is then not that of the stranger at our door but that of the strangeness found at home with us. We thus have also to welcome ourselves as an other. Inexorable plurality on the one side, impenetrable solitude on the other. A struggle for transparency on the one side, a culture of opacity on the other. Translation is confronted with these two genuine challenges. But whether it is a question of a translation from one language to another or of translation internal to one's own language, in both cases it is a question of saying the same thing differently, without ever being sure that one has said the same thing twice, owing to the lack of a means to measure the equivalence of messages assumed to have the same meaning.

The immense resources of the labor of translation make the hospitality of language in the broadest sense a powerful model beyond the sphere of language properly speaking. To support this thesis, we need to adopt the movement proposed above from plurality to intimacy. Translation is from end to end the remedy for plurality in a world of dispersion and confusion.

This is true first of all on the very plane of the literary, cultural, and spiritual productions of the great linguistic families. We need only to think of the translation of the Hebraic Torah into Greek with the Septuagint, of St. Jerome's translation of the Bible into Latin, of its translation into German by Luther. Entire cultures have been born from these frontier crossings that were at the same time far-reaching linguistic transgressions. On the other side of the world, Buddhism passed from Sanskrit to Chinese, crossing another linguistic abyss. The same victory is found on the plane of the genesis of philosophical and scientific concepts: Cicero literally created a learned Latin by translating Greek philosophical idioms. We ourselves are the heirs of these discoveries. Without the impact of Arabic and Hebrew transmitters, what would the knowledge of Greek philosophy be for the Latin-influenced West? The literary languages of Renaissance Europe themselves arose from the elevating of vernacular languages from their village settings to the level of the Latin of the clergy. Kant always notes in Latin his conceptual breakthroughs in German. In our own day, French philosophical language has uprooted itself from its Cartesian sufficiency only through translating the German of Kant, Hegel, Nietzsche, and Heidegger and, to a lesser degree, the English of the seventeenth and eighteenth centuries.

The foreign origin of a translation ought not to make us forget the losses that are the price of a naïve belief that concepts can simply be transferred from one language to another, with no impact from the facticity of the target language. What I have said about the labor of translation internal to a language may help us to overthrow this illusory belief in the innocence of the concept. The metaphorics that gives rise to concepts works beneath our abstractions like a kind of silent hermeneutics. This work of translation internal to a language is often sharpened by the translation from one language to another. The borrowings that are the result continue, as said, to draw languages where they do not want to go, at the price of a certain violence exercised on the genius they claim for themselves. When this immanent work is brought to light, the dilemmas left in silence clearly proclaim themselves: must we, in translating, seek to produce a substitute text that will dispense with the need for any knowledge of the original? Or, on the contrary, ought we to seek to convey the asperities to the point of making reading the translation difficult? Professional translators are well aware of these dilemmas, which bring us to the practical alternative of translation as the ambiguous serving of two masters that is condemned to betray both in turn. Equivalence without identity, owing to the lack of any absolute criteria, leaves us with a judgment of taste—and the arbitration of retranslation.

This struggle with plurality, its failures and successes, continues in spheres more and more distant from that of work properly speaking applied to language and languages. Translation functions as a paradigm by which to expand the problematic. Humanity, I said, only exists as fragmented. In this regard, historical communities, with their dominant ethnic, cultural, juridical, political, and religious features, can be compared to heterogeneous linguistic conglomerations concerned to protect their identity when confronted by such diversity. I speak here of "blocks" of meaning in order to talk about these organic wholes constituted on the basis of founding texts that make these organic wholes spread far beyond their luminous centers.

In the religious domain, the great Christian confessions of East and West do not reduce to dogmatic propositions, to articles of faith; they are more like linguistic wholes proposed for adhesion to the heart and mind and will. These idioms, with their internal rules of interpretation, are offered like foreign languages to those on the outside: blocks of meaning, blocks to be translated. The understanding that can transfer from one confessional whole to another involves a double work of translation: from my to your language but also internal to my language to make room within myself for another way of formulating problems and at the same time reformulating in another way the very terms of age-old conflicts. Beyond the technical means used to reduce the difficulties encountered by interpreters better or worse trained for the work of translation, there is the spirit of translation consisting in transporting oneself into the sphere of meaning of the foreign language and in welcoming the other's discourse into the sphere of the target language, at the price of the double betrayal already spoken of. Here, too, to translate is to retranslate.

Expanding the sphere of examination, I want to speak in the same way about the relations between philosophy and religious belief as a kind of translation. These are the great textual ensembles that meet and meet again in my reading, giving rise, through a mutual interpretation, to attempts at translating one ensemble into the other; for example, at the level of foundational texts, between the Psalms of David and Greek tragedy, between the Wisdom writings, such as Job, Ecclesiastes, and the Song of Songs, and pre-Socratic and Socratic themes.

Expanding even further the realm of translation to the dimension of those great cultural wholes often designated by a proper name, I want to extend this notion of a "block" of meaning, itself resulting from a translation internal to the frontier between the metaphor and the concept, to these organic wholes, which are constituted, as I say in my essay on authority and its "enunciative" component, in terms of founding texts and are expanded into artistic creations, political utopias, and so forth. Thus, we speak of the medieval scholastic mind, of the spirit of the Renaissance,

of the Age of Enlightenment, of the heritage of the French Revolution, of the Romantic aspect of modernity. The "task of translation," to use Walter Benjamin's well-known title, is to restate
with the semantic resources of one's own culture what has been
said elsewhere about such a cultural label.

Someone may ask, at the end of these long excursuses, which
go well beyond the twists and turns of translation theory, what all
this has to do with the just. But we have never stopped speaking
of it! To translate is to do justice to a foreign intelligence, to in-
stall the just distance from one linguistic whole to another. Your
language is as important as mine. This is the formula for equity-
equality, the formula for recognized diversity. What is more, the
tie to the idea of justice is perhaps most concealed, but strongest,
in renouncing the dream of a perfect translation that I refer to at
the end of my essay. I speak there of the mourning that has to be
carried out for the idea of perfection. This mourning is the strict-
est existential condition to which the desire to translate is invited
to submit. The work of translation, like the work of memory, does
not happen without this work of mourning. It makes acceptable
the idea of an equivalence without identity that is the formula for
justice in the field of translation.

II

The essays gathered in part III under the title "Exercises" illustrate the "little ethics" of *Oneself as Another* at its terminal phase
of practical wisdom. Judgment is at work there in determinate re-
gions of moral practices, principally in the areas of medicine and
judicial punishment. It is a question, therefore, of two regional
ethics, where the grammatical plural "ethics" derives from the
grammatical singular "ethic" that fits at the foundational level of
moral reflection, in traversing the plane of moral and juridical
obligation. If the plural form underscores the plurality of regional
ethics, this is because everyday life proposes a plurality of empirical situations to which these practices and institutions correspond,
principally in terms of suffering and conflict, regardless of any organization of practices or institutions. These are boundary situations in the sense given this phrase by Karl Jaspers and Jean Nabert,

independently of each other, an inevitable condition that action is confronted with and that is shared by innumerable situations taken as contingent, unrepeatable, yet equally as constraining. They all underscore the passivity, the fragility, the vulnerability that our analyses of responsibility have encountered more than once as its object or underside. Yet if they have in common always existing and always being "suffered," they are irreducibly distinct and quite simply multiple, as popular feeling confirms. It is only the practices they give rise to that give them an occasion to be talked about, formulated, communicated, understood.

I have placed at the head of this last series of essays a lecture, "The Difference between the Normal and the Pathological as a Source of Respect," given before different audiences: psychiatrists, educators, all confronted by those who have to deal with psychic handicaps. Indeed, it is starting from the biological plane, and more precisely the pathological situation, that respect, taken as the virtue common to both morality and law, is to be exercised. In the reflections of Georges Canguilhem on the normal and the pathological I found a decisive handhold for my thesis that it is the very difference between two realms of life, between two relations opposed to health, that calls for respect. This conclusion is perceived only at the price of a patient preparation concerning successively the relation of the living being to its milieu, reformulated in terms of confrontation, of "making sense of . . . ," then of the status of illness as a lack, a deficiency, a powerlessness, another form of organization in relation, to be sure, to a "narrowed setting," yet one bearing positive values as alternatives to those of health. This reevaluation of illness, from the biological to the institutional plane, lies at the source of an argument directed against any depreciation of the ill themselves and against the prejudices leading to their exclusion. In this way, a corrective is brought to the tendency, which can be spotted even in my own more speculative essays, to characterize vulnerability as a mere lack, as a pure deficit. If illness bears values, which we can organize following Canguilhem at the vital, the social, and the existential levels, it is not just the autonomy of a person that has to be taken as a source and object of respect, but this vulnerability itself or illness adds the note of the pathological to that of passivity. In its difference in relation to the normal and on the basis of the values attached to this difference, the pathological is worthy of esteem and respect. In this way, justice can be done to those pathologically impaired people faced with prejudices that lead to their social exclusion.

In the next essay, "The Three Levels of Medical Judgment," the problematic of the just is taken up from the perspective of judgment, more particularly in terms of one species of judgment, medical judgment. The term "judgment" designates at the same time an assertion characteristic of the practice under consideration, here medical prescription, and the taking of a position exercised by the protagonists, healers on the one side and patients on the other.

It is ordering such judgment in terms of three levels—prudential, deontological, and teleological—that provides the basic structure for this essay. The reader will readily discern here the reverse order of the three terms I used to articulate moral experience in the little ethics of *Oneself as Another.* The study placed at the head of this volume proposes another form of organization that makes the deontological point of view move to the fore, to stand between an upstream ethic, arising out of a grounding reflection, and downstream ethics, arising out of concern for practical application of moral and juridical rules. Still, it was fitting in an essay dealing with regional ethics and centered on the therapeutic (clinical) orientation of bioethics to begin its inquiry on the plane closest to actual practice, the plane of prudential judgment, where this is understood in the sense of the Latin and medieval *prudentia* as translating the *phronesis* of Greek tragedy, that virtue of a sensible person.

Therefore, it is from the agreement to render care as a pact based on trust that my analysis begins. This face-to-face relation between a patient and a physician itself is the result of suffering, one of the boundary situations referred to above. Starting from this level, precepts are formulated that imply a certain know-how and the personal involvement of the protagonists. It is these precepts that give content to the prudential judgment and set it on the way toward the deontological judgment.

As for the deontological approach characteristic of the Kantian approach to morality, I see it as contributing to the different functions assigned to medical judgment on the juridical, as well as the moral, level. At their head stand the rules of medical deontology that apply in every therapeutic situation: confidential sharing of the medical secret, the right to know the truth about one's case and one's treatment, the exercising of informed consent. Next come the coordinating rules that are organized as a code of professional ethics for the medical profession. Finally, come the rules capable of arbitrating among the conflicts that are born at the crossroads where medical deontology runs up against obligations stemming from other than therapeutic considerations: the interests of scientific knowledge on the plane of experimentation and concern for public health as it affects institutional organization and public expense.

It is at the boundaries of this critical use of judgment in conflictual situations that the implicit deontology of medical codes links up in depth with the teleological order of a basic ethic. Here is a case that verifies my thesis in my first lecture that the requirements of a basic ethic formerly borne by a typology of virtues and the exhibiting of leading examples are today so covered over that only regional ethics offer them a space to manifest themselves in the form of sage advice appropriate to uncertain, urgent situations. This is certainly the case in the medical realm. It is through the "unspoken" parts of the code that the masked ultimate interests of bioethics and the law applied to life and to living creatures advance, sometimes in the service of individuals, sometimes of society. In this way a long history of solicitude finds itself condensed and summarized into the lapidary and sometimes ambiguous formulas of our codes. They are meant to thematize the points of convergence in the fundamental convictions of the consensus proclaimed by advanced democratic societies.

The tie to the theme of the just does not then here reduce to the proximity that judgment as an intellectual act has to justice. It is also expressed in justice itself, which this judgment aims at on all three levels. Finally, the concern for the intersecting interests of the individual and of society finds itself placed under the guardianship of the conception of justice that presides over the social and political relations at work in advanced democratic societies. Yet this conception of justice really only authorizes the spirit of compromise among those spiritual families that together

continue to contribute to refounding the social pact in these societies. This is why I thought it appropriate to refer in concluding to the formulas I borrow from John Rawls concerning an
"overlapping consensus" and the recognition of "reasonable disagreements." It is in these terms that the just finds itself directly
implicated in the unspoken part of our codes.

"Decision Making in Medical and Judicial Judgments" is meant
to expand the field of judgment. This double approach is not unexpected inasmuch as, from my first chapter, my plea in favor of
applied ethics has been based on the idea of a diversity of regional
ethics. The plurality of domains of application ought in this respect to be explored beyond the pairing of medicine and the judiciary, as far as the problematic of judgment allows. From the
same angle could be considered historical judgment concerning,
for example, singular causal implication as developed by Max
Weber and Raymond Aron[11] and political judgment as applied to
criteria of "good government," to use Charles Taylor's expression.
However, in every case it is judgment in the sense of subsumption
that is at issue, it being understood that between the rule and the
case the movement can be from the rule to the case (determining judgment) or from the case to the rule (reflective judgment,
which rules over the whole realm of the *Critique of Judgment*, but
which Kant limited to aesthetic judgment and teleological judgment as applied to organized wholes).

The differences between these two types of judgment proceed
from the duality of limit situations that give rise to them: suffering on the one side and conflict on the other. The initial situations
are fully comparable: discussion in the medical office, on the one
hand, and the trial process in a courtroom, on the other. The terminal acts are also comparable: medical prescription, penal sentence. The two sorts of judgments are opposed in terms of their
functions. Medical judgment joins the protagonists in the agreement to provide care; judicial judgment separates the antagonists in
the trial process. Yet we can also speak of differences affecting the
initial and terminal situations in terms of variations of distance: to
conjoin, to disjoin. These variations in turn can be seen as opposed

11. See Ricoeur, *Time and Narrative*, 1:183–92.

yet complementary figures of a just distance. On the one side, the pact to give care does not dissolve into a confusion of roles and the fusion of persons but preserves the distance of respect; on the other, the sentence that places the aggressor and the victim in distinct places does not abolish the human bond of consideration due to individuals among themselves. This search for a just distance places this whole essay, like the others, under the sign of the just.

Having said this, I want to emphasize two points here where this essay may have something new to contribute. The first one has to do with the progression on the scale of judgment from the level of a basic ethic to that of regional ethics; the second, with the treatment of the in-between covered by the work of judgment from the level of norms to that of concrete situations. Adopting the now-familiar progression from the prudential to the deontological, then to the teleological planes, but in the reverse order from that adopted in *Oneself as Another*, I note that the central pillar for ethical rules constitutive of the pact to give care in the medical order (as I have spelled this out in the preceding essay) now appears flanked by two adjacent pillars structured by weighty rules: that of biological and medical sciences on the one side and that of the politics of public health on the other. The pairing of the medical and the judicial finds an initial verification here. The central act of the trial process is itself backed up on one side by a juridical knowledge base that serves as a doctrinal base for jurists and on the other side by legal rules claiming authority or judicial power, as well as by measures stemming from the penal policy determined by the politics of the state. In this way, a framework comparable to that of the medical act can be discerned in the judicial and penal order.

As for the second innovation, it has to do with the medial phase of the operation of judging. Above I limited myself to comparing the initial situations of the private medical consultation and the trial process with their terminal situations. And I related their differences and resemblances to the originary duality of suffering and conflict. What remains to be explored is the kinship at the intermediary level of operations joining the initial situations of judgment to its end states. These operations join knowledge or norms to concrete situations of judgment. In this, I return to the discussion outlined in *Oneself as Another* and dealt with at greater length in *The Just,* under the heading of argumentation and interpretation in judicial judgment. In the latter work I also discussed the controversy over the general problematic of normativity arising within the framework of the transcendental pragmatics inaugurated by Karl-Otto Apel and developed more explicitly by specialists in legal theory such as Robert Alexy.[12] My concern for the parallelism between the medical and the judicial orders in the present essay has to be set against this background. The idea proposed is that the dialectic of argumentation and interpretation is more readable on the judicial plane than on the medical one because it is codified through a known procedure and distributed among a plurality of roles: the parties in the trial, lawyers, judges, and jury. In this way, decision making in the medical order gains from being compared with its judicial parallel. In particular, we better understand the elevating of medical deontology from the rank of bioethics to the more legal one of "biolaw" governing the legal aspects of any right to life or of a living creature—and, through its prolongation, the turn today to the legal system as it applies to the medical relation. This is why it is important when the time comes to recall from what initial situations the whole process begins: suffering on one side, conflict on the other. Nor is it a matter of indifference if we interweave the near-term and long-term ends inscribed in these situations: healing, on the one hand, satisfaction, on the other. Is it going too far to suggest that the long-term ends of care and of the trial link up in something like a therapeutic of the body and of the social body?

The theme of "Justice and Vengeance" imposed itself at the crossroads of two lines of inquiry: on the one hand, a long meditation on incapacities, forms of fragility, of vulnerability, which together signal the passivity of the capable human being, the subject of acting and suffering; on the other, my having sought to take into account in *The Just* the limits and failures of the enterprise of justice, considered principally in terms of its penal expression. The resistance of the spirit of vengeance to the meaning of justice stands out clearly in the two large problematics that my earlier essays sought to address. The point of this essay comes after a

12. See, for example, Ricoeur, *The Just,* 109–26.

rehearsal of the gains we owe to the elevating of the virtue of justice to the rank of an institution: the tutelage of the state, the writing down of laws, the setting up of courts, the codification of the trial process and its rules, the conducting through language of that ceremony up to the pronouncement of the word of justice, which sets each person in his or her just place, on the basis of a just distance between the author of the tort and his or her victim.

Now it is punishment, its sentence and specific violence, that comes to the fore with what Hegel called in a broad sense the administration of justice. Violence comes up in the first place on the occasion of Max Weber's definition of the state as having the monopoly on legitimate violence. Violence is further legitimated rather than justified by the belief whose status I discuss in my essay devoted to the basic categories of Weber's sociology.

Violence is named a second time with regard to the threat of coercion that gives the decision of justice its ability to impose itself through force. Here we touch on the major difference between morality and the law: morality is sanctioned only by reprobation that is wrongly called condemnation; the law is sanctioned by punishment, in other words, by the sentence. Pascal's brilliant reflections on the dialectic of justice and force in this regard are well known. What follows from them is the setting in parallel of a scale of penalties with one of infractions following a rule of proportionality meant to be rational. In this way we come to the terminal act of the trial process recognized through its double face of stating what is just and of inflicting the penalty through the sentence.

It is at this point that we come to the troubling problem of the resurgence of vengeance at the heart of the very exercising of the act of justice. The sentence makes someone suffer. It adds suffering to suffering and thus places the stamp of violence on a speech act that claims to state the law.

Someone may object that we ought not to speak too quickly of a return of vengeance on the occasion of the inflicting of a penalty. It is the satisfaction, as is said, given the victim by the condemnation of the offender that gives license to inevitable, and in many respects legitimate, vindictive feelings. These feelings have to do with the subjectivity of the victim who receives recognition of his rights and, as much as possible, compensation for his misfortune. But, the argument continues, this subjective manner of receiving satisfaction is not part of the meaning of the penalty as a kind of punishment. Only the merited character of the penalty counts for its meaningfulness and, as a result, justifies the painfulness of the penalty.

I understand this argument. It satisfied rational thinkers as demanding as Kant and Hegel. It has to be understood as a reply to a purely pragmatic consideration whose echo can be found in my essay when I invoke as a simple fact the absence of any alternative to the deprivation of liberty, admitting that unfortunately we have no viable project for abolishing our prisons. I would add today that it is not for the lack of anything better—like something left over—that we have to affirm the duty to preserve for prisoners the possibility of their being reintegrated into the community of free citizens. This obligation does not merely correspond to the respect, the consideration, owed to prisoners as human beings; even less does it stem from mere commiseration. It is part of the very meaning of any penalty; it constitutes its end. In this sense, it has to be incorporated into the argumentation that seeks to dissociate the satisfaction of the victim, in the juridical sense of satisfaction, from the vindictive feelings that make up the other sense of satisfaction. Every measure having to do with prison reform finds its place in such reasoning, such as the pragmatic considerations having to do with rehabilitation that I referred to in the essay in *The Just* titled "Sanction, Rehabilitation, Pardon."[13] However, I do not for all that repudiate the final argument of the present essay according to which there are only pragmatic solutions to the dilemma of justice and vengeance, in the sense that this project of rehabilitation arises from the ensemble of private and institutional efforts placed under the sign of practical wisdom. What violence that will for a long time remain in the practice of justice stems from the fragility, the vulnerability, of all the enterprises of that capable human being whom I have characterized as an acting and suffering being.

To conclude part III, I chose the essay "The Universal and the Historical." This lecture, addressed to a wide audience outside

13. Ibid., 133–45.

France, proposes a final run through the three levels of moral reflection, taken not just from the perspective of their interconnectedness but in terms of the confrontation of the universal and the historical at each of the levels considered. This difficulty has haunted the preceding analyses. With regard to the dialectic of autonomy and vulnerability, I noted that autonomy offers features of universality more relevant than does vulnerability, which moreover modulates its originary passivity through the cultural circumstances that history unfolds. As both presupposition and task, autonomy raises a claim to universality that is part of its constitution in principle, whereas the signs of vulnerability are inscribed in a history of passivity that confers upon vulnerability an irreducible historicity.

This redoubling of the paradox of autonomy and vulnerability on the plane of its conceptual apprehension has to affect those moral doctrines most concerned about coherence. Thus it was that I proposed in the setting of the "Readings" placed in the middle of this volume to reread Charles Taylor's *Sources of the Self* in light of the dialectic of the universal and the historical. The connection between the self and the good is posed there as the universal that structures the whole undertaking. Yet the traversal that, from the school of inwardness (itself endowed with a distinct development), leads, through the rationalism culminating in the Enlightenment, to Romanticism and life and environmental ethics is an eminently historical one. If there is a highly dialectical concept here, it is surely that of modernity, understood in turn as a project with a universal pretension and as the name of an era, in both cases designating itself as marking the break between the new and the old, the ancient, the out-of-date.

This dialectic of the universal and the historical is reconstructed in the final essay in this volume at the three successive levels of a basic ethic, moral obligation, and practical wisdom. The reevaluation of the Kantian heritage by Rawls, on the one hand, and by Apel and Habermas, on the other, provides the occasion for reformulating the transition from moral obligation to practical wisdom and regional ethics in terms of the correlation between the universal and the historical. Insofar as these ethics arise from eminently historical situations, such as suffering and conflict, they express themselves in propositions marked by historical cultures.

The tragic dimension of action is the place where the universal and the historical overlap and intersect.

Is it not this same dialectic, confronting the universal and the historical, that confers on "just," understood in terms of the force of the neuter adjective, its fundamental dynamic?

1. Studies

From the Moral to the Ethical
and to Ethics

Specialists in moral philosophy do not agree on how to apportion the meanings of the two terms "morality" and "ethics."[1] Etymology is no help in this regard, inasmuch as one of the terms comes from Latin, the other from Greek, and both refer in one way or another to the domain of moral behavior. Yet, if there is no agreement concerning the relationship between these two terms, whether it be hierarchical or some other form, there is agreement about the necessity for both terms. Seeking to orient myself as regards this difficulty, I propose taking the concept of morality as the basic term, assigning it a double function: that of designating, on the one hand, the region of norms, in other words, of principles about what is permitted and what prohibited, and, on the other, the feeling of obligation associated with the subjective aspect of the relation of a subject to such norms. Here, for me, is the fixed point, the hard core of what is at issue. And it is in relation to it that we have to determine our use of the term "ethics." I next see the term "ethics" as splitting in two, one branch designating something like the upstream side of norms—I shall speak of an anterior ethic—and the other branch designating something like the downstream side—what I will call posterior ethics. The general thrust of my presentation will consist in a double argument. On the one hand, I want to show that we have need of

1. The reader who knows my "little ethics" in *Oneself as Another* should see the present essay as something more than a clarification and something less than a *retractatio,* as the writers of late Latin antiquity would put it. Let us say it is a "rewriting." For those who do not know the earlier text, let me assure them that the present essay can be read on its own.

such a split, divided, differentiated concept of ethics, the anterior ethic pointing to the rootedness of norms in life and desire, the posterior ones aimed at inserting norms into concrete situations. I shall add a complementary thesis to this principal one: namely, that our only way to take possession of what precedes the norms intended by the anterior ethic is to make their contents appear on the plane of practical wisdom, which is that of the posterior ethics. In this way, the use of a single term—ethics—to designate the two sides of norms will be justified. Therefore, it is not by chance that we sometimes designate by "ethics" something like a meta-ethic, a second-degree reflection on norms, and sometimes positive practices that invite us to use the term in the plural and to accompany it with a qualifying adjective, as when we speak of medical ethics, legal ethics, business ethics, and so on. What is surprising is that this sometimes abusive and purely rhetorical use of the term "ethics" to designate regional ethics does not succeed in abolishing the noble sense of the term, reserved for what we can call a fundamental ethic like that of Aristotle's *Nicomachean Ethics* or Spinoza's *Ethics*.

I shall begin therefore with what shall appear *in fine* as the intermediary region between the anterior and the posterior ethics, the realm of norms. As I said above, I take this sense of the concept of morality as the principal reference and hard core of the whole problematic. The best starting point in this regard is to consider the predicate "obligatory" attached to what is permitted and what is forbidden. In this regard, it is legitimate to begin like G. E. Moore from the irreducible character of the relation of "ought" to "is." This predicate can be stated in several ways depending on whether it is taken absolutely (you must do this) or relatively (this would be better than that). But in both uses, the "ought" is irreducible to a fact. By assuming this, philosophers are only taking into account common experience, according to which there is a moral problem because there is something that ought to be done or that would be better to do than something else. If we now consider that this predicate can be associated with a wide variety of action sentences, it is legitimate to make the idea of norm more precise through that of a formalism. In this regard, Kantian moral philosophy can be taken, in its broadest sense, for an exact account of our common moral experience, one which holds that the only thing that can be taken as obligatory are maxims of action that can satisfy a test of universalization. Still, for all that, it is not necessary to take duty as the enemy of desire. The only candidates for the title of obligatory that are excluded are those that do not satisfy the stated criterion. In a minimal sense, the connection between obligation and formalism implies nothing more than a strategy of purgation aimed at preserving the legitimate uses of the predicating of obligation. Within these strict limits, it is legitimate to assume the categorical imperative in its most somber form: "Act only according to the maxim that says that you can at the same time will this maxim to become a universal law." This formula does not tell us how to discover such maxims, that is, proposed actions that would give a content to the form of duty.

Thus, the other side of the normative comes into play, namely, the positing of a subject of obligation, an obliged subject. Here we have to distinguish the imperative that applies to a subject obliged to fulfill such an obligation from the predicate "obligatory" that applies to actions and maxims of action. The imperative, as a relation between commanding and obeying, has to do with the subjective side of the norm, which we can call practical freedom, whatever may be said about the relation of this practical freedom to the idea of free causality over against determinism on the speculative plane. Moral experience requires nothing more than a subject capable of imputation, if we understand by "imputation" the capacity of a subject to designate itself, himself, or herself as the actual author of its, his, or her own acts. In a language less dependent on the letter of Kantian moral philosophy, I will say that a norm—whatever utility it may or may not have—calls for a being capable of entering into a practical symbolic order as that norm's counterpart, that is, one capable of recognizing in norms a legitimate claim to govern behavior. In turn, the idea of imputability, as a capacity, allows itself to be inscribed in the long enumeration of capacities through which I characterize what I will call the "capable human being" on the anthropological plane: capacities to speak, to act, to narrate. Imputability adds to this sequence the capacity to posit oneself as an agent.

If we now bring together the two halves of my analysis, namely, the objective norm and subjective imputability, we obtain the mixed concept of autonomy, auto-nomy. I will say that morality requires as a minimum the mutual positing of the norm as the *ratio cognoscendi* of the moral subject and imputability as the *ratio essendi* of the norm. To speak of autonomy is to posit the mutual determination of the norm and the obliged subject. Morality presupposes nothing more than a subject capable of positing itself in positing the norm that posits it as subject. In this sense, we can take the moral order to be self-referential.

FUNDAMENTAL ETHICS AS ANTERIOR ETHIC

Why, someone may ask, require of a moral philosophy of obligation, concerning which we admit that it is sufficient unto itself, that it be in this sense self-referential, a fundamental ethics, what I am calling here an anterior ethic to distinguish it from the applied ethics that diversify the other side of ethics, posterior ethics? The necessity of such a move is more easily seen if we start from the subjective side of moral obligation, from the feeling of being obligated. This marks the stitch between the realm of norms and that of life, of desire. As I said above, formalism does not entail a condemnation of desire. It neutralizes it as a criterion of evaluation applied to the maxims of action offered to moral judgment, the critical function being limited by Kant to the criterion of universalization. Yet the question of motivation remains intact, as the great chapter in Kant's own *Critique of Practical Reason* devoted to the question of respect, under the general heading of rational motives, bears witness. Respect, in my opinion, constitutes only one of the motives capable of inclining a moral subject to "doing his duty." It would be necessary to lay out the whole gamut, were this possible, of moral sentiments, as Max Scheler began to do in his *Formalism in Ethics and Non-formal Ethics of Values:* for example, shame, modesty, admiration, courage, devotion, enthusiasm, and veneration. I would give a place of honor to one strong sentiment, something like indignation, which is a negative intending of others' dignity as well as one's own dignity. Negatively, refusing humiliation expresses the recognition of what makes the difference between a moral and a physical subject, a difference called dignity, where dignity is an evaluative measure that our moral feeling directly grasps. The order of moral sentiments thus constitutes a vast affective domain irreducible to pleasure and pain. Perhaps we even need to go so far as to say that pleasure and pain as unmarked moral sentiments become morally qualified by their connection to some specifically moral sentiment, something that current language ratifies by speaking of moral pain and of the pleasure of doing one's duty. Why do we not like to do good to others? Why do we not take pleasure in acknowledging the dignity of history's humiliated ones?

What do the moral sentiments stitch together? The realm of norms and moral obligation, on the one hand, that of desire, on the other. This realm of desires was the object of a precise analysis in the opening chapters of Aristotle's *Nicomachean Ethics*. There we find a discourse structured in terms of *praxis,* something sorely lacking in Kant. Everything turns on the concept of *prohairesis,* the capacity for rational preference. This is the capacity to determine "this is worth more than that" and to act according to this preference. The concepts that precede it in the dialectical order, such as liking and disliking, or those that succeed it, such as deliberation, gravitate around this key concept. The intentional object of this conceptual chain is constituted by the predicate "good," which we may be tempted to oppose too rapidly to that of "obligation," which governs Kantian ethics. In my opinion, there is no need to oppose these two types of predicates. They do not belong to the same reflective level. The first one quite clearly belongs to the plane of norms, but the second one belongs to a more basic order, that of the desire that structures the whole of the practical field. That this capacity was rapidly absorbed in the context of Greek culture into an enumerating of excellences of action under the name virtues should neither surprise us nor hold us back. It should not surprise us insofar as we pass easily from rational preference to the idea of virtue by the intervention of the idea of *hexis* (*habitus,* "habit"), where virtue consists essentially in a way of acting under the guidance of rational preferences. The transition between the limited aims of practices (crafts, lifestyles, and so on) and the intending of a good life is ensured by the mediating concept of the *ergon,* the "task"—which orients a human life considered as a whole. The task of being human overflows and envelops every partial task that assigns a good intention to every practice. As for the enumerating of these excellences of action, which are the virtues, this must not bar the horizon of meditation and reflection. Each one of these excellences picks out its intended good against the background of an open-ended intention magnificently designated by the expression of a "good life" or, better, "living well." This open horizon is inhabited by our life projects, our anticipations of happiness, our utopias, in short by all the changing figures of what we take as signs of a fulfilled life. We shall return below to the question of the fragmentation of the ethical field by the distinct contours of the enumerated virtues. Projected against the horizon of a good life, these excellences are themselves open to all the kinds of rewriting found in a *Treatise on Virtues*, which I shall return to in the final part of this essay.

If it is in Aristotle that I find the most clearly outlined lineaments of such a fundamental ethics, I do not renounce the idea of finding something equivalent in Kant himself. Not only are the two approaches, which for didactic reasons get encapsulated under the labels of teleology and deontology, not rivals inasmuch as they belong to two distinct planes of practical philosophy, but they overlap at some significant points. The most noteworthy of these points is indicated by the Latin concept *voluntas,* which unfolds its history in a continuous manner from the medieval thinkers to the Cartesians, the Leibnizians, up to Kant himself. To be sure, this concept of the will, in which we can see the Latin heir of the Greek rational preference, is strongly marked in our cultural history by the Christian meditation on the bad will, on evil, a meditation that contributed to splitting apart modern and ancient moral philosophy. Yet the tie between a voluntary intention and the intending of a good life has not been broken. How could we forget the declaration that opens Kant's *Grounding for the Metaphysics of Morals:* "There is no possibility of thinking of anything at all in the world, or even out of it, which can be regarded as good without qualification, except a *good will.*"[2] To be sure, the remainder of this work leads to a drastic reduction of the predicate "good" to being a norm and to the criteria of universalization that validate it. But this reduction presupposes in a problematic way the preconception of something that would be the goodness of a good will.

2. Kant, *Grounding for the Metaphysics of Morals,* 7.

This preconception is in no way exhausted by its deontological reduction, its reduction to duty. One sign of resistance to this formalism is given in chapter 3 of book 1 of the *Critique of Practical Reason* where Kant takes into account the question of "The Incentives of Pure Practical Reason," that is, the "subjective principle," says Kant, of the determination of the will of a being whose reason is not already, in virtue of its nature, in necessary conformity with the fundamental law. I have already referred to this theme of moral sentiments. We need to return to it. What is at issue under this heading? What has "influence over the will," what inclines it to place itself under the law, or, as I said above, to enter into a symbolic order capable not only of constraining it to action in conformity to the law but of structuring, of informing, action? It is in terms of this second aspect—its structuring capacity—that moral sentiment indicates an empty place in the theory of praxis which, after Aristotle, is not really fully unfolded until we come to Hegel, principally in his *Philosophy of Right*.

A strong bond, which the scholarly tradition has obscured, thus joins the *prohairesis* of the *Nicomachean Ethics* and the vow to "live well" that crowns it to the concept of a good will in the *Grounding for the Metaphysics of Morals* and that of respect in the *Critique of Practical Reason*.

Allow me to add a final argument in favor of the subterranean kinship between these two approaches to the problem of a fundamental ethics that the tradition has frozen with the labels "teleological" and "deontological" ethics. This argument is drawn from the ultimate recourse Kant makes to the idea of the good in his *Religion within the Boundaries of Mere Reason*. This recourse seems discordant as regards a moral philosophy reputed to be hostile to the idea of the good, especially since we find it in a work that drew the most reproachful judgments against its author. That the idea of the good should return in the essay on radical evil should not surprise us. The problem posed by evil is, indeed, that of an inability to do good—a wound, an open sore at the heart of our wish to live well. The occasion for this recourse to the idea of the good is remarkable: at the moment of distinguishing radical evil from the intolerable idea of original sin, it becomes urgent to put up a block against the accusation that threatens to put the idea of a good will completely out of play. Kant does so by declaring that the propensity (*Anhang*) to evil does not affect the disposition (*Anlage*) to the good, which in turn makes possible the whole enterprise of a regenerating of the will that sums up the whole idea of "religion within the boundaries of mere reason." Thus, we rediscover the concept of a good will at the end of Kant's works, under the prodding of a meditation on evil, that is, precisely the theme that, in the wake of Christianity, was supposed to have divided the moral philosophy of modern and ancient philosophers.

That the moral philosophies of the ancients and moderns can rejoin, can recognize each other, and mutually greet each other in this concept is a possibility that stems neither from ethics nor from moral philosophy but from a philosophical anthropology that would make the idea of capacity one of its central concepts. The phenomenology of capacities that, for my part, I develop in the chapters of my *Oneself as Another* that precede my "little ethics" prepares the ground for that properly ethical capacity imputability, the capacity to recognize oneself as the actual author of one's own acts. This imputability can be associated in turn with the Greek concept of rational preference and the Kantian one of moral obligation. Indeed, it is from the focal point of this capacity that the "Greek" wish to live well arises and from where opens the "Christian" drama of the incapacity to do the good by oneself without an approbation coming from above, giving the "courage to be," another name for what has been called a disposition to the good, which is the very soul of the good will.

POSTERIOR ETHICS AS THE SITES OF PRACTICAL WISDOM

The moment has come to argue in favor of the second presupposition of this essay, namely, that the sole means of giving visibility and readability to the primordial ground of ethics is to project it onto the postmoral plane of applied ethics. This is the enterprise that in *Oneself as Another* I called practical wisdom.

In Kant as well as in Aristotle we can find signs of the necessity for this transfer from an anterior ethic to posterior ethics. Indeed, it is noteworthy that Kant should have believed it necessary to complete the stating of the categorical imperative by formulating three variations of the imperative that, when stripped of the terminology that scholarly expositions have carved in stone, orient obligation in the direction of three spheres of application: the self, others, the city. The first analogy between moral and natural law, following the first formulation, is aimed, within a philosophy that opposes ethics and physics, at underscoring the kind of regularity that brings together the legality of the moral realm and that of the physical one, the self-constancy over time that presupposes the respect for one's given word upon which rest promises, contracts, agreements, treaties. Ipseity is another name for this self-constancy. It is the formula for moral identity as opposed to the physical identity of what is always the same. To be sure, self-constancy represents only the subjective component of a promise and has to be put together with the respect for others in the exchange of expectations that concretely make up the promise. It is this other component of the promise that is signaled by the second formulation of the Kantian imperative, which requires that the person, in myself and in others, be treated as an end in itself and not merely as a means. Yet respect, as I suggested above, only constitutes one of the configurations of moral sentiment. I have proposed calling the structure common to all these dispositions favorable toward others that underlie the nearby relations of intersubjectivity "solicitude." We ought not to hesitate to include among these relations care for oneself, as a self-reflexive figure of this care for others. Finally, the obligation to hold oneself to be both subject and legislator in the city of ends can be interpreted in a broad sense as the general formula for relations having to do with citizenship in a state governed by the rule of law.

In turn, these still-general formulas which distribute the imperative into a plurality of spheres—self-constancy, solicitude for the neighbor, participation in sovereignty as a citizen—become concrete maxims for action only when taken up, reworked, and rearticulated in regional, applied ethics such as medical, legal, business, and environmental ethics in what is an open-ended series.

Aristotle's "Greek" ethics opposed a comparable program of multiplication and dispersion to fundamental evaluations placed under the sign of "virtue." His *Nicomachean Ethics* unfolds in a back-and-forth fashion between virtue and virtues. Reduced to itself, the discourse on virtue, even though constructed on the substantial ideas of reasonable preference and polarized by the idea of the good life, tends to close in on one formal feature common to every virtue, namely, the character of being the "mean," the craggy, just middle that separates each virtue into an excess and a default. As a result, only the rational reinterpretation of the figures of excellence in actions allows us to give a body, a substance, to the bare idea of virtue. This is why the enumeration of typical situations of practice and their corresponding excellence follows. In this regard, courage, temperance, liberality, kindness, and justice are the quintessential product of a shared culture, enlightened by a great literary tradition—Homer, Sophocles, Euripides, along with the masters of public speaking and other wise teachers, whether professional or not. The letter of these small treatises, which we read today with such pleasure, ought not, however, to arrest the movement of reinterpretation begun by these texts from the heart of their own culture. The understanding we still obtain, through reading these profiles of virtue, ought to invite us not only to re-read these treatises but to rewrite them to the benefit of a modern doctrine of virtues and vices.

Aristotle himself gave one key to these rereadings and rewritings in setting one intellectual virtue apart from those virtues he calls ethical: *phronesis*, which became "prudence" in Latin, which we may take as the matrix for all posterior ethics. It consists in a capacity, the aptitude, for discerning the right rule, the *orthos logos*, in difficult situations requiring action. The exercise of this virtue is inseparable from the personal quality of the wise human being—the *phronimos*—the sensible person.[3] There is a close tie between prudence and "singular things." In this sense, it is in applied ethics that the virtue of prudence is put to the test of practice. And in this regard, the same *phronesis* that is supposed to operate at the interior of the everyday practice of virtues ought also to preside over the reinterpretation of the table of virtues in the wake of modern treatises on the passions.

I would like to propose two examples, the one taken from the medical, the other from the judicial order, of such a redeployment

---

3. The distinction between fairness and justice offers a noteworthy example of this passage from the general norm to the right maxim in circumstances where the law is too general or, as we say today, in regard to difficult, or hard, cases.

of practical wisdom in regional ethics. Each of these applied ethics has its own rules, but their phronetic kinship, if I may be allowed such an expression, preserves a remarkable formal analogy between them at the level of forming judgments and making decisions. On both sides, it is a question of passing from a knowledge base constituted in terms of norms and theoretical knowledge to a concrete decision in some situation: a medical prescription in the one case, a judicial sentence in the other. And this application takes place through a singular judgment. The difference in situations, however, is considerable. On the medical side, it is suffering that gives rise to asking for care and the concluding of an agreement that binds the ill person and the physician. On the judicial side, the typical initial situation is one of conflict. It gives rise to a demand for justice and finds its rule-governed application in the trial court. Hence the difference between the two outcomes: prescription, sentence. Yet the progression to judgment is similar on both sides. The agreement to give care concluded between a physician and a patient can be placed under different sorts of rules. In the first place are those moral rules assembled in the code of medical ethics. There we read such rules as the obligation to preserve privacy, the right of the sick person to know the truth about his or her case, the requirement for informed consent before undertaking any risky treatment, and so on. Next come rules stemming from biological and medical knowledge, which the treatment in a particular clinical situation puts to the test of reality. Finally, there are administrative rules operating at the level of public health that govern the social treatment of disease. Such is the threefold framework for the concrete medical act leading to a concrete decision, the prescription and, in moving from one plane to another, the medical judgment or phronesis.

It is this movement that judgment in the judicial order allows us to articulate better inasmuch as it is so rigorously codified. The frame, I said, is the trial process. This makes clear the operations of argumentation and interpretation that lead to making the final decision, the sentence, also called the judgment. These operations are apportioned to multiple protagonists and governed by a strict procedure. Yet, as in the medical judgment, the stake is the application of a judicial rule to a concrete case, the case in question, in litigation. The application consists both in adapting the rule to the case, by way of qualifying the act as a crime, and in connecting the case to the rule, through a narrative description taken to be truthful. The argumentation that guides the interpretation of the norm as much as of the case draws upon codified resources for public discussion. But the decision remains singular: this crime, this accused, this victim, this sentence, all of which are crystallized in the word of justice pronounced in a singular situation.

These are the structural resemblances between two processes for applying a rule to a case and for the subsumption of a case under a rule. They are what ensure the resemblance between the two modes of decision making in the medical and the judicial realms. At the same time, these resemblances illustrate the movement from the anterior ethic, which is more fundamental than the norm, to applied ethics, which exceeds the resources of the norm.

To which feature of this fundamental ethic does medical ethics give visibility and readability? To solicitude, which asks that help be given to anyone in danger. But this solicitude is not made manifest except by traversing the filters of the medical secret, the patient's right to know about his or her case, and informed consent—all rules that confer an applied deontology on the agreement to give care.

As for the decision making that ends with the sentence in the setting of the judicial process, it incarnates in a concrete formulation the idea of justice that, short of any positive law, stems from the wish for a good life. One of my theses in my little ethics in *Oneself as Another* was that the ethical intention, at its deepest level of radicality, is articulated in a triad wherein the self, the nearby, and the distant other are equally honored: to live well, with and for others in just institutions. If medical ethics bases itself on the second term of this sequence, judicial ethics finds in the desire to live in just institutions the requirement that binds together judicial institutions and the idea of a good life. It is this wish to live in just institutions that finds visibility and readability in the word of justice pronounced by the judge in the application of norms that pertain to the hard core of private and public morality.

To conclude, we can take as equivalent the following two formulations. On the one hand, we can take morality as the plane of reference in relation to which a fundamental ethic that is anterior to it and an applied ethics that is posterior to it are defined. On the other hand, we can say that moral philosophy in its unfolding of private, juridical, and political norms constitutes the transition structure that guides the movement from the fundamental ethics to applied ethics, which gives moral philosophy visibility and readability on the plane of praxis. Medical and judicial ethics are exemplary in this regard, inasmuch as suffering and conflict constitute two typical situations that imprint praxis with a tragic stamp.

Justice and Truth

What I am going to propose is purely exploratory in nature. Its long-term aim is to justify the thesis that theoretical and practical philosophy are equal in rank, neither being a first philosophy in relation to the other but both being "second philosophy" in relation to what has been characterized by Stanislas Breton as a "meta-" function.[1] But it is not of this assuredly hypothetical metafunction that I want to speak today, but rather what I have called the equality in rank of these two second-order philosophies. To take hold of this thesis I propose taking the ideas of justice and truth as regulative ideas of the highest rank on the condition of standing second in relation to the metafunction. The goal of my argument will be attained if it can demonstrate two things: (1) that these two ideas can be posited independently of each other, the first figure of their equality; (2) that they intertwine in a strictly reciprocal way, the second figure. First, then, we must think justice and truth apart from each other; next, we need to think them in terms of a reciprocal or intersecting presupposition.

There is nothing revolutionary about this undertaking. It is situated in line with speculation about transcendental categories, their distinction and their mutual convertibility. By placing ourselves under this ancient patronage, at the same time we make apparent the absence of the idea of the beautiful in our enterprise,

---

1. In the centenary number of the *Revue de métaphysique et de morale,* I offered a plea in favor of this reformulation of metaphysics in terms of this "metafunction," wherein are conjoined the "Great Kinds" of Plato's last dialogues and Aristotelian speculation on the plurality of meanings of Being and of being. See my "From Metaphysics to Moral Philosophy."

an absence whose mending would no doubt call for a comparable meditation concerning the irreducibility of this category and its interweaving with the other two. In this sense, my inquiry suffers from a recognized and acknowledged limitation.

The immediate objection this undertaking encounters has to do with the replacement of the good by the just at the summit of the practical order. To which I reply that as a first approximation these two eminent predicates can be taken as synonyms. Their actual relation, which I already want to characterize as dialectical, will appear over the course of my argument. For the moment, let me indicate that it will turn out to be easier (for a purely dialectical argument) to justify, on the one hand, the claim of the just to occupy the summit of the practical hierarchy and, on the other hand, its imbrication in the pursuit of truth as itself constituting a practical project, or let us say a theoretical practice. The modern character of a reevaluation of the tradition about transcendentals will consist in this twofold justification, a reevaluation bearing on their distinction and their mode of convertibility.

As a first step, I shall take the idea of justice for my reference and plead in favor of the supremacy of the just, thought about apart from the true, in the hierarchy of regulative ideas of the practical order. Second, I shall undertake to demonstrate in what specific way the just in a way enrolls the true in its circumscription.

SUPREMACY OF THE JUST IN THE PRACTICAL FIELD

In preparing the first stage of my analysis, I thought of John Rawls's assertion at the beginning of his *Theory of Justice* that "justice is the first virtue of social institutions, as truth is of systems of thought."[2] Two things are simultaneously affirmed here: the disjunction between justice and truth, and the pairing of justice and institutions. The second part of his thesis seems to compromise the ambition of the first part, which is to promote justice to the summit of practice. It will be important therefore to show in what way the two halves of the thesis are interdependent.

2. Rawls, *Theory of Justice*, 3.

I shall try to demonstrate the first part of Rawls's definition using resources from the part on ethics in my *Oneself as Another*, with an eye to ensuring the eminent status of justice. I propose two intersecting readings of the structure of morality. A horizontal reading will lead me to derive the constitution of the self from the following threefold structure: the wish for a good life, with and for others, in just institutions. A vertical reading will then follow the ascending progression that, starting from a teleological approach guided by the idea of living well, traverses the deontological approach where the norm, obligation, prohibition, formalism, and procedures dominate, to find its end on the plane of practical wisdom which is that of *phronesis*, of prudence as the art of a fair decision in situations of uncertainty and conflict, hence in the tragic setting of action. According to this intersecting reading, justice finds itself situated at the intersection of two axes, since it first figures in third place in the threefold structure in which I have joined the terms, and it remains the third category named when this threefold structure is transposed from one plane to another. Justice can thus be taken as the highest category of the practical field if we can show that there is a progression on the horizontal plane from the first to the third term of the basic threefold structure, and equally on the vertical axis, where the idea of justice culminates in that of fairness. This is the thesis I now want to argue for in spelling out the kind of progression that operates along these two axes.

The triad that applies to the horizontal axis does not consist of a simple juxtaposition of the self, the neighbor, and the more distant other. This progression is in fact that of the dialectical constituting of the self. The wish to live well roots the moral project in life, in desire and a sense of what is lacking, as the grammatical structure of wishing indicates. But without the mediation of the other two terms, this wish for a good life would lose itself in the nebulousness of different figures of happiness, without being able to claim equality with the well-known Platonic idea of the good that Aristotle liked to make fun of. I readily admit that the short circuit between the wish for a good life and happiness is the result of misunderstanding the dialectical constitution of the self. This dialectical constitution means that the path to carrying out the wish for a good life passes through the other. My formula from *Oneself as Another* is in this sense a primitive ethical formulation that subordinates the reflexivity of the self to the mediation of the otherness of the other. But the dialectical structure of this wish for a good life would remain incomplete were it to stop with the other of interpersonal relations, with the other known in friendship. What is still lacking is the progression, the unfolding, the coronation constituted by the recognition of the other who is the stranger. This step from the nearby to the distant other, of the apprehension of the near as distant, if you will, is also the step from friendship to justice. The friendship of private relationships stands out against the background of the public relation of justice. Before any formalization, any universalization, any procedural treatment, the quest for justice is for a just distance among all human beings. This just distance is a mean between the too little distance belonging to so many dreams of a fusion of emotions and the excess of distance that underlies arrogance, distrust, and hate of the stranger as someone unknown. Thus, I see in the virtue of hospitality the most apt emblematic expression of this cultivating of a just distance.

In relation to this search for a just distance we can begin to think about the first tie between justice and institutions. The most general function of any institution is to ensure the *nexus* between what is one's own, the nearby, and the distant in something like a city, a republic, a commonwealth. In this still-undifferentiated sense of an institution, this *nexus* can be said to be "instituted," that is, established.

Before considering the progression from the idea of justice on the vertical axis that leads to the preeminence of practical wisdom and, with it, the idea of justice as fairness, let me make a comment about the relationship between kindness as a good and justice. This relation is not one of identity or of difference. Such goodness characterizes the deepest aim of desire and stems in this way from the grammar of wishing. Justice as a just distance between the self and the other, encountered as someone distant, is the fully developed figure of this goodness. Under the heading of justice, the good becomes a common good. In this sense we can say that justice develops the goodness that it encompasses into itself.

Yet the moral primacy of the idea of justice is not fully recognized except at the end of the second axis of the constitution of morality. Under the sign of the norm, the governing category of the deontological point of view, justice passes through the test of universalization, of formalization, and of procedural abstraction. In this way it is brought to the level of the categorical imperative. Transposed to the formal plane, the internal progression of the triad of what is one's own, what is near, and what distant, rejoins the three formulations of the Kantian imperative, which Kant presents in the *Groundwork*. When so transposed to the plane of the norm, this basic triad becomes that of the autonomy of the self, respect for the humanity in the person of oneself and others, and the projection of the city of ends in which everyone would be both subject and legislator.

It is in relation to the task of establishing this city of ends that the tie between institution and justice can be articulated a second time. It can be represented by the notion of "orders of recognition" proposed by Jean-Marc Ferry in his *Les puissances de l'expérience*. These designate the systems and subsystems among which our multiple allegiances find themselves apportioned. And it is at this level that the discussion can be pursued between the upholders of a unitary conception of the principles of justice, on the model of Rawls's *A Theory of Justice*, at the price of a dramatically procedural reduction of these principles, and the upholders of a pluralistic conception of instances of justice, such as Michael Walzer and the communitarians. Even if we break things into "spheres of justice," to use Walzer's terminology, the idea of justice remains the highest regulative idea, if only as a rule of vigilance concerning the boundaries of each of these spheres, indicated by the passion for domination that tends to transgress them. And across the procedural rules that preside over the division of roles, tasks, and burdens, we continue to hear claims of the most disfavored in the cases of unequal distributions. In this way, the filiation of justice according to the norm and justice starting from something wished for is markedly evident.

A few words still need to be said about the way in which the passage from the deontological point of view to that of practical wisdom leads to an ultimate transformation in the idea of justice. This has to do with the difficult decisions that have to be made in circumstances marked by incertitude and conflict under the sign of the tragic dimension of action, whether it be a question of a conflict among norms of apparently equal weight, of a conflict between respect for a norm and solicitude for the persons involved, of a choice that would not be one between black and white but between gray and gray, or, finally, of a choice where the line between the bad and the worst is not clear. Stating the law in the singular circumstances of a trial, hence within the framework of the judicial form of institutions of justice, constitutes a paradigmatic example of what is meant here by the idea of justice as fairness or equity. Aristotle defined it in the closing pages of his treatise on justice in his *Nicomachean Ethics:* "this is the nature of the equitable: it is a corrective to the law, where the law is not clear because of its generality" (1137b12–13). This text allows us to see that it is not only when faced with what Ronald Dworkin calls "hard cases" that justice needs to be fair, but in all those circumstances where moral judgment is placed in a singular situation and where the decision is marked by the stamp of some innermost conviction.

This is the point where the course of justice reaches completion. It can be taken as the highest practical rule insofar as it is both the last term of the ternary relation initiated by the wish to live well and the last term of the move from level to level that ends with practical wisdom. As for the relation to the good, it can be summed up in the formula proposed in our examination of the basic threefold structure: the good designates the rootedness of justice in the wish to live well, but it is the just that, in unfolding the double—horizontal and vertical—dialectic of this avowal, places the stamp of prudence on goodness.

THE IMPLICATION OF THE TRUE IN THE JUST

The time has come to say in what sense truth is implicated in justice. It does not seem to me that it would be a helpful path to look for truth on the side of the different successive statements that mark out the discourse we have been presenting, whether it is a question of the initial threefold structure or the chain of teleological, deontological, and prudential points of view. To be sure, someone might well ask me if I take what I have said here to be true. But to take it as true would consist in nothing more than a reiterating of such practical propositions along with a yes of assent to them. And this would have no other source than the force of the self-positing of the wish to live well as a practical, not a theoretical, instance. The rule of justice in terms of the three successive assertions I have proposed, culminating in the idea of the just as equitable, as fair, has no other truth than its force as an injunction. In this sense, I distance myself from those Anglo-American moral philosophers who have pleaded for the idea of a moral truth. I understand their reasons for doing so. They want to preserve moral propositions from a subjective or collective arbitrariness, or from a naturalistic reduction of so-called moral facts to social or biological facts. However, the threat of the arbitrary is warded off first by the dialectical constitution that carries the good to the level of the just thanks to the mediation of the nearby or distant other. It is warded off a second time for the same reason that protects moral reflection from any naturalistic reductions. This reason is nothing other than the preservation of the difference between what Charles Taylor rightly calls "strong evaluations" and natural facts or events. The correlation that he establishes in the first part of his *Sources of the Self* applies straightaway to the self-affirmation of the self and its orientation among the different figures of the good. The self and the good are simultaneously and mutually constituted. Therefore, there is no supplementary or distinct truth that needs to be sought for the injunction of the good and the just.

But if a truthful dimension is to be sought for the ideas of goodness and justice, it lies in another direction than that attached to the idea of a moral truth. Instead, we have to look on the side of the anthropological presuppositions of the entry into the moral order. These presuppositions are the ones in virtue of which human beings are held to be capable of receiving the injunction of the just. It is a question therefore about what human beings are in relation to their mode of being, what they have to be if they are to be a subject open to a moral, juridical, or political problematic or, let us more broadly say, one of values. Let me illustrate my thesis by the difference in status that Kant establishes between the idea of imputability and that of autonomy. Imputability comes from the *Critique of Pure Reason*. It is an existential proposition that figures in the thesis of the Third Cosmological

Antinomy and an implication of the affirmation that human beings can make things happen in the course of the world, can introduce beginnings into the course of the world. This is another
name for the free spontaneity in virtue of which action is open
to praise or blame, because some human being is said to be its
actual author (*Urheber*). It is this assertion of imputability and
not of autonomy that, thanks to its belonging to the theoretical
field, is capable of truth. Autonomy is of another order. It rests
on the connection between freedom and the law following an a
priori implication that practical reason makes manifest. Whatever may be said about the well-known *factum rationis* by which
Kant characterizes the implication constitutive of autonomy, he
does not base autonomy, as a practical category, on imputability,
as a "physical" category, in a nonreductionistic sense of the term.

I want next to show how this Kantian idea of imputability can
be distributed over the three teleological, deontological, and prudential levels to which successively belong the three figures of justice we have considered as the wish, the norm, and the prudential
judgment. There are three figures of imputability to which correspond three modes of truth.

On the teleological level of a wish for a good life in just institutions are the existential modes of the capable human being, recognized by way of the different answers to the question *who?* Who
speaks? Who acts? Who recounts? Who holds him- or herself
responsible for the course of his or action? Such answers are all
affirmations having to do with abilities. I can speak, act, recount,
recognize myself accountable for the effects of acts for which I
acknowledge myself to be the author. In short, the existential
theme correlative to the wish to live well is the self-affirmation of
the capable human being. This idea of a capacity is therefore the
first figure of imputability, as an existential proposition.

And this presupposition can be said to be true. But in what
sense of true and false? To say something is true admits a polysemy correlative to the domain considered. The significant break,
which follows from an analysis I draw from Jean Ladrière, passes
between action and natural phenomena placed under laws said
to be laws of nature, following subsumption rules corresponding to different types of explanation. Action, on the contrary,
is understood as the theme of a narrative. This is putting things

quickly, too quickly, but it brings me to my principal assertion, namely, that the truthful dimension that has to do with those powers that specify the general idea of a human capacity is *attestation*. I talked at length about the epistemic status of attestation in *Oneself as Another*, and Jean Greisch has generously helped me clarify what still remained equivocal in my recourse to this key idea. Essentially, it is a belief, a *Glauben*, in a non-doxic sense of this term, if we keep the term *doxa* for a lesser degree of *episteme* in the order of natural phenomena and also in that of those human facts open themselves to being treated as observable facts. The requirement for verification and the test of refutability correspond to this sense of the idea of truth, following Karl Popper. But the belief belonging to attestation is of another nature. It has to do with confidence. Its contrary is suspicion, not doubt, or it is doubt as suspicion. It cannot be refuted but can be challenged. And it can be reestablished and reinforced only by a new recourse to attestation, eventually aided by some gracious acts.

This is the first correlation between justice and truth. My wish to live in just institutions is correlative with the attestation that I am capable of this wish to live well, which distinguishes me from other natural beings.

A second correlation between an existential judgment and an evaluative one is found at the deontological level, where strong evaluations take on the form of the formal, universal, procedural norm. The technical notion of imputability referred to by Kant within the framework of the Third Cosmological Antinomy corresponds to this plane, hence as the theoretical contrary of the practical idea of autonomy. I propose making this new use of imputability more precise by specifying it in terms of another sort of capacity that I have already articulated in terms of the capacity to act. The idea of this capacity of another order was suggested to me by Thomas Nagel's *Equality and Partiality*. He says that it is the capacity to adopt two standpoints with respect to ourselves or to others. Let me cite this passage from his book, entirely written in the vocabulary of capacity:

> Most of our experience of the world, and most of our desires, belong to our individual points of view: We see things *from here*, so to speak. But we are also able to think about the world in abstraction

from our particular position in it—in abstraction from who we are. . . . Each of us begins with a set of concerns, desires, and interests of his own, and each of us can recognize that the same is true of others. We can then remove ourselves in thought from our particular position in the world and think simply of all those people, without singling out as *I* the one we happen to be.[3]

This capacity therefore does not have to do with the order of action, following the analogy of action that I proposed in *Oneself as Another*. It refers more to the old Socratic adage concerning the examined life. This presupposes anthropologically the capacity to accomplish the act of abstraction that puts in place what Nagel calls "an impersonal point of view," taking up a theme first stated in his *View from Nowhere*. In this regard the capacity to juxtapose personal and impersonal points of view with respect to one's own life is the ontological presupposition of the Kantian imperative. We can see without difficulty how the existential assertion and moral obligation intertwine:

> But since the impersonal standpoint does not single you out from anyone else, the same must be true of the values arising in other lives. If you matter impersonally so does everyone.[4]

In this way, we arrive at the assertion: "every life counts and none is more important than any other." Is this an assertion stemming from the order of truth or from that of the just? An assertion or an obligation? I would say that it is a mixture of the orders of fact and right. But the fact here is nothing other than the capacity to adopt the impersonal point of view; better, the capacity to negotiate between the personal and the impersonal points of view. Yet we are already within the sphere of moral judgment with what Charles Taylor would call the strong evaluation included within the judgment of importance according to which every life counts and none is more important than any other. The capacity to adopt the impersonal point of view thus is not distinguished from the capacity to balance the judgments of importance that we all make about everyone else. The ethical significance of the assertion is certainly dominant and hardly differs from the second formulation of

3. Nagel, *Equality and Partiality*, 10.
4. Ibid., 11.

the Kantian imperative, any more than from Rawls's second principle of justice: to ameliorate the minimal share in the case of unequal distributions. Yet the frankly moral proposition that makes respect an unconditional obligation is based on the ontological presupposition that individuals are capable of the impersonal point of view that opens the moral horizon of the equalitarian principle of the theory of justice. Impartiality as the capacity to transcend the individual point of view and equality as the obligation to maximize the minimal share are combined in a mixed judgment that one can do what one ought and ought to do what one can.

This division of the judgment into an "I can" and a "you must" is essential to the evaluation we can make of equalitarian utopias. For the dramatic aspect of the conflict between standpoints is played out at the level of capacities and not that of obligations. At the level of capacities, there remain two points of view, and the conflict has to do with what we can and cannot do. The ability to feel the suffering of others, to sympathize with them, does not have to do with the order of commandment but with that of a disposition. And human beings are divided within themselves between these two points of view, which stem less from the capacity than from the ability to make compromises. It is precisely because moral and political behavior has to take varying abilities to compromise into account that the virtue of justice is a virtue. Considered from the point of view of the open conflict between our two points of view, such behavior aims, as Plato saw better than did Aristotle, at restoring unity there where our capacities leave us divided within ourselves. Let me cite Nagel again:

> The question is, how can we put ourselves back together? The political problem, as Plato believed, must be solved within the individual soul if it is to be solved at all. This does not mean that the solution will not deal with interpersonal relations and public institutions. But it means that such "external" solutions will be valid only if they give expression to an adequate response to the division of the self, conceived as a problem for each individual.[5]

Perhaps you are struck as I was by the fact that this return from the imperative of respect to the capacity of impartiality not only

5. Ibid., 16.

leads to giving a kind of ascetic anthropological dimension to morality but, by pointing out the conflictual situation connected to the confrontation between points of view, gives the moral demand for equality a new depth that points Kant's—and even Aristotle's—theory of justice back to Plato at that point where the division that justice aims to correct runs through each individual, divides each soul. It is thanks to the anthropological consideration of these two points of view that the decisive question becomes clear: "How to rediscover our unity. That is the question."

To conclude these remarks devoted to the intersection of the point of view of truth and that of the normative, I will say that the connotation of truthfulness attached to the assertion of a capacity for impartiality is still, as it was at the ethical stage of morality, a question of a truth of attestation, with its double character of belief opposed to suspicion and confidence opposed to skepticism. Attestation has only been elevated to a higher degree at the same time that morality has passed from the wish for a good life to the requirement for universality. The rule to universalize the maxim receives the support of the belief that I can change my point of view, raise myself from the individual to the impersonal point of view. I believe that I am capable of impartiality at the price of a conflict between the two points of view of which I am capable.

What truth claims do we find connected with practical wisdom? This is the question with which I shall end this section of my remarks. I propose that we concentrate for a moment on the epistemological aspect of the procedures for the application of the norm to a particular case, taking as our touchstone the test represented by the formation of a judgment about what Dworkin has called hard cases in the setting of the law court. Hence it is within the juridical sphere that we shall linger for a moment, but I hope to show that the tribunal is not the only place where the analysis we are going to consider applies. The analysis of the penal judgment shows that what we can call an application of the law consists in something other than the subsumption of a particular case under a rule. In this regard, the practical syllogism consists in the didactic packaging of a quite complex process of adapting to each other two parallel processes of interpretation: the interpretation of the facts of what happened, which in the final analysis is of a narrative order, and the interpretation of the norm with regard to the question of figuring out what formulation, at the price of what extension, even what invention, is capable of "sticking" to the facts. This process involves a back-and-forth movement between two levels of interpretation—the narrative of the facts, the juridical reasoning about the law—to the point where what Dworkin calls a point of equilibrium is produced, which we can characterize as a mutual "fit" between two processes of interpretation, one narrative, the other juridical. Establishing this fit that makes up the application of the norm to the case presents, from the epistemological point of view, an inventive and a logical face. The inventive face has to do as much with the construction of the narrative chain of causes and effects as with the legal reasoning. The logical face has to do with the structure of argumentation stemming from a logic of the probable.

What kind of truth is at issue here? It is no longer in terms of capacity that we have to formulate it, but rather in terms of convention. It is a truth that fits, that is, a kind of characteristic situational sense of what is obvious that merits being called a conviction, an inner conviction, even if the decision is made in the judge's chambers. Can we speak then of objectivity? No, not in the constative sense of this term. It is a question rather of the certitude that in this situation this is the best decision, what has to be done. It is not a matter of constraint; the force of this conviction has nothing to do with a factual determination. It is the sense *hic et nunc* of what obviously fits, of what ought to be done.

We have taken an example drawn from the judicial sphere, but I would like to suggest that several other disciplines intertwine interpretation and argumentation in a comparable fashion and that these disciplines also have their hard cases. I think first of all of medical judgments when confronted with extreme situations, principally those having to do with the beginning and end of life. I also have in mind historical judgment when it is necessary to evaluate the respective weight of individual actions and of collective forces. Finally, I shall mention political judgment when the head of a government is confronted with the obligation to establish an order of priority among heterogeneous values whose arrangement will lead to a program for good government. In all these disciplines, the same logic of the probable consolidates the risky search for a conviction that will authorize making a moral judgment in some particular situation. We can then rightly speak of a justness added to justice.

We have considered three levels of truth, corresponding to the three levels of imputability. And in each case it was a question of what we could call a truthfulness implied in the moral judgment.

Have I succeeded in making plausible my initial thesis that the true and the just are of equal rank, even if in a second movement they mutually imply each other? My argument will remain incomplete so long as I have not demonstrated that truth, in turn, which has an autonomous status within its own order, fulfills the constitutive course of its own meaning only with the help of justice.

Autonomy and Vulnerability

The announced title for my contribution to our seminar this year—"Who Is the Subject of Rights [*droit*]?"—contains the question that encompasses all the perplexities we are going to have to confront this year.[1] The subject of rights is both the major *presupposition* of every juridical investigation and the *horizon* of judicial practice. It is this paradox that I want to set before you during this hour. To give this paradox its full force, in considering the movement between a condition of possibility and a task, I propose taking as my guide the pair autonomy and vulnerability, which you have placed at the head of the list of contributions this academic year. Autonomy is indeed the prerogative of the subject of rights, but it is vulnerability that makes autonomy remain a condition of possibility that judicial practice turns into a task. Because as a hypothesis human beings are autonomous, they must become so. We are not the first people to be confronted with this paradox. For Kant, autonomy appears in two places: first, in the *Critique of Practical Reason*, as the a priori connection between freedom and the law, freedom being the *ratio essendi* of the law, while the law is the *ratio cognoscendi* of freedom; it also appears a second time in a more militant piece, *What Is Enlightenment?* There autonomy

1. This was the opening lecture for a seminar at the Institut des hautes études sur la justice, presented 6 November 1995. It was first published in A.-M. Dillens, ed., *La philosophie dans la cite: Homage à Hélène Ackermans*, Publications des facultés universitaires Saint-Louis, 73 (Brussels: Publications des facultés universitaires Saint-Louis, 1997), 121–41; then again in *Rendiconti dell'Accademia nazionale dei lincei* (Rome, 1997), 585–606; and in A. Garapon and D. Salas, eds., *La justice et la mal* (Paris: Odile Jacob, 1997), 163–84.

is the task for political subjects called on to escape their state of tutelage, of "minority," with the cry *sapere aude*, "dare to think for yourself!" It is from the perspective of this paradox that I want to speak of the idea of a project of autonomy.

Here is how we shall proceed:

Degree by degree, I am going to formulate the paradox of autonomy and vulnerability. For the requirements of this analytic task, I am going to examine in succession different degrees of the idea of autonomy and set each stage in correspondence with a specific figure of vulnerability, or, as I prefer to say, of fragility. I hope in this way to make clear why there is a paradox, and why the human condition contains such a paradox. Paradox, after all, shares the same situation of thought with the antinomy, that is, that two contrary theses equally resist being refuted and have therefore to be held in common or both be abandoned. But while the terms of autonomy belong to two different universes of discourse, the terms of our paradox meet in one and the same universe of discourse. Thus, in the old antinomy of freedom and determinism, the thesis comes from the moral universe and the antithesis from the physical universe under the banner of determinism. Philosophy can only divide them and confine each to its own order. But this is not the case with the paradox of autonomy and fragility. They are opposed to each other in the same universe of thought. It is the same human being who is both of these things from different points of view. What is more, not simply opposed to each other, our two terms go together: the autonomy in question is that of a fragile, vulnerable being. And this fragility would be something pathological if we were not called on to become autonomous, because we are already so in some way. Here we have the difficulty we have to confront. We can assume that a paradox like this will not allow for a speculative solution, unlike an antinomy (one more difference between them), but calls for a practical mediation, a militant practice like that conveyed by Kant's *sapere aude*. But whereas Kant was addressing himself to enlightened human beings—in a state of "voluntary servitude," to recall a phrase of La Boétie—the adverse term we have to consider over against autonomy presents passive features not comparable beyond the human sphere and, let me quickly add, not comparable beyond the social and political sphere. This precision adds something to our difficulty. If Kant could still treat complacency about being in tutelage as a voluntary choice, as a bad maxim of action, and hence attack it in the name of universal features of humanity, the figures of vulnerability or fragility that we are going to consider bear particular marks, common to our modernity, that force us to combine considerations on the modern condition and even the extremely contemporary one with features that can be taken, if not as universal, at least as long term and very long term, following the example of the prohibition of incest. Hannah Arendt already ran into this epistemological difficulty where the fundamental and the historical clash when she was writing *The Human Condition*.[2] It is not one of the least aspects of this paradox that there is more of the fundamental on the side of autonomy, at least in what it presupposes, whose contemporary indications are precisely what disturb us and press us to shift autonomy from the plane of the fundamental toward that of the historical.

Here then is the order that I propose to follow in composing the idea of the project of autonomy degree by degree. As in the text I placed first in my collection *The Just*, precisely under the title "Who Is the Subject of Rights?" I shall begin as far away as possible from the ethico-juridical plane, where the idea of autonomy reaches its full deployment; that is, I shall start from the level of philosophical anthropology, where the general question can be summed up in the following terms: What kind of being is a human being that he or she can give rise to the problematic of autonomy? By proceeding in this way, we start from those features least marked by contemporary changes, hence from features best anchored in our common human condition. And at each stage I shall point out corresponding features of fragility, in order to sharpen and progressively draw together the paradox of the idea of a project of autonomy.

I shall begin therefore—with no more delay—with the theme of the capable human being concerning which we shall see later the extension to the ethico-juridical through the idea of imputability.

The strength of this vocabulary concerning capacities, power, strength, was recognized by Aristotle as *horexis*, by Spinoza as

---

2. Unfortunately, her book was translated into French with the title *Condition de l'homme moderne*, no doubt in order to offend André Malraux!

conatus. I like to invoke Spinoza not only because he defined every finite substance by its effort to exist and preserve itself in being but because he situates the concept of potentiality in his *Theological-Political Treatise* as a direct extension of his ontology of *conatus*, opposing it to the *potestas* of Hobbes and Machiavelli. From a phenomenological point of view, this capacity to do something is expressed in the multiple domains of human intervention through the mode of different abilities: the ability to speak, to act on the course of things and to influence other protagonists of an action, the ability to gather one's own life into an intelligible and acceptable narrative. To this bundle of abilities we shall have later to add that of taking oneself for the actual author of one's acts, the heart of the idea of *imputability*. But before taking up the correlative modes of incapacity that make up the basis of fragility, which can thus be called basic, it is important to indicate the connection between the content of an affirmation indicated by the notion of being able to do something and the very form of the applicable affirmation. Power, I will say, affirms itself, declares itself. This connection between affirmation and power needs to be emphasized. It governs all the reflexive forms by which a subject can designate him- or herself as the one who can. But this simple, direct affirmation of a power to act already presents a noteworthy epistemological feature that cannot be proven, demonstrated, but can only be attested. This is indicative of a kind of belief that unlike the Platonic *doxa* is not some inferior form of *episteme*. Like the Kantian *Glauben*, which the author of the first *Critique* says, in the well-known introduction to that work, that he has put in place of *Wissen*, this is to accredit a practical conviction, a confidence in one's own capacity, which can be confirmed only through being exercised and through the approbation others grant to it (the word "sanction" finds its first connotation here, that of approbation). Attestation/sanction thus upholds the ability to act in language. Its contrary is not doubt but suspicion—or doubt as suspicion. And we overcome such suspicion only by a leap, a *sursum*, that other people may encourage, accompany, assist by having confidence in us—by an appeal to responsibility and autonomy, which we shall rediscover later to be the place of all pedagogy, all education, be it moral, juridical, or political. So let us take this connection between affirmation and ability to act as something to build on.

Remaining faithful to my claim never to lose sight of the paradoxical character of my theme for discussion, let me now say something about the corresponding figures of fragility. If the basis of autonomy can be described in terms of the vocabulary of ability, it is in that of inability or a lesser ability that human fragility first expresses itself. It is first as a speaking subject that our mastery appears to be threatened and always limited. This power is never complete, never fully transparent to itself. All psychoanalysis stems from this. But in a juridical perspective, we cannot overemphasize this major incapacity. Does not the law rest on the victory language gains over violence? Let me recall here Eric Weil's introduction to his *Logique de la philosophie* and the alternative he proposes there: violence or discourse. To enter the circle of discourse as one with legal expertise is to enter the domain of agreements, contracts, exchanges, and, in a more striking manner for you judges, the universe of the trial process, that is, of the debate made up of a confrontation of arguments, a war of words. What immediately comes to mind is the fundamental inequality among human beings when it comes to mastering such language, an inequality that is not so much a natural given as a perverse cultural effect, once the inability to speak well results in effectively being expelled from the sphere of discourse. In this regard, one of the first forms of the equality of opportunity has to do with equality on the plane of being able to speak, explain, argue, discuss. Here the historical forms of fragility are more significant than the basic, fundamental ones, having to do with finitude in general, which means that no one ever completely masters the use of language. These acquired, cultural, and in this sense historical acquisitions call for more thought than does any talk about the finitude of language, which could lead us to other important considerations having to do with the plurality of languages, translation, and other difficulties concerning the use of language. The picture becomes even more complex if we take into account the connection between affirmation and ability. The confidence I place in my power to act is a part of this very power. To believe that I can is already to be capable. The same thing applies to the figures of inability and in the first place to those having to do with an inability to speak. To believe oneself unable to speak is already to be linguistically disabled, to be excommunicated so to speak. And it is just this dreadful handicap—of an incapacity redoubled by a fundamental doubt concerning one's ability to speak, and even tripled by a lack of approbation, sanction, confidence, and aid accorded by others to speak for oneself—that you as attorneys and judges are confronted with: being excluded from language is a handicap that we can well call basic.

I shall not say more here about these inabilities that redouble the modes of our being unable to do something. I prefer instead to concentrate on the ability and inability to speak that constitute one of the major stakes in those professions like yours and my own that depend on language. I shall confine myself to a rapid discussion of those fragilities in the order of action that are directly connected to a pedagogy of responsibility. Here the incapacities humans inflict on one another, on the occasion of multiple interactions, get added to those brought about by illness, old age, and infirmities, in short, by the way the world is. They imply a specific form of power, a power-over that consists in an initial dissymmetric relation between the agent and the receiver of the agent's action. In turn, this dissymmetry opens the way to all the forms of intimidation, of manipulation, in short to those kinds of instrumentalization that corrupt service relations among humans. Here we need to take into consideration the kinds of unequal distribution of the ability to act, especially those that result from hierarchies of command and authority in societies based on efficiency and competition like our own. People do not simply lack power; they are deprived of it. In modern societies where activity, occupation, employment, and work tend to be confused with one another, it is principally in regard to perverted relations of work, leisure, and unemployment that a sociology of action would be required in order to give a precise content to an anthropological theme like the one Hannah Arendt develops to deal with the relation between labor, work, and action in her *Human Condition*. It is here above all that the historical is by far what is most significant in comparison with the fundamental, the existential.

I shall not speak further about the idea of the capable human being and the pairing of capacities and incapacities, whence comes the most elementary form of the paradox of autonomy and vulnerability. Instead, I want next to consider two corollaries of our basic theme, which will point the way toward the ethico-juridical components of this same paradox.

It seems to me that it is difficult to speak of autonomy without also talking about identity. But we can do so from two different points of view: First of all, from the point of view in relation to time, where we speak of a *narrative identity*, and then from the perspective that marks the singularity of *personal identity*, which cannot be replaced by something else.

I shall speak quickly about narrative identity, having dealt with this topic at length elsewhere. And I will do so by placing the principal accent on the fragile side of this temporal structure of identity.

Let me recall the conceptual network in which I have formulated this notion of a narrative identity. In general terms, under the heading of identity we seek to spell out those features that allow us to recognize something as being the same. But in doing so, we in fact pose two different questions, depending on the way in which we take one and the same word. Applied to things, the word "same" in its first sense is equivalent to seeking a permanence in time, an immutability of things. This first sense is important here inasmuch as, if I can put it this way, we are like a thing ourselves in some ways. I have in mind the permanence of our genetic code or our fingerprints. This structural permanence has a corollary: the identity of the same thing over the course of some development—the acorn and the oak tree are one and the same tree. In this sense, we can recognize ourselves in paging through a photo album, from childhood to adulthood. What we call our character corresponds closely to this first sense of identity. But as soon as we pass to the psychological domain of sense experience, desires, and beliefs, we are confronted with a variability that led philosophers such as Hume and Nietzsche to call into question the existence of a permanent me that fits the criteria for sameness. Moral philosophers, on their side, have deplored the instability of moods, passions, convictions, and the like. And yet we cannot stop with this negative verdict. In spite of change, we expect other people to vouch for their acts by being the same people who did something yesterday and who must today account for them and, tomorrow, bear their consequences. But is it a question here of the same kind of identity? Must we not, in taking promises as our model—the basis for every contract, agreement, pact—speak of something like self-constancy despite changes, a constancy in the sense of keeping one's word? Here is where I suggest, following others, including Heidegger, that we should speak of "ipseity" rather than of sameness. But as I have suggested, there is also an *idem*, a "same" in us as a fulcrum for identification, in a sense of this latter word that is more apparent in English than in French. To take this dialectic of *ipse* and *idem* into account, I propose that we take as our guide the narrative model of a character who, in ordinary narratives, whether fictional or historical, is emplotted along with the story told. What we can call a narrative coherence, an idea to which Dworkin appeals in his work on jurisprudence, combines the concordance of the ongoing plot and the discordance of the peripeteia, such as changes in fortune, reversals, upheavals, unexpected events, and so forth. If today I return to this notion of a narrative identity, it is because it gives the paradoxes with which we began, those of capacities and incapacities, a new dimension owing to the introduction of time into their description. Narrative identity is something claimed, something like a mark of power. And it also declares itself as a kind of attestation. But it is also a term for impotence through the admission of all the signs of vulnerability that threaten any such narrative identity. Our paradox is not only stretched out over time, it takes on specific forms that have to do precisely with the threat that time brings. Then we can see the claim for an identity divest itself of its narrative mark and claim the kind of immutability we have placed under the *idem* heading. We are well aware of the kind of ravages that provoke this confusion between the two senses of identity, as when ideologists try to clothe the historical claim to identity with the prestige of immutability, in order to remove such identity from the bite of historical time. Yet we must not allow ourselves to get caught by the fascination of this pitfall of confusing ipseity and sameness, which leads to excessive claims. Nor must we lose sight of the opposite possibility, that of an inability to attribute some identity to someone or something because we have not acquired the ability to apply what I have called narrative identity. If politicians often get caught up in excessive claims, those of a substantial identity that overlooks history, jurists run the greater risk of having to deal with individuals who are incapable of constructing a narrative identity, of identifying themselves not only through some history but with some history. One German author likes to say, *"Die Geschichte steht für den Mann"*—a person, a human being, is his or her history. The handling of one's own life, as a possibly coherent narrative, represents a high level competence that has to be taken as one of the major components of the autonomy of a subject of rights. In this regard, we can speak of an education for narrative coherence, an education leading to a narrative identity. To learn how to tell the same story in another way, how to allow our story to be told by others, how to submit the narrative of a life to the historian's critique, are all practices applicable to the paradox of autonomy and fragility. Let us say therefore that a subject capable of leading his or her life in agreement with the idea of narrative coherence is an autonomous subject.

I have referred to the first sense of the idea of identity, that of its relation to time. But narrative identity is not the whole thing as regards our problematic of autonomy. So I want to say something about the second sense, that of singularity. I link this to the idea of a perspective that cannot be substituted for. Here we assuredly have a major implication of the idea of autonomy: dare to think *for yourself*. You, and not someone else in your place. The paradox here has to do, not with the temporal dimension, the test of time, but with the confrontation with other perspectives, the test of alterity.

I want to emphasize and, if I may, plead for this paradox, over against those forms of discourses in favor of alterity that have taken on a disheartening banality. Alterity is in fact a problem inasmuch as it leads to a fracture in a reflexive relation of the self to itself, which has its moral and psychological legitimacy on the plane that institutes and structures the human person. There must first be a subject capable of saying I am capable of taking the test of the confrontation with the other. In this regard, I start from a level lower than that of the Cartesian *cogito*, from that enigmatic "interconnectedness of life" of which Dilthey speaks, which makes a human life something that cannot be substituted for by another. This why we have to start deeper down than with consciousness, and all the more so for that reason from reflection, in order to give full force to the idea of the unsubstitutability of persons. The best illustration of this singularity is provided by the untransferable character of a memory from one person to another person. Not only is our actual experience unique, but we cannot exchange our memories. It was in this sense that Locke made memory the criterion of identity. All the degrees of self-reference that fall under the heading of reflection are based on this untransferable singularity of the prereflexive soul—for example, that we can reflexively double the attestation to all our abilities to act and designate ourselves as the one who "can." I shall call self-esteem the ethical form that clothes this claim to singularity. All the forms of fragility that affect this claim to singularity proceed from the collision between this claim and the different forms of social pressure. In this respect, we can speak of an open conflict between reflexivity and alterity. The rights of alterity also start deep down, however. They come with language, which was addressed to us before we began to speak. Language is what elevates human desire to the rank of a demand. It is what permits memory, whose unsubstitutable, incommunicable character I have spoken of, to base itself on narratives told by others and to borrow from that store of memories that constitutes the collective memory of which Maurice Halbwachs, in his last work, risked saying that individual memory constitutes only one aspect, one perspective. The crucial moment in the confrontation between reflexivity and alterity is represented by the split at the interior of the very concept of identification. On the one side, we identify ourselves by designating ourselves as the one who speaks, acts, remembers, imputes action to him- or herself, and so on; on the other, to identify oneself is to identify with heroes, emblematic characters, models, and teachers and also precepts, norms whose field extends from traditional customs to utopian paradigms, which, emanating from the social imaginary, remodel our private imaginations, sometimes following those ways that Pierre Bourdieu describes in terms of an insidious inculturation and symbolic violence. Freud saw the superego as developing in a similar way, following its double valence as repressive and structuring.

We need to follow to its extreme form the protestation of singularity, of solitude, of autonomy, of self-esteem, that is raised by the I/me and confront it with the claims of alterity pushed to the point of the domination of the stranger over one's own self.

These are indeed two poles: the effort to think for oneself and the domination or rule by the other. The identity of each person, and hence his or her autonomy, is constructed between these two poles. It is the task of education to bring about an interminable negotiation between our seeking singularity and the social pressure that is always capable of reconstituting those conditions that the Enlightenment called a state of minority.

These, then, are the two transitions that I propose to intercalate between our anthropological considerations under the heading of the capable human being and the more properly ethico-juridical approach to the problem of autonomy. I want to place this latter under the aegis of the idea of imputability, the classical ancestor of our modern notion of responsibility.

At first view, we take a qualitative leap in passing from the idea of capacity to that of imputability. By even mentioning this heavy term, action finds itself immediately placed under the idea of obligation, as either the obligation to compensate for a tort in civil law or as suffering a punishment in penal law. The idea of obligation is so pregnant that we willingly grant that subjects are responsible for, capable of answering for, their acts only insofar as they are capable of placing their action, first taken in the sense of an obligation to follow a rule, then in the sense of bearing the consequences of any infraction, tort, or offense.

I did not want us to begin to explore this pathway of obligation without a guide. This is why I have suggested that we ought to explore the resources of the notion of imputation, which is richer than that of obligation. In the idea of imputation we first come upon the idea of rendering an account—*putare, computare*. To impute in its most general sense is to assign to a person's account a blamable action, a fault, hence an action confronted as a precondition with an obligation or a prohibition that this action breaks. The idea of obligation is not absent, but the initial accent is on the act of assigning an action to someone's account, as the grammar of the word indicates. The Latin *imputabilitas* was translated into German, for example, as *Zurechnungsfähigkeit* or as *Schuldfähigkeit*. We can see here the filiation of the idea of imputability with that of responsibility: is not being responsible in the first place to "respond," to answer the question "who did this?" which calls for the avowal *ego sum qui fecit*. To be responsible is first of all to answer *for* my acts, that is, to admit that they belong on my account. This genealogy is interesting in that it allows us to place the vocabulary of responsibility along the path that extends the idea of capacity from which we began. Imputability is the capacity to be taken as responsible for one's acts as having been their actual author. We are, therefore, not far here from the vocabulary of capacity. The expression of such responsibility conjoins two more primitive ideas: the attribution of an action to an agent and the moral, generally negative qualification of an action. In this regard Kant was not far removed from his "natural law" predecessors. In the *Metaphysics of Morals* he defines *Zurechnung* (*imputatio*) in the moral sense as the "judgment by which someone is held to be the *Urheber* (*causa libera*) of an action (*Handlung*) which is thus called a *Tat* (*factum*) and falls under the laws." The conceptual interconnections here are clear: attribution of an action to someone as its actual author, assignment of it to the author's account, and submission of the action to approbation or disapprobation (which is the initial sense of the idea of a sanction), judgment, condemnation, and so on. In this way the purely juridical idea of the obligation to repay, from which we began, is not lost sight of but comes at the end of our path, at the end of the list.

The question that then comes to mind has to do with the connection between the idea of taking someone to be the actual author of an action and that of placing the action under some obligation. At bottom, this is the sense of the synthetic operation found in Kant's idea of autonomy, which joins *auto* and *nomos*, oneself as author and the law that obliges. Kant limits himself to taking this connection to be a synthetic a priori judgment but also adds that the awareness we have of this connection is a "fact of reason," which is a way of saying that it is an irreducible given of moral experience. However, I think we can reflect back before this ligature, by drawing on the resource of a phenomenology of moral experience, which we can ask to make apparent the place where the force of this connection coincides with the vulnerability imposed by the fact that the idea of autonomy occupies two apparently contradictory positions: that of being a presupposition and that of being a goal to attain, that of being both a condition of possibility and a task.

The primary experience that I would draw from this phenomenology can once again be described using the vocabulary of capacity.

We shall concentrate on the experience having to do with our capacity to submit our action to the requirements of a symbolic order. I see in this capacity the existential, empirical, and (as we shall say) historical condition for binding a self to a norm, something we have seen is signified by the idea of autonomy. Let us consider in turn the symbolic dimension of this order and the normative dimension of the symbolic system. I have chosen the adjective "symbolic" because of its capacity to encompass within a single emblematic notion the different ways in which language can give figure to obligation: as an imperative, to be sure, an injunction, but also as counsel, advice, shared customs, founding narratives, the edifying lives of heroes of the moral life, the praise of moral sentiments, including—besides respect—admiration, veneration, guilt, shame, pity, solicitude, compassion, and so on. Furthermore, the term "symbolic" recalls through its etymology that the figures of obligation operate as signs of recognition among the members of a community. We shall return later to this shared aspect of the symbolic order. But first I want to say more about the symbolic order, having considered its symbolic aspect.

The term "order" conceals the greatest difficulty for ethico-juridical philosophy, namely, the status of the authority attached to this symbolic order, that which even makes it an order. Authority implies several different characteristics. First of all is that of antecedence: order precedes us, each of us taken one by one. Next is superiority: we place it or rather find it "above" us, at the head of our preferences. Here we touch a sense of the "better" that makes desires and interests, in short, one's own preferences, withdraw to a lower rank. Third, authority appears as external to us, in the sense that, even if given a Platonic concept of reminiscence, it requires someone like Socrates to awaken it, a real stingray, or a teacher of justice as severe as the prophets of Israel, to enjoin us, in short, a wise teacher. You will recall that the big question in the early Socratic dialogues is whether virtue can be taught. In this regard, the teacher-disciple relation is the one external relation that does not imply either a pact of servitude or one of domination. It is through a purely moral alterity that such things are communicated, transmitted—principally across generations, by filiation, we might say in a broad sense. This threefold characterization turns the moral phenomenon as a whole into an enigma: for whence comes the authority that is always already there? As we know, some contemporary thinkers, political philosophers, for the most part, see the democratic era as beginning with the loss of transcendent guarantees, leaving it up to a contract and procedures to take on the difficult task of making up for this missing foundation. But I would like to note that even those who charge democracy with this demiurgic task, once they move to the phenomenological level, cannot avoid situating themselves beyond such a foundation and assuming the phenomenon of authority, with its threefold structure of antecedence, superiority, and exteriority; one does not even have to point out, following one of Gadamer's important insights, that no superiority imposes itself unless it is recognized as such. Yet it remains the case that what is recognized is precisely the superiority of authority, to which allow me to add an anteriority that continues to endure, an exteriority that is compensated for by a movement of internalization. Yet this reciprocity does not abolish the vertical dissymmetry whose enigma, we know, troubled Hannah Arendt when it came to distinguishing the authority of power. Power, she said, is born in the present from the will to live together. Authority "augments" this by coming from further off, from the ancients, as though all authority proceeded from a prior authority with no assignable beginning date. Here we should probably stick with the plane of moral phenomenology. Rather than alleging some artificial foundation that has to fall to the performative contradiction Karl-Otto Apel speaks of, would it not be better to admit a plurality of foundations, as Rawls does in his last work? Rather than a lack of foundation, we should acknowledge an acceptable form of plurality applicable at least to what he calls constitutional or liberal democracies, a pluralism made viable by an overlapping consensus concerning moral sources compatible in this way with those reasonable practices which Rawls speaks of in terms of reasonable disagreements.

These admittedly tentative remarks help to open the way to meditation on the fragility of the symbolic order. What we must say is that the authority of the symbolic order is both the very site of the strongest connection between the self and the norm and the very principle of its fragility. The vulnerability that stands in counterpoint to responsibility can be summed up in the difficulty that everyone has in inscribing his or her action and behavior into a symbolic order, and in the impossibility a number of our contemporaries have in comprehending the meaning and necessity of this inscription, principally those whom our sociopolitical order excludes. If we have been able to see in this capacity something that we presume every human being is capable of as human, now it is in terms of incapacity that we have to speak of the corresponding fragility. But while we could describe the positive capacity with the resources of a moral phenomenology relatively independently of considerations having to do with a sociology of action and more precisely a sociology of the relationship of obligation in contemporary societies, it is impossible to refer to the incapacities that afflict contemporary moral behavior, especially its most fragile forms, without giving more weight to the history of mores than to the eidetics of imputation. It is as though each person's competence were more stable than his or her performance, which, by definition, can be in deficit in relation to the competence being considered.

In this regard, we can take as a trustworthy guide through the meanderings of the sociology of moral action what I have said about the multiple figures taken by the symbolic function and about the implications of the very idea of a symbolic order. These considerations can be of great help to judges called upon, not only to qualify infractions juridically, but to include into the very act of judging—unlike their Anglo-American confreres—the degree of the accused's capacity to situate him- or herself in relation to a symbolic order. The judge must therefore take into account deficits at the very level of the figuration of obligation: a weak sense of the injunction, a loss of the sense of the pertinence of some founding narratives, a weakened influence of the seduction of heroes of the moral life, a poor discernment of one's moral feelings, or a loss of energy from what Charles Taylor calls "strong evaluations," and so forth. It is not my task here to take up this diagnostic, which stems from a discipline that I want only to rub shoulders with, in considering the epistemological difficulties of such an enterprise. I shall allow myself, however, to affirm that it is not possible to make sense of the contemporary crisis in the idea of authority, as the epicenter of all the shocks to the landscape of current morality, unless our moral sociology takes as its guide those features of the phenomenon of authority that a good phenomenology can reveal.

What sociology by itself is capable of doing, either through research or otherwise, is to study the kinds of reception, transmission, and internalization of the codes of some symbolic order in
terms of a given milieu, age-group, sex, and the like; in short, the
sociology of what Socratic thinkers would place under the heading
of the teaching of virtue, a theme that we know they approached
with circumspection when prodded by the Sophists. Whatever
may be said about the details of analysis of our moral incapacities,
which the judge, like the psychiatrist, must take into account, it
will not be a surprise if we see case studies and situations converg-
ing on the same focal point, the loss of credibility of traditional
sources of authority. I have already referred in this regard to the
discordant interpretations of politicians and jurists concerning the
task imposed on contemporary democracies by the crisis of legitimation that simultaneously strikes both the political and the juridical spheres. But we need to move beyond both the sociology
of action and the phenomenology of moral experience when we
take a stand about the remedies for this crisis, hesitating between
a heroic substitution of convention for conviction or a patient reconstitution of a consensus of a different, less dogmatic, less univocal, and hence more deliberately pluralistic type, meant to knit
together traditions and innovation. If taking such a position regarding fundamental questions goes beyond the competence of
the phenomenology of moral experience that I have recommended
and begun to practice, this phenomenology does come into play as
soon as jurists or politicians, basing themselves on a given symbolic
order, ask how we can give a content to the ideas of a "foundational
authority," of "institutions with which one can identify," or "functions that sanction and reintegrate" people (phrases I take from the
chapter headings of Antoine Garapon's *Le gardien des promesses*).

In such a case, the same moral phenomenology from which earlier I borrowed the description of the primary experience of entry
into a symbolic order will be able to help us in this reconstructive
phase that follows any diagnostic of the characteristic incapacities affecting the contemporary moral conscience.

Nor have we exhausted all the implications of the idea of a
symbolic order. What I called, more or less in passing, the entry
into the symbolic order—or, if you prefer, the passage from competence to performance—can be facilitated by other resources of

the idea of a symbolic order that we have not yet considered in our diagnostic and that I have chosen to keep in reserve for this moment of my analysis that most clearly comes close to something therapeutic. I shall point out three such features of the notion of a symbolic order that complement and serve as a remedy to the rigors of the idea of authority, the privileged site of the force and the fragility of moral and juridical obligation.

A bit earlier, I recalled one of the origins of the term "symbol": the symbol as a sign of recognition. In effect, a symbolic order is something that has to be shared. Here we touch on a feature that distances us from orthodox Kantianism inasmuch as this gives a monological version of the connection between the self and the norm within the core of the idea of autonomy, holding the added requirement to respect humanity as part of respect for the law for the second formulation of the categorical imperative. That the symbols of any ethico-juridical order stem from a shared understanding is a point on which universalist thinkers such as Habermas and Alexy and communitarians like Walzer and Taylor agree, before dividing over the boundaries between the universal and the historical. In this sense, the authority attached to a symbolic order immediately has a dialogical dimension. We might in this regard take up again the Hegelian concept of recognition to speak of this communalization of moral experience. To be capable of entering into a symbolic order is to be capable of entering into an order of recognition, of inscribing oneself in a "we" that distributes and apportions the authority of the symbolic order.

In the second place there is the concept that an important American philosopher, Thomas Nagel, puts at the summit of the ethical life, the concept of impartiality, which he defines by the capacity to take two points of view, that of our interests and that of the higher point of view that allows us to adopt in our imagination the perspective of the other person and to affirm that every other life is worth as much as our own. In this sense, this concept offers a counterpart to the perspectivism referred to earlier in regard to the idea of personal singularity. Nagel does not deny such perspectivism. On the contrary, he fights energetically for the theme dear to him of "two points of view" on the field of conflicts that give moral life its dramatic intensity. And in this sense, Kant presupposed this capacity to raise oneself to an impartial point of view when he demanded that moral subjects submit their maxim to the test of the rule of universalization. If I may put it this way, he presupposed our ability to do our duty. Whatever may be said about the irreducibility of the principle of impartiality which Nagel takes for granted, I prefer taking it as a complement to the shared understanding I just referred to. Nagel's principle would then constitute the solitary face of moral effort, the victory over unilateralness. But can this heroic side do without the aid that every moral subject finds in the shared values of some common symbolic universe?

It is the complementarity between a shared understanding and the capacity of impartiality that gave me the idea to place these two practical modes of entry into the symbolic order at a point of intersection—the idea of a just distance between singular points of view against the backdrop of a shared understanding. Like Antoine Garapon, I am convinced that this idea of a just distance occupies a strategic place in the conceptual structure of a philosophy of law centered on the judicial function. For both of us, this idea of a just distance also governs the third-person position assigned to judges between the parties involved in a dispute in a trial process, as well as the holding at a distance, in space and time, of the facts in the case to be judged, in order to remove them from the overly immediate emotions arising from the visible suffering and the call for vengeance proffered by the victims, which themselves may be reinforced by coverage in the media. There is also a just distance between the victim and the offender set up by the pronouncement of the law. This is meant to preserve a place within the continuity of public space for the condemned person who is thereby also excluded from it. This idea of a just distance is all the more valuable in that it brings together the juridical and the political fields, and more precisely the problem of democracy. The dream of a direct democracy, a current rage of the media, implies a mistrust of the institutional mediations characteristic of a representative democracy as much as do the cries for expeditious justice coming from public opinion that the media take up with tears in their eyes and as a cry for blood. In this sense, the conquest of a just distance has to do both with those things that fall under the competence of the courts and with the citizen in each of us.

We can conclude by repeating what I have said in my introduction about how autonomy and vulnerability paradoxically intersect in one and the same universe of discourse, that of the subject of rights. Let me just add the following comment: lacking a speculative solution, a pragmatic one still remains open to us, one that rests on a practice of mediations. I have given a foretaste of this with my discussion of the dialectic between basic capacities and incapacities, then in terms of the pitfalls of narrative identity and the conflicts between singularity and sociality and, finally, at greater length, by evoking the help to be found along the path of the entry into symbolic orders in which the figure of the rule of law appears. Multiple practical mediations exist between the two poles of our paradox: autonomy as a condition of possibility and as a task to be accomplished. I have referred to a few of them regarding the incapacities that afflict our capacity to act. They stem from a kind of education. I have referred to others in regard to the contradictions of narrative identity. They stem from a critical approach to the relation between memory and history.

The Paradox of Authority

I hesitated in entitling my contribution—perhaps it should have been "The Enigma of Authority" or even "The Aporia of Authority": the enigma, because something opaque remains in the idea of authority following its analysis; the aporia, because there is a kind of unresolved contradiction tied to the difficulty, even the impossibility, of legitimating authority in the final instance.[1]

Nevertheless, as a first approximation, the notion of authority is relatively easy to define. The *Robert* dictionary says, "the right to command, the power (recognized or not) to impose obedience." Authority, therefore, is a species of power, the power to command. This immediately underscores the dissymmetrical, hierarchical aspect of a notion that brings face-to-face those who command and those who obey. But what a strange power that rests on a right, the right to command, which implies a claim to legitimacy. The question is not disturbing so long as some existing power finds itself already legitimated. This is the case for those about whom we say that they exercise an authority. At most, we expect them to have such authority, that is, the capacity to make themselves obeyed. For example, we speak of civil servants who lack authority. But we take refuge in individual or social psychology when we elude the question of legitimacy concealed behind this capacity. Those most cloaked with authority start to babble if one asks them where they get such authority. Generally, they answer by

1. This lecture was first presented at a conference in Lyons in November 1996, then published in *Quelle place pour la morale?* (Paris: Desclée de Brouwer, 1996), 75–86.

indicating a higher authority than their own, an individual or institution placed above them, which we call an authority for that reason, meaning the already-established organs of power: a legislative, administrative, judicial, or military authority. The term "authority" then refers to an existing, "positive" institution, incarnated in its authorities, that is, those people who exercise power in the name of the institution. This is why we rightly call them constituted authorities. If we speak further of the authority of the law, in order to account for the obligatory force of some act of a public authority, we have just about covered all the definitions of authority, the meanings that together make up the polysemy of this term. Broadly speaking, these definitions suffice for a civil servant ordinarily covered by one or another institutional authority and the people who incarnate it. The civil servant can give orders because he himself obeys and because above him sits a, so to speak, naked authority, as in the first definition: the right to command, the power (recognized or not) to impose obedience. But the insidious question comes to mind, which need not be a malicious one: whence comes such authority in the last instance?

In fact, we have surreptitiously passed from the substantive form to the verb, from substantive, already established, already instituted authority to the act of authorizing. This is an interesting shift, which by way of a synonym leads to what is essential in the verb "to accredit," which all our dictionaries associate with the idea of authorizing. Why is this shift so interesting? Because it directs our gaze toward the blind spot in the definition of authority, which does not lie in the words "power," "command," or "obey," but in the words "right to . . ." What is more, it conceals itself in the perfidious parenthesis in the *Robert* that speaks of a recognized or unrecognized power to impose obedience.

The pair "command" and "obey," as indicating a given structure of interaction, thus finds itself redoubled by another pair, one that passes from fact to right. On the one side, we have the right to . . . on the part of the one who commands, a right that exceeds the simple capacity to make oneself obeyed inasmuch as it confers the legitimacy without which the power to make oneself obeyed would reduce to the bare fact of domination. On the other side, what do we find? Recognition by a subordinate of the superior's right to command. Let us look again in the *Robert*. A recognized or unrecognized power. With this "or not," doubt insinuates itself at the very heart of our definition. It is this polarity of legitimacy and recognition that we are going next to transcribe using the vocabulary of credit, suggested a moment ago by the definition of the verb "to authorize": to cover with authority, accredit. The doublet that will interest us therefore is accredit-credit, where the term "credit" is pivotal.

In fact, it is this pair that introduces us to the denseness of the enigma. Without this double reference to creditability on the side of the one who commands and credence on the side of the one who obeys, we would be incapable of distinguishing authority from either violence or persuasion, as Hannah Arendt notes at the beginning of her essay "What Is Authority?" to which I shall return in a moment.[2] Authority does border on violence as the power to impose obedience, that is, as domination. But what distinguishes it from violence is precisely the creditability attached to its character of legitimacy, at least its claimed legitimacy, and, over against it, the credit or credence attached to its recognition or nonrecognition or the right of my superior—as an institution or an individual—to impose obedience on me. The nuance is more delicate concerning the role of persuasion, for there is persuasion in the communication of creditability, hence also rhetoric. But, as Arendt observes, persuasion "presupposes equality and works through a process of argumentation" (93). But authority conserves some sense of hierarchy, of a vertical dissymmetry, between those who command and those who obey. The recognition of superiority is therefore what tempers domination by distinguishing it from violence, but also from persuasion.

Our discussion is now framed by the precision brought by the pair creditability and credit or credence, which are constitutive of the recognition or nonrecognition of the power of authorities to impose obedience on their subordinates. We must now try to push closer to the hard core, or opaque heart, of the process of legitimation by which authority accredits power on the condition that such credit is available to it or not.

Why then is the question of such a fiduciary relation between creditability and credence so troubling, so disturbing? Because,

2. Arendt, "What Is Authority?" in *Between Past and Future*, 91–141.

whoever we are, subordinates or in charge (or, as one says, cloaked with authority), we do not really know what authorizes this authority. The question has perhaps always existed, but today we have the feeling of being caught up in a crisis of legitimation, or let us say of a deaccreditation of authority, authorities, institutions, and persons—a crisis emphasized by a general reticence to give credence, that is, recognition, to any superiority, be it of an individual or an institution as being invested with a power to impose obedience. This feeling is so strong that Arendt's essay can begin with this avowal: "In order to avoid misunderstanding, it might have been wiser to ask in the title: What was—and not what is—authority?" (91). To which she adds: "authority has vanished from the modern world." Perhaps, but if authority is a thing of the past, then a mixture of violence and, more or less fraudulent, persuasion seems to have replaced it. But is this really the case? Has not authority rather transformed itself, even while preserving something of what it had been? It is this second hypothesis that I want to explore and argue for.

To have some chance of succeeding we need first to agree about what has been lost. I have found some aid, if not for resolving the problem, at least for posing it correctly in a work by Gérard Leclerc, *Histoire de l'autorité*. He too begins by saying that "authority is not what it was; it was once a principle of legitimation of forms of discourse; today it signifies the mode of existence of legitimate forms of power" (7). I shall retain from this as a working hypothesis the idea that there are two foci of legitimation: the one that Leclerc calls an enunciative authority; the other, institutional (which accounts for his subtitle). On the one side, therefore, we have the symbolic power, either of an enunciator or of an "author," to engender belief, to persuade, through a text, an assertion; to be persuasive, to engender belief. On the other side, there is the power connected with an institution, namely, the "legitimate power that an individual or a group has at its disposal to impose obedience on those it claims to direct" (7). We are still within the framework of our initial definitions. We have simply split in two the place of origin of the process of legitimation—on the one side, discourse, as the source of symbolic power; on the other, the institution, as the source of legitimacy for those who exercise authority within it. But does Leclerc's thesis hold once we change domains by passing from what we could call a "scriptural" authority to one that would no longer be, he says, a philosophical concept, but a sociological one? Drawing on Arendt, who sees in authority an originally political concept, whose origin she situates clearly in Rome, that is, ancient imperial Rome, I want to suggest the idea that what has taken place is not the replacement of an authority that was largely enunciative by one that is only institutional, at the risk of an overall delegitimation, but rather the replacement of one historical configuration determined by a pairing of enunciation and institution by another configuration of the same two terms. What is true about Leclerc's thesis is that in the authority that has disappeared there was a prevalence of heralded authority. But there has never been a purely enunciative authority with no institutional authority, and today there is no purely institutional authority without the contribution, the symbolic support, of some enunciative order—this is what I want to suggest.

The ideal type of a dominantly enunciative authority that once was but today no longer exists is medieval Christendom. And the ideal type of what is said to have succeeded and replaced it is the Enlightenment, more exactly the Enlightenment of the French Lumières, who placed themselves in fact on the same enunciative terrain as did the ideal type of medieval Christendom. However, our crisis is still more complicated than that in that the ideal type of the French Enlightenment thinkers itself has lost much of its creditability, as contemporary talk about postmodernity bears witness. The result is that our crisis is double (or, if you will, doubly dense, two staged): we are reexperiencing in a way the crisis of the deaccrediting of the ideal type of medieval Christendom by way of the crisis of the delegitimizing of what followed from this loss of creditability of the ideal type of Christendom. Before we take up this complicated history, let me emphasize one point. I am not identifying Christendom, as a historically dated configuration, with Christianity, inasmuch as this latter is not exhausted, and has not exhausted its specifically religious creditability, in the production of the particular historical configuration that we call Christendom. I would say of this latter that its ideal type was as much a dream as an actual reality. This is why I speak of it as an ideal type. And therefore we must say of it, not only that it no longer exists, but that it never was historically what it claims to have been. Furthermore, if we take the ideal type of Christendom at the eve of its decline, at the dawn of the appearance of that other corpus of enunciative authority, Diderot and d'Alembert's *Encyclopedia*, we need to recognize that at that time this model was already moribund, already condemned to death by its very sclerosis.

That the authority of the ideal type of Christendom was predominantly an enunciative one is clear in light of the acknowledged authority assigned to the biblical writings and to the tradition founded on them. Still, a few features do need to be emphasized that indicate the vulnerability of this model to the blows coming from the camp of the *philosophes*. In a word, the model functioned as already instituted, as a model that had forgotten the history of its own establishment. Thus, the canonization of scripture was an event that had already occurred and that, for a long time, was taken as given, implying a clean break between the sacred texts, accompanied by their authorized commentaries, and the remainder of profane literature. As for the authority of the scriptures, it itself was assimilated once and for all to the inspiration of the Holy Spirit, God himself being taken as their author. Any new assertion therefore was found in advance to be classifiable either as orthodox or as heretical. What is more, a list of classical texts from pagan antiquity was drawn up and placed in a relation of subordination to the sacred texts. These were themselves authorized *auctoritates*.

This authority of scripture and what depended on it was intertwined with the institutional authority of the church, which in the seventeenth and eighteenth centuries was itself an established authority removed from any legitimate challenge. The ecclesiastical *magisterium* controlled the development of tradition, whose authority was added to that of scripture. It even controlled any new pronouncements, whose orthodoxy only it was capable of evaluating. Through the institutional network of universities and its clerics, the church controlled the production of thought by establishing theology to be the predominant mode of discourse, in relation to which the words of pagan teachers such as Aristotle and other *auctoritates* were discourse authorized by the ecclesial authority.

I have emphasized to the point of caricature the aspect of being already instituted that made the idea of tradition the favored target of the *philosophes*. But, without injustice, we can present the enunciative and institutional authority that together make up the largely nostalgic ideal type of Christendom as a fossilized model, which, as I have already said, forgot and so to speak erased the history of its own genesis while also repressing its original creative aspects, which were capable of resurfacing after the calling into question of this ideal type by the *philosophes*. In fact, some of these resources were actually liberated by this critique: for example, reserves of meaning connected with the very formation of the New Testament and the birth of the early church, or the riches linked to a buried pluralism, sometimes tributary to deviances of all sorts which had occurred as much on what I have called the enunciative as the institutional plane. But it is not this aspect of things that I want to emphasize, but rather the following. I want to introduce a serious corrective to the preceding picture, where the enunciative and the institutional authority seem to stem from a single base. In one sense, this is true in that the ecclesiastical institution declared itself and still declares itself today to be founded on scripture. We can ask, however, whether the institutional authority of the church as actually shaped by history was not the beneficiary of an origin distinct from this scriptural authority.

We need first to note the circular relationship that was established between the ecclesiastical institution and the sacred text, once the institution destined to become the church had delimited the canon of scripture and continued to decide in authoritative fashion on what subsequently was to be taken as orthodox or heretical, to the point where this institutional authority would manage its tradition, the seat of its symbolic power, with no further appeal possible. However, there was something still more important, something I want to take up here in referring to Hannah Arendt's essay "What Is Authority?" We may ask with her whether ecclesiastical authority was not also the heir and beneficiary of a strictly political origin of authority, the Roman *imperium*. This question is important because, if this were so, and it is so in the sense that the church that calls itself Roman Catholic does draw a part of its authority from a political model, then we can ask if the decline of properly scriptural authority, in other words, the decline of the creditability of the sacred texts and their authors, did not leave vacant the part of authority issuing from the Roman *imperium*, once freed of its union with the properly religious authority of the church. And we can also then ask whether this part of authority was not thereby made available for other durable investments, owing to which we find ourselves situated today at the end of the theological-political age. This is what I want to suggest in conclusion to this lecture.

That political authority has a distinct root is attested to by the whole history of sovereignty. The claim to authority on the part of the city is at the heart of the political philosophy of the ancient Greeks, as much in Plato as in Aristotle. The government of human beings requires a factor of stability, of durability, capable of exceeding the transitory existence of individuals and of supervising the replacement of generations. The *politeia* was to be such a source of stability, of security for persons and goods, capable of giving validity to the laws. Yet there is something paradoxical about this in both Greek and Roman thought. The paradox lies in the project of establishing a hierarchy among free people. This paradox was already brought to its most virulent point in Greek political philosophy. This is why neither the word nor the issue of authority was Greek, but Roman. The Greeks had only metaphors, all inappropriate, to speak of this paradox of a hierarchy among equals: the helmsman in his ship, the master of slaves, the physician, the head of the household, the orator, the potter, the *sophos*. In his *Politics*, Aristotle says that every political body is composed of those who govern and those who are governed. But he did not know how to make this accepted idea agree with his other assertion that the city is a community of equals to the profit of what is potentially the best life. Political regimes might differ depending on their form of government, which could depend on one, some, or the multitude. But the origin of the power to command remained the enigma of political life, of the *bios politicos*. As Arendt notes, "The grandiose attempts of Greek philosophy to find a concept of authority which would prevent deterioration of the polis and safeguard the life of the philosopher foundered on the fact that in the realm of Greek political life there was no awareness of authority based on immediate political experience" (119). This perception, this "immediate political experience," was something that only the Romans had, under a figure with a sacred character: the figure of the *foundation*, of the founding of the *urbs*, of the founding of Rome, *ab urbe condita*. This is why there could exist many Greek cities and even a whole *diaspora* of cities, but there was only one Rome, whose singular, unique holiness Virgil and Titus Livy celebrated. It even turns out that the connection of this foundation to its past was called precisely *religio* by these authors. Arendt cites here book 43, chapter 13, of Livy's *Annales:*

> While I write down these ancient events [*vetustas res*], I do not know through what connection [*quo pacto*] my mind grows old [*antiquus fit animus*] and some *religio* holds [me] [*et quaedam religio tenet*]. (121)

You can see the density of the enigma, which is proportional to the density of this experience, which we can call the experience of the energy of a founding, which in a way authorizes itself and its great age. The tradition of authority is identical with the authority of tradition in the sense of a transmission from the origin of the foundation itself, from the founding event. This legitimation was to be denounced as mythical, yes. But, precisely, the question is whether this authority does not proceed from a founding myth, the myth of a founding event, connected to that of founding characters, such as Moses, Lycurgus, Solon. The paradox of authority then is constituted as combining anteriority, exteriority, and superiority. The very word *auctoritas* in Latin, which has no Greek equivalent, carries within its etymology something of the aura of this founding, for the verb *augere* means "to augment." What has the power to augment is the energy of such a founding. Thus, Livy speaks of *conditores*, of founders as *auctores*. And this augmentation can be perceived in the famous formula that Cicero cites in *De legibus* 3:12–28: "while power [*potestas*] resides in the people [*in populo*], authority [*auctoritas*] rests with the Senate [*in senatu*]." By this term, "senate," the Romans meant the transmitters of this founding energy. The *auctoritas majorum*, the authority of the ancients, gives the present condition of ordinary people its weight, its gravitas.

I have said enough to suggest that in the past authority did not have a unique focal point in the sacred texts claimed by a revealed religion, nor even in the ecclesiastical institution that claimed to be founded by these scriptures. It also had a distinct political focus, that is, for us Westerners, a Roman source that was also religious but in the sense of the fiduciary connection immanent in the tradition that bears the founding energy. This is the source of the hypothesis that the Catholic Church itself is Roman, not only through Peter, but because Peter was brought to Rome, the seat of the *imperium* and of the political origin of institutional authority. This episode of historical Christianity thus makes sense as a fusion of the *auctoritas* of the Roman foundation and the authority of the instituted church, held to be founded in the scriptures. It was thanks to this conjunction that the Roman church could, over the course of its history, rein in the antipolitical and anti-institutional tendencies of primitive Christian faith. What is more, once the Roman Empire collapsed under the blows of the barbarians, the Roman church could save the heritage of the *imperium* and perhaps, without knowing it, preserve it for adventures other than the ecclesiastical one beyond the age of Enlightenment and for the time of decline we see today as the relentless foe of the ideal type of Christendom. In this way, the suggestion of a double origin of the ideal type of Christendom clarifies the fate not only of this ideal type but also of its ferocious adversary, the French Lumières, who proclaimed themselves through the *Encyclopedia* as a kind of anti-Bible.

If we turn now to their ideal type, we must say that the *philosophes* shared the illusion of the defenders of Roman Catholic orthodoxy when they were at the threshold of its decline that the authority to be combated was par excellence one of a discourse and that it had to be fought against principally on this ground. It was left to the thinkers of the French Revolution to attack the institutional authority of the Ancient Regime on the properly political plane. Thus, it was neither fortuitous nor surprising that the Roman models should have sprung up again at the moment when the power of the people was threatened and in search of augmentation, of *auctoritas*.

What justifies this hypothesis of a double root to institutional authority is the fact that despite the medieval dream of a unity of authority, the duality of monarchical and ecclesiastical power remained insurmountable. At best the two powers and the two corresponding authorities mutually supported each other, the ecclesiastical one offering its unction to the monarch, while the political realm offered the sanction of the secular arm in return. Unction plus sanction could ensure the practical functioning of an internally divided theological politics.

But let us dwell for a moment on the ideal type of the Lumières at the precise point of its principle of authority. We must not think that there was nothing in common between the orthodoxy of a Bossuet and the subversion of this orthodoxy connected with the diffusion of Diderot and d'Alembert's *Encyclopedia*. In his history of authority, Gérard Leclerc devotes two long chapters to the crisis of authority in terms of his approach, which is centered on symbolic, discursive, scriptural authority, in short, enunciative authority. There we find the history of "the ancients, rediscovered, then lost again" (139)—Erasmus, Montaigne, the Reformation, Descartes and the Cartesians, Pascal and Port-Royal, Spinoza, the condemnation of Jansenius (the author of *Augustinus*), and the Quarrel of the Ancients and the Moderns—which all unfolds in the sphere of enunciation, of writing and printing, of reading, apart from the double instance of ecclesiastical unction and political sanction. In this sense, the façade appeared to be intact for a long time. The ideal type of Christendom could remain unshakable in the eyes of the upholders of the dominant orthodoxy even when they were placed on the defensive.

This is why it is not out of place to oppose the ideal type of the Enlightenment—at least of the French Lumières—term by term to that of Christendom at the end of the eighteenth century. It is worth noting that the *Encyclopedia* did not overlook the distinction between two kinds of authority: political authority and authority "in discourse and in writings." Leclerc, who points this out, notes that the article on political authority signed by Diderot is a presentation of natural law political theory (219). But he then adds: "but this does not really concern us." He is partially correct to make this division, inasmuch as for the *Encyclopedia* the essential scene has to do with authority "in discourse and writings." And it is on this plane that a new figure of enunciative authority takes shape, one that does not authorize itself on the basis of the absolute transcendence of a sacred text in relation to other utterances and to public opinion, but which is based on the creditability of the author. Let me cite here this passage from the article on authority in the *Encyclopedia* that Leclerc does hang on to:

> I understand by authority in discourse the right one has to be believed in what one says: thus, the more one has the right to be believed on his word, the more authority he has. This right is founded on the degree of learning and good faith one recognizes in the person speaking. Learning [*science*] prevents one from fooling himself and prevents error that can arrive through ignorance. Good faith prevents one from fooling others and represses the lie that malignancy seeks to accredit. Therefore, it is Enlightenment and sincerity that are the true measure of authority in discourse. These two qualities are essentially necessary. The most learned and most enlightened of men does not merit being believed if he is deceitful; nor does the most pious, most saintly of men if he speaks about what he does not know. (215)

A polar opposition is put in place in a radical way in the sense that the word "authority" had been captured by ecclesiastical authority and identified with tradition, an opposition where reason— or the right of reason—is opposed to authority. Thus, we can set our two ideal types in parallel term by term. To the medieval hierarchy of the sciences, dominated by theology, stands opposed the dispersion of articles in dictionaries arranged in terms of an anarchical alphabetical order. The articles on theology are prudently orthodox but reduced to a common level by the play of cross-references, of the "intertextuality of words, statements, and knowledge" (217). The perfidious subtlety of this is even admitted by Diderot in his article entitled "Encyclopedia"!

> When necessary, they also produce a quite contrary effect. They set notions in opposition to one another. They attack, shake, secretly overturn ridiculous opinions that no one would dare insult openly. (218)

As we can see, authority can and must change places, but it remains inexpugnable as having a fiduciary connection. Our initial definition in terms of creditability and credence continues to come to the surface. We will have to recall this in concluding.

Having said this, the argument over political authority has to take place elsewhere, in terms of censorship and the freedom of

thought, expression, and publication. The whole of Enlightenment Europe was caught up in this battle for what Kant called
Öffentlichkeit, "publicity," as the antitype of "ecumenical" ecclesiastical control. This is the scene of institutional authority properly
speaking, of the authority of the state.

How did the French Revolution deal with the question of authority, and what heritage did it leave us concerning authority?
It has to be said that its message is unclear. On the one hand, we
have a strong vow to admit just one source of power, that of the
people, of the people taken as one indivisible, unified will, that of
a sovereign people. And the French Revolution had its proponents
in this regard. Pierre Nora was right to begin the volumes he edited entitled the *Lieux de mémoire* with their mad idea of starting
the calendar over again at year zero. Everything is wiped away
and one starts again from nothing. In Arendt's vocabulary, this
is the power of the people without the authority of the ancients.
Or, we could say, it is authority as stemming from power, where
this power is itself identified with the general will. In philosophical terms, it is the political equivalent of autonomy on the moral
plane. It is freedom giving itself the law—whence the recourse
made to a contractual model whose function is, in effect, to re-
absorb authority into power. We can even speak in this regard of
a self-referential authorization: the "people" authorizes itself. But
does this parallel with moral autonomy really hold? Is not this
latter itself filled with obscurity, as indicated by Kant's difficulty
when he is forced to treat the ground of the synthetic a priori
judgment by which freedom gives itself a law but where this law
stems from freedom as a "fact of reason" (*factum rationis*)?

What would be the political equivalent of this *factum rationis*?
This is the difficulty that every contractual theory of the origin of
political power and of sovereignty runs up against.

Speaking historically, the conditions for the exercise of a self-
grounding of sovereignty turn out to be draconian: it requires, as
Rousseau stated in his *On the Social Contract*, distinguishing the
one and indivisible general will from the sum of individual wills.
Furthermore, it is necessary to take this general will not only as
enlightened but as infallible, inerrant (which is why in France, until recently, there has been no appeal beyond our criminal courts,

whose decisions were held to be made in the name of an infallible people). However, above all else, the Revolution never succeeded in giving a historical equivalent to this ahistorical social contract, in the form of a constitution capable of giving revolutionary power stability and the capacity to endure over time. This is what Hegel denounced in his *Phenomenology of Spirit* when he condemned the Terror as freedom without law. Rousseau himself glimpsed the difficulty of inscribing the social contract in historical time in having to make recourse to the figure of a founding legislator. To legitimate the principle is one thing; to inscribe this legitimacy in actual facts is another, as we have known ever since Machiavelli, who was fascinated, not by the question of legitimation, but rather by that of founding and, more precisely, by that of the founder, the pivot point of any pragmatics of authority. Here is where the problem of the authority of the ancients reappears. It was not by chance that the figures of republican and imperial Rome taken as models or paradigms returned forcibly during the Revolution. It is as though the history of authority was functioning as a distinct, cumulative source, one capable of giving a then-current, momentary, fragile, and perishable power the aura that its novelty could not ensure but that the great age of the past history of authority alone could confer on power in the present. One recent author, Guglielmo Ferrero, whom Emmanuel Le Roy Ladurie cites in an essay in the journal *Commentaire,* even maintains that the thesis of the great age of authority alone can account for all authority.[3] In fact, a revolution that outlived its wars of conquest became established and has endured because it was able to transform its own age into an argument for authority. For myself I am pretty willing to believe that no power is assured of stability and endurance unless it succeeds in capitalizing on the earlier history of authority for its own benefit.

Can we rest with this? Can we allow foundational myths, myths of great age, to replace the rational need for legitimation? Can we resign ourselves to eliminating from the definition of "authority" the factor of recognition by virtue of which the creditability of power is dialectically balanced by the act of accrediting it? If it is

---

3. Le Roy Ladurie, "Sur l'histoire de l'état moderne," citing Guglielmo Ferrero, *Pouvoir, les génies invisibles de la cité* (Paris: Livre de Poche, 1988).

this fiduciary connection that makes the ultimate difference between authority and violence at the very heart of the hierarchical relation of domination, to what then do we finally give credit? To authority per se, to the great age of power, to the authority of tradition weighed against the tradition of authority? I admit that I am not satisfied with this, in spite of Talleyrand's cynical words cited by Le Roy Ladurie that "a legitimate government . . . is always one whose existence, form, and mode of action are consolidated and consecrated by a long succession of years and, I willingly add, by an ancient prescription. . . . The legitimation of sovereign power is the result of the ancient state of possession" (620). Or should we turn toward a more radical solution, like that of Claude Lefort and his school, who assume the lack of a foundation as the fate of democracy along with all the weaknesses inherent in what we have called a self-authorization? Here I resist and refuse to yield. Or ought we, taking advantage of the very idea of credit, like the later Rawls, admit a multiple foundation, a diversity of religious and secular, rational and Romantic traditions, that mutually recognize one another as cofoundational under the double auspices of the principle of "overlapping consensus" and the "recognition of reasonable disagreements"? Within such a framework with this double principle a role may be found for the authority of the Bible and that of ecclesiastical institutions—but not in such a way as to give rebirth to the lost paradigm of Christendom. It would be a question, rather, of Christian communities taking up, without any hang-ups, their part in this cofoundation in open competition with other, heterogeneous traditions, which themselves are reinvigorated and driven by their unkept promises. Finally, and this final remark should not be taken as insignificant, a place has to be reserved for dissensus and for the right to respond to the offer of creditability on the part of any authorities in place by a refusal to grant credit to them. This calculated risk, which should be recognized as having a supportable marginal role, is, after all, part of the very idea of "credit," of accrediting.

The Paradigm of Translation

Two different ways of access to the problem posed by the act of translation present themselves: either to take the term "translation" in the narrow sense of the transference of a verbal message from one language to another or to take it in a broader sense as a synonym of "interpretation" that applies to the whole range of meaning within one and the same linguistic community.[1]

Both approaches have arguments in favor of them. The first one, chosen by Antoine Berman in his *Experience of the Foreign*, takes account of the obvious fact of the plurality and diversity of languages. The second, followed by George Steiner in *After Babel*, is directly addressed to the overall phenomenon that Steiner sums up as follows: "to understand is to translate." I have chosen to begin with the former, which brings to the fore the relation between what is familiar and what foreign and thus leads to the latter through the difficulties and paradoxes that arise from translating one language into another.

Let us begin, therefore, from the plurality and diversity of languages and note a first fact: it is because humans speak different languages that translation exists. This fact is the diversity of languages, to recall the title of a work by Wilhelm von Humboldt.[2] But this fact is at the same time an enigma. Why not a single language, and why so many languages, five or six thousand according to ethnologists? Every Darwinian criterion of utility and

---

1. This was a lecture given at the Faculté de théologie protestante de Paris in October 1998, then published in an issue of *Esprit* (June 1999) devoted to translation.

2. Humboldt, *On Language: On the Diversity of the Human Language Construction and Its Influence on the Mental Development of the Human Species.*

adaptation in the struggle for survival is put to flight. This uncountable multiplicity of languages is not only needless, it is a problem. If the exchange of messages within a community is ensured by the ability to learn a language, some language, the exchange beyond one's own linguistic community is rendered impracticable at the limit by what Steiner calls "a harmful prodigality." Still, the enigma not only is the interference in communication, that the myth of Babel, which I shall have more to say about later, calls "dispersion" on the geographical plane and "confusion" on that of communication, but also has to do with other features having to do with language. In the first place there is the considerable fact of the universality of language. "All humans speak"—here is a criterion of humanity alongside those of tools, institutions, and burial practices. Let us understand by language the use of signs that are not things but that stand for things, the exchange of signs in interlocution, the major role of a common language within a community that identifies itself as a community. What we have then is a universal competence denied by its local performances, a universal capacity denied by its fragmented, disseminated, dispersed actualization—whence those speculations, first at the level of myth, then at that of the philosophy of language, that inquire into the origin of this dispersion and confusion. In this regard, the myth of the Tower of Babel, which is brief and confused in its literary form, tends to make us think of an earlier, presumably lost linguistic paradise beyond its offering itself as a guide to this labyrinth. This dispersion and confusion is then seen as an irremediable linguistic catastrophe. In a moment, I want to suggest a more helpful reading as regards our originary condition as human beings.

But before that, I want to speak of a second fact that must not be masked by the first one, the diversity of languages; I refer to the fact, which is just as important, that one has always translated. Before there were professional translators, there were voyagers, merchants, ambassadors, spies, which means a lot of bilingual and polyglot people! Here we touch on a feature more noteworthy than any deplored incommunicability: the very fact of translation presupposes that every speaker has the aptitude to learn and use languages other than his or her own. This capacity seems to go with other, more dissimulated features having to do with the use of language, features that will lead me, in concluding, to the neighborhood of intralinguistic procedures of translation—or, to anticipate, to the reflexive capacity of language, this always-available possibility of talking about language, of setting it at a distance and thus treating our own language as one language among others. I shall hold this analysis of the reflexivity of language for later and concentrate here on the simple fact of translation. Humans speak different languages, but they can learn languages other than their maternal tongue.

This simple fact has given rise to an immense amount of speculation that gets caught up in a ruinous alternative that we need to get beyond. This paralyzing alternative is that the diversity of languages expresses a radical heterogeneity, and hence translation is theoretically impossible; languages are a priori untranslatable into one another—or translation as a fact is explained by a common basis that makes possible this fact of translation. But then we must either seek to rediscover this common basis, which is the search for an original language, or seek to reconstruct it logically, which is the quest for a universal language. Whether original or universal, this absolute language should be able to be demonstrated in terms of its phonological, lexical, syntactical, and rhetorical tables. I repeat the theoretical alternative: either the diversity of languages is radical, and thus translation is impossible in principle, or translation is a fact, and it is necessary to establish its possibility in principle by an inquiry into its origin or by a reconstruction of it as a fact in terms of its a priori conditions of possibility.

I want to suggest that we need to get beyond this theoretical alternative of translatable versus untranslatable and substitute for it another, practical alternative, stemming from the very exercise of translation, the alternative of fidelity versus betrayal, even while admitting that the practice of translation always remains a risky operation looking for its theory. At the end, we shall see that the difficulties of intralingual translation confirm this embarrassing confession. Recently I participated in an international meeting on interpretation and I listened to a presentation entitled "Theoretically Hard and Practically Easy" by the analytic philosopher Donald Davidson.

This is also my thesis regarding translation considered in terms of its two (extra- and intralinguistic) sides: theoretically incomprehensible but actually practicable, at the high price we are going to consider—the alternative of fidelity versus betrayal.

Before setting out along the way of this practical dialectic of fidelity versus betrayal, I would like very briefly to lay out the reasons for the speculative impasse arising from the clash between the alternative of untranslatable or translatable.

The thesis about untranslatability is the conclusion reached by one school of ethnolinguistics, that of Benjamin Lee Whorf and Edward Sapir, which set out to demonstrate the non-superimposable character of the different ways of carving up things that form the bases on which different linguistic systems rest. There is a phonetic, articulatable way of carving things up at the basis of phonological systems (vowels, consonants); a conceptual one governing lexical systems (dictionaries, encyclopedias); a syntactical one at the basis of different grammars. There are numerous examples. If one says *bois* in French, one groups together the ligneous material and the idea of a small forest. But in another language, these two meanings may be separate and grouped into different semantic systems. On the grammatical plane, it is easy to see that the systems of verbal tenses (present, past, future) differ from one language to another. There are languages in which one marks, not the position in time, but the accomplished or unaccomplished character of an action, and there are languages without verbal tenses where the position in time is indicated by adverbs equivalent to "yesterday," "today," "tomorrow," and so forth. If you add the idea that each linguistic carving up of things imposes a worldview, an idea that I do not agree with, by saying, for example, that the Greeks constructed ontologies because they had the verb "to be," which functions both as a copula and as asserting existence, then it is the overall ensemble of human relations among the speakers of a language that turns out not to be superimposable on the means by which the speaker of another language understands himself in understanding his own relation to the world. We must then conclude that this misunderstanding exists in principle, and that translation is theoretically impossible and that bilingual people must be schizophrenics.

We are tossed up therefore on the other bank. Since translation exists, it must be possible. And if it is possible, this is because, beneath the diversity of languages, there exist hidden structures which either bear the traces of a lost original language that needs to be rediscovered or which consist of a priori codes, universal or, as some say, transcendental structures that need to be reconstructed. The first version, that of an original language, has been professed by different forms of gnosis, by the Kabala, by hermeticisms of every kind, to the point of producing such poisonous fruits as the plea for a so-called Arian language, held to be historically fruitful, in opposition to Hebrew, reputed to be sterile. Olender, in his book *The Languages of Paradise,* with the frightening subtitle *Arians and Semites, a Providential Pair,* denounces the perfidious anti-Semitism to be found in what he calls a "scientific myth." Yet, to be fair, we must also say that the nostalgia for an original language has produced the powerful meditation of a Walter Benjamin in "The Task of the Translator," where the "perfect language" and the "pure language" (his expressions) figure as a messianic horizon of the act of translation, in secretly ensuring the convergence of idioms when these are brought to the peak of poetic creativity.[3] Unfortunately, the practice of translation receives no help from this nostalgia turned into an eschatological expectation. And perhaps we shall have to mourn this vow of perfection in order to take up without inebriation, in all sobriety, the translator's task.

The other version of a search for unity, not in the direction of an origin in time but in that of a priori codes, is more hardheaded. Umberto Eco has devoted some useful chapters to these efforts in his *Search for a Perfect Language.* It is a matter, as Bacon emphasized, of eliminating the imperfections of existing natural languages, which are the source of what he calls the "idols" of language. Leibniz will give form to this exigency with his idea of a universal symbolic system, which is aimed at nothing less than being able to compose a universal lexicon of simple ideas, completed by a summary of all the composition rules applying to these veritable atoms of thinking.

In this we come to the question of confidence—and, in this sense, the turning point in our meditation. We need to ask why this attempt fails and why it has to fail.

There are certainly some partial results on the side of Chomsky's school of generative grammar, but a total failure on the lexical and phonological sides. Why? Because it is not the imperfections

3. Benjamin, "The Task of the Translator," in *Illuminations,* 69–82.

of natural languages but their very functioning that is anathema. Simplifying to an extreme what is a very technical discussion, let me point to two pitfalls. On the one side, there is no agreement about what would characterize a perfect language at the lexical level of primitive ideas that enter into composition with one another. This agreement would presuppose a complete homology between the sign and the thing, with nothing arbitrary about it, therefore more broadly a complete homology between language and the world, which would be a tautology, a privileged carving up of things decreed as the figure of the world, something that is an unverifiable claim, given the absence of an exhaustive inventory of every spoken language. The second pitfall is even more formidable. No one can tell us how to derive natural languages, with all their peculiarities, which I shall speak more of later, from the presumably perfect language. The gap between the universal language and any empirical tongue, between what is a priori and what historical, seems to be unbridgeable. Here is where my concluding reflections on the work of translation within a single natural language will be most helpful in bringing to light the infinite complexities of these languages, which means that in each case one has to learn how such a language works, including the case of one's own language. So we have my brief summary of the battle that opposes the land of relativism, which leads to the conclusion that translation is impossible, to the formalism of the study, which fails to found the fact of translation on a universally demonstrable structure. Yes, we need to confess, from one language to the next, the situation is indeed one of dispersion and confusion. And yet translation is part of a long litany of "in spite of all that." In spite of fratricide, we campaign for universal fraternity. In spite of the heterogeneity of idioms, there are bilingual, polyglot people, interpreters and translators.

How, Then, Do They Do It?

I earlier announced a change in orientation. Leaving behind the speculative alternative of translatability versus untranslatability, let us, I said, take up the practical alternative of fidelity as opposed to betrayal.

To get us started along the way of this reversal I want to return to the interpretation of the myth of Babel, from which I do not want to end up with the idea of a linguistic catastrophe inflicted on human beings by a god jealous of their success. We can also read this myth, like all other myths of beginnings that take account of irreversible situations, as the assertion of an originary separation apart from any condemnation. We can begin, at the beginning of Genesis, with the separation of the cosmic elements that permits order to emerge from chaos, continued by the loss of innocence and the expulsion from the Garden, which also indicates the accession to adulthood and responsibility, to come next to fratricide, the murder of Abel, which makes fraternity itself an ethical project and not a simple given in nature, something that will be very interesting for our rereading of the Babel myth. If we adopt this line of reading, which I share with Paul Beauchamp, the Old Testament exegete, the dispersion and confusion of tongues announced by the myth of the Tower of Babel serve to crown this history of separation by extending it to the very heart of the use of language. This is how we are, how we exist, dispersed, confused, and called to what? Well, to translation! There is an after Babel, defined by the task of the translator, to recall the already-cited title of Walter Benjamin's well-known study.

To give more force to this reading, I will recall along with Umberto Eco that the narrative in Genesis 11 is preceded by 10:31–32, where the plurality of languages seems to be taken as a simple given fact. Here are those verses in André Chouraqui's translation:

> Behold the sons of Shem and their clan, their tongue, their land, their people.
> Behold the clans of the sons of Noah, their movements, their land, their people: from them all the peoples of the earth split up following the Flood.

These verses sound like a kind of enumeration expressing a simple benevolent curiosity. Translation then would be a task, not in the sense of a constraining obligation, but in the sense of something to be done if human action is to continue, to speak as Hannah Arendt, who was a friend of Benjamin's, does in her *Human Condition*.

What follows next is the narrative we call the myth of Babel:

And for the whole earth: a single lip, a unique speech.
And here was their departure for the Orient: they find a canyon
in the land of Shinar, they establish themselves there.
They say, each to the next: Let's go, let us make bricks, bake
them in the flames. And the brick becomes stone for them,
bitumen, mortar.
They say, let's go, let us build a city and a tower. Its head: in the
heavens. Let us make a name for ourselves, so that we not be
dispersed over the face of the earth.
Yahweh descends to see the city and the tower the sons of men
have built.
Yahweh says: yes, a single people, a single lip for all of them:
but look what they have begun to do! Now nothing will prevent
them from doing what they intend to do.
Let's go. Let us descend. Let us confuse their lips, a man will no
longer understand the lip of his neighbor.
Yahweh disperses them over the face of the earth. They stop
building their city.
Which is why it proclaims its name: Bavel, Confusion, for there
the lip of the whole earth is confused and from there Yahweh
disperses them over the face of the whole earth.
Behold the generations of Shem, Shem, a hundred years old,
begets Arpakhsad, two years after the Flood.
Shem lives, after begetting Arpakhsad, five hundred years. He
begets sons and daughters.

As we can see here, there is no recrimination, no regret, no accusation. "Yahweh disperses them over the face of the earth. They
stop building." They stop building! This is a way of saying: that is
how it is. Well, well, that is how it is, as Benjamin liked to say.
Starting from this reality of life, let us translate!

To talk about the task of translating, I would like now, following Antoine Berman in *The Experience of the Foreign*, to turn to the
desire to translate. This desire goes beyond constraint and utility.
There is certainly a constraint. If one wants to engage in commerce, voyages, negotiations, even spying, one needs messengers
who speak other people's language. As for the utility, it is patent.
If one wants to economize on learning other languages, one will
be content to discover translations. After all, this is how we have

access to the Greek tragedies, to Plato, to Shakespeare, Cervantes, Petrarch and Dante, Goethe and Schiller, Tolstoy and Dostoevsky. Constraint and utility, yes. But there is something more tenacious, more profound, more hidden: the desire to translate.

It is this desire that has motivated German thinkers after Goethe, the great classic, and Humboldt, already mentioned, from the Romantics and Novalis, the Schlegel brothers, and Schleiermacher (who translated Plato, let us not forget), up to Hölderlin, who translated Sophocles, and finally Walter Benjamin, his heir. And behind this crowd, stands Luther, the translator of the Bible, Luther and his strong will to "Germanize" the Bible, held captive by St. Jerome's Latin.

What did these people impassioned about translation expect from their desire? What one of them called "enlarging" the horizon of their own language—and what they all called *Bildung,* that is, both configuration and education, and in the first place, if I may put it this way, discovery of their own language and its fallow resources. Here is what Hölderlin had to say: "What is one's own has to be learned just as much as what is foreign." But then, why must this desire to translate be paid for at the price of a dilemma, the dilemma of fidelity or betrayal? Because there exists no absolute criterion of good translation; for such a criterion to be available, one would have to be able to compare the source and target texts to a third one that would bear the identical meaning that was held to circulate between the former and the latter. The same thing would have to be said in both cases. Just as in Plato's *Parmenides,* there is no third man between the idea of man and the individual man (Socrates, as it turns out), and there is no third text between the source text and the target text. Whence the paradox, before the dilemma: a good translation can only aim at a presumed *equivalence,* not one founded on a demonstrable *identity* of meaning. An equivalence without identity. This equivalence can only be sought for, worked out, presumed. And the only way to criticize a translation—which one can always do—is to propose another one presumed, or claimed, to be better or different. And this, by the way, is what happens among professional translators. As for the great texts of our culture, we live essentially on their retranslations continually taken up again. This is the case for the Bible, for Homer, for Shakespeare, for all the authors previously mentioned, and for philosophers, from Plato right up to Nietzsche and Heidegger.

Inundated with retranslations, are we better prepared to resolve our dilemma of fidelity versus betrayal? In no way. The risk that one takes with the desire to translate, and that marks the encounter with the foreigner in his own language, is insurmountable. Franz Rosenzweig, whom our colleague Hans-Christoph Askani takes as a "witness to the problem of translation" (which is how I would translate the title of Askani's book), gave this test the form of a paradox.[4] To translate, he said, is to serve two masters: the foreigner in his foreignness and the reader in his desire to appropriate. And before him, Schleiermacher broke this paradox into two propositions: to bring the reader to the author and to bring the author to the reader. For my own part, I will risk applying the Freudian vocabulary to this situation and speak of the work of translation, in the sense that Freud spoke of the work of memory, of mourning.

The work of translation is accomplished through overcoming intimate resistances motivated by fear, even by hate, of the foreigner, perceived as a threat to our own linguistic identity. But there is also a work of mourning, applied to the very ideal of a perfect translation. This idea has not only nourished the desire to translate and sometimes the joy of translating but also caused the misfortune of Hölderlin, broken by his ambition to meld German and Greek poetry into a hyperpoetry wherein every difference in idioms would be abolished. And who knows whether it is not this ideal of a perfect translation that, in the final analysis, leads to the nostalgia for an original language or to the idea of mastering language by means of a universal language? To give up the dream of perfect translation is to admit the unsurpassable difference between what is peculiar to us and what is foreign, so that the test of the foreign always remains.

This brings me back to my title: the paradigm of translation.

It seems to me that translation poses not just an intellectual, theoretical, or practical labor but also an ethical problem. To bring the reader to the author and the author to the reader, at the risk of serving two masters, is to practice what I would like to call

4. Askani, *Das Problem der Übersetzung.*

"linguistic hospitality." It is the model for other forms of hospitality that I see as akin to it. Are confessional traditions, religions, not like foreign languages to one another, with their lexicons, grammar, rhetoric, and style, which have to be *learned* in order to begin to make sense of them? Does not eucharistic hospitality assume the same risks of fidelity and betrayal, but again with the same renouncing of a perfect translation? I will go no further here with these risky analogies and questions.

But I do not want to end without having said something about the reasons why we must not neglect the other half of the problem of translation, namely, you may recall, translation within the same linguistic community. I want to show, at least succinctly, that it is this work applied to itself within the same language that reveals the profound reasons why the gap between a presumed perfect, universal language and what we call natural languages, in the sense of not being artificial ones, is insurmountable. As I have already suggested, it is not the imperfections of these natural languages that one wants to eliminate, but their very functioning along with their peculiarities. And it is the work of internal translation that precisely reveals this gap. Here I link up with the declaration that governs Steiner's *After Babel*. After Babel, to understand is to translate. What is at issue here is more than a simple internalization of our relation to the foreigner, thanks to Plato's adage that thinking is a dialogue of the soul with itself, an internalization that would turn internal translation into a mere appendix to external translation. It is a question of an original exploration, one that lays bare the everyday procedures of a living language, those that mean that no universal language can succeed in reconstructing such an unlimited diversity. It is in fact a question of getting close to the arcana of a living language and, with this, making sense of the phenomenon of misunderstanding, which, according to Schleiermacher, gives rise to interpretation, for which hermeneutics provides the theory. The reasons for the gap between a perfect language and a living one are exactly the same as these causes of misunderstanding.

Let me begin from one massive fact characteristic of the use of our languages: *it is always possible to say the same thing in a different way.* This is what we do when we define a word by another word in our lexicon, like every dictionary does. Peirce, in his semiotic theory, places this phenomenon at the center of language's reflexivity about itself. But it is also what we do when we reformulate an argument that was not understood. We say that we will explain it, that is, unfold it. To say the same thing in another way—*to put it another way*—is what the translator of a foreign language does. Thus, we rediscover at the interior of our linguistic community the same enigma of the same, of the same meaning, the undiscoverable identical meaning, supposed to make equivalent two versions of the same statement. This is why, as we say, we can't cope with this. And, often, we aggravate the misunderstanding with our explanations. At the same time, there is a bridge from internal translation, as I will call it, to external translation; that is, within the same community, understanding requires at least two interlocutors. They are not foreign to each other, to be sure, but already others, close others, if you will. This is why Husserl, speaking about the knowledge of others, called the everyday other *der Fremde*, the stranger, the foreigner. There is a stranger in every other. It is in terms of more than one person that one defines, reformulates, explains, that one seeks to say the same thing *in a different way*.

Let us take another step in the direction of the arcana that Steiner speaks of and returns to again and again. What are we working with when we speak and address our words to another person?

With three sorts of units: *words*, that is, the signs found in the lexicon; *sentences*, for which there is no lexicon (for no one can say how many sentences have been or will be said, either in French or in any other language); and, finally, *texts*, that is, sequences of sentences. It is the making use of these three things (the first one emphasized by Saussure, the second by Émile Benveniste and Roman Jakobson, and the third by Harald Weinrich, Hans-Robert Jauss, and other theorists dealing with the reception of texts) that is the source of the gap in relation to any presumed perfect language and the source of misunderstandings in everyday usage and, in this regard, the occasion for multiple competing interpretations.

Let me say two words about words. Each of our words has more than one meaning, as we see in our dictionaries. We call this their polysemy. The meaning is delimited in each case by use, which essentially involves sifting out the part of the meaning of a word that fits with the rest of the sentence and that works with it to convey what is being expressed and offered in exchange. It is the context in each case that, as we say, decides the meaning that a word takes on in such a circumstance of discourse. Beyond this, disputes over the meaning of words can be endless: what did you mean to say? It is the interplay of question and answer that either clears up or muddies these interactions. For there are not only patent contexts but hidden ones and what we call connotations, not all of which are intellectual, but some emotional, and not all of which are public, but some belong to a class, a group, even to a secret circle. For example, there is the whole margin dissimulated by censorship, the forbidden, the unsaid, crisscrossed by the figures of the hidden.

With this recourse made to the context, we have passed from the word to the sentence. This new unity, which in fact is the first unit of discourse, for the word comes from the sign which is not yet discourse, brings with it, in the final analysis, new sources of ambiguity having to do principally with the relation of the signified—what one says—to the referent—that about which one speaks, the world. A big program, as the other says! Short of a complete description, we have only points of view, perspectives, partial worldviews. This is why we are never finished explaining ourselves, with words and sentences, explaining ourselves to others who do not see things from the same angle as we do.

Then texts come into play, those interconnections of sentences which, as the word suggests, are "textures" that "weave" discourse into greater or longer sequences. Narrative is one of the most noteworthy forms of these sequences, and is particularly interesting for our inquiry inasmuch as we have learned that one can always recount things in another way by varying the emplotment. But there are also all kinds of other texts, where one does something other than narrate, for example, argue, as in moral philosophy, law, and politics. Here rhetoric comes in with its figures of style, its tropes, metaphors, and other devices, and all those language games in the service of innumerable strategies, including seduction and intimidation at the expense of any honest concern to convince oneself or the other.

From this follows everything that we might call translationology concerning the complicated relations between thought and language, the spirit and the letter, and the endless question: should we translate the words or the meaning? All the difficult questions concerning translation from one language to another find their origin in this reflection on language through language, which is why Steiner says that to understand is to translate.

Now I come to what Steiner takes to be most important and which tends to turn our inquiry in the opposite direction from that of the test of the foreign. He looks at uses of speech that intend something other than the truth or the real, that is, not only the manifestly false, the lie—even though to speak is to be able to lie, dissimulate, falsify—but also everything that we can classify as other than real: let us say the possible, the conditional, the optative, the hypothetical, the utopian. It's crazy—we must say—what one can do with language: not only say the same thing in another way but say something that is other than what is. Plato talked about this—with much perplexity—through the figure of the Sophist.

But it is not this figure that might most derail the order of our inquiry. It is the propensity of language for the enigma, the hermetic, the secret, in short, for noncommunication. Here is where we get what I would call Steiner's extremism, who, out of a hatred for idle chatter, conventional use, and the instrumentalization of language, is led to oppose interpretation to communication. The equation between understanding and interpreting then gets closed in on the self in the secret wherein we rediscover the untranslatable, which we thought to have set aside to the benefit of the fidelity versus betrayal pairing. We find ourselves back at the search for the most extreme form of fidelity. But fidelity to whom and to what? Fidelity to the capacity of language to preserve the secret in the encounter with its propensity to betray it. Fidelity, therefore, to oneself rather than to others. And it is true that the complex poetry of a Paul Celan does come close to being untranslatable, by coming close to the unspeakable, the unnamable at the heart of his own language, as much as lying in the gap between two languages.

What ought we to conclude from this sequence of reversals? For myself, I remain, it must be said, perplexed. I was led, it is true, to privileging beginning from the gate of the foreign. Were we not set under way by the fact of human plurality and by the double enigma of the incommunicability of idioms and translation in spite of this? And then, without the test of the foreign, would we be sensitive to the strangeness of our own language? Finally, without this test, are we not threatened with the bitter fate of enclosing ourselves in a monologue, left alone with our books? All honor, therefore, to linguistic hospitality!

But I also can see the other side, that of the work of language on itself. Is it not this work that gives us the key to the difficulties regarding translation *ad extra*? And if we had never drawn near to the country of the unsayable, would we ever understand the meaning of the secret, of the untranslatable secret? And do not our best exchanges, in love and friendship, preserve this quality of discretion—of secrecy and discretion—that preserves distance in proximity?

Yes, there are indeed two ways of taking up the problem of translation.

11. Readings

Otfried Höffe's *Principes du Droit*

Principes du droit is the fourth work of Professor Otfried Höffe to be made available to French readers.[1] In 1985, they had already welcomed his *Introduction à la philosophie pratique de Kant,* where he proposed an overall reading of Kant's practical philosophy, considered thematically and methodologically, without overlooking the philosophy of justice, the philosophy of history, or the philosophy of religion. In 1988 followed the translation of a critical presentation of political philosophy written by American philosophers, with the title *L'état et la justice: John Rawls et Robert Nozick.* This work was the complement to another wide-ranging work, *La justice politique,* whose French translation was published in 1991. Kant was noticeably absent from this discussion but tacitly present throughout the argument. Here now is a volume where Kant's transcendental perspective is first presented, then confronted with its principal adversary, utilitarianism, recognized to be the dominant current in contemporary juridical and political thought, then with those systems that claim in varying degrees to be Kantian even though they reject theses that Höffe takes to be inseparable from the Kantian perspective. The subtitle of the German original—*Ein Kontrapunkt der Moderne*—well conveys the author's main thesis, which is not meant to defend every nook and cranny of Kant but rather to claim a modest, yet inexpugnable place for the Kantian perspective. The word "counterpoint" expresses both a concession on the plane of evaluating

1. There is an English translation by Mark Migotti: *Categorical Principles of Law: A Counterpoint to Modernity.*—Tr.

the forces in play on the battlefield considered—Kant alone, is over!—and a conviction: Kant's adversaries and emancipated heirs cannot really carry through on their programs without doing justice to the Kantian moment of autonomy and to the categorical imperative, at least not if they claim to give a moral basis to their theory of justice or of the state.

However, Kantianism cannot claim to occupy the place spoken of in the symphony that constitutes modern juridical thinking unless it makes itself the object of a reevaluation, even a reformulation, aimed at determining what in it merits being defended under the rubric of "categorical principles" in the controversy with the "modern." It is through a rigorous work of sorting out and placing into a hierarchy what lies at the heart of Kant's practical philosophy that this new work of Höffe's distinguishes itself from his earlier *Introduction à la philosophie pratique de Kant*, and thanks to it the discussion begun in *L'état et la justice* and especially in *La justice politique* can be taken up again in relation to new interlocutors and to more openly Kantian arguments. If Höffe does not claim to raise his counterpoint to the level of an alternative position, it is because the conditions for entering into discussion with his adversaries are already present in Kant himself. Thus, this whole work is meant to demonstrate that the "categorical" moment in Kant, which appears in the German title, *Kategorische Rechtsprinzipien*, works only in connection with the noncategorical, that is, the empirico-pragmatic component of modern juridical culture. We will not stretch things too much if we say that the role of counterpoint, formerly held by the empirical-utilitarian current of Kantian discourse, is now to be held by the transcendental at the heart of practical philosophy, considered in terms of its overall method and theme.

This concern to circumscribe what merits being taken as categorical explains the order followed in this work: the first part is devoted to the foundational question; the second part considers the best-known examples—the prohibition of suicide and lying, the forbidding of false promises, the duty to assist others and to cultivate one's own talents. The third part is devoted to those who have tried to reform Kant.

I have referred to a double strategy of sorting things out and setting them into a hierarchy. The latter dominates the first part;

the former, the second and third parts. One has to have a hierarchy in order to sort things out. In this regard, it is of the highest importance to distinguish between a first moral philosophy (the fundamental ethics of the *Groundwork of the Metaphysics of Morals* and the Second Critique) and a second one (that of the *Metaphysics of Morals*) and to distinguish, beginning with the former, centered on the categorical imperative in general (which will be opposed later to the juridical imperatives of the Doctrine of Justice), a level that we can call a semantic one in the sense that it deals with the meaning of the concept of the moral (the good will, an obligation applying to every reasonable being, an imperative for every finite creature such as ourselves) and a level of normative ethics that deals with the criteria of moral philosophy, first of all in terms of the fundamental form of the general law stemming from the rule of universalization, then under the three subformulations known as the three Kantian imperatives. No less important is the distinction, within the second moral philosophy, between a general and a particular part. It is the general part that is at the center of the discussion in this book. It comprises, side by side and with the same categorical force, the juridical imperative in the singular (which governs the Doctrine of Justice) and the categorical imperative of virtue in the singular (which governs the Doctrine of Virtue). The particular part deals with the categorical principles in the plural, which are juridical on the one side (for example, the prohibition of false promises) and moral on the other (the prohibition of suicide and so forth).

Therefore, it is under the heading of the second moral philosophy, in its general part, that the categorical juridical imperative in the singular is situated, which merits being defended against every attempt to reject it, but also against any attempted revision. It constitutes the hard core of what deserves to be called a juridical ethics. The title *Metaphysics of Morals*, attached to the second moral philosophy, opened by this juridical ethics, strictly parallel to that of virtue, has to be defended inasmuch as it points to nothing less than its nonempirical positing. But then it has to be stripped of its theoretical, nonpractical additions having to do with the noumenal human person and it has to be dissociated from what stems from a wholly other problematic, that of the dialectic of practical reason, prolonged by its postulates about

God, immortality, and the free will. As we can see, the sorting out begins by differentiating among things.

The important thing, therefore, is to situate correctly juridical ethics and its categorical imperative in the singular. It is to this, and to this alone, backed by the preceding semantic analysis, that the principle of utilitarianism, which seeks to promote the greatest happiness for the greatest number, has to be opposed. On the other hand, certain mergers with Aristotle are justified inasmuch as the differentiation within the categorical leads us to the threshold of substantial, albeit still categorical, principles. In this sense, Höffe's book stems from a critique of critique, which, in a nonnegative sense of the term, consists in an evaluation of the legitimate scope of Kant's first-order critique and an inspection of its limits. If there is one accusation that this second-order critique can bring against Kant, it is that he aimed too high and claimed to reach an exclusive position, at the same time making impossible the wished-for counterpoint by handing himself over to the charge of anachronism—whence the title of the first part of Höffe's text: "Counterpoint or Anachronism?" Höffe undertakes to refute this alternative. In this regard, the recognition that anthropological elements make up part of the categorical moment in Kant's execution of his program but without any concession constitutes one of the most noteworthy achievements of this book.

Let us limit ourselves here to what deals directly with juridical ethics, whose place within the Kantian architectonic was mentioned above, along with the formulation of its categorical imperative in the singular.

This latter is stated in the following way in the introductory section to the Doctrine of Right:

> Any action is *right* if it can coexist with everyone's freedom in accordance with a universal law, or if on its maxim the freedom of choice of each can coexist with everyone's freedom in accordance with a universal law.[2]

We can get rid of the charge of moralism if we observe the threefold limitation intrinsic to this imperative. In the first place, liberty means liberty of action, hence the capacity to intervene in a field of

2. Immanuel Kant, *The Metaphysics of Morals*, in *Practical Philosophy*, 387.

interaction. Furthermore, the principle governs only external leg-islation, as the phrase "coexist with" indicates. Finally, it requires only legality, in the sense of the semantics of obligation, that is, conformity to the rule, not morality in the strict sense of obedience to duty as a duty, in other words, conviction (*Gesinnung*). Yet these three limits do not affect the transcendental condition itself that is expressed in the phrase "in accordance with a universal law." This requirement entails nothing other than the capacity for equal ap-plication to everyone's will. When we have understood that the re-quired universality governs only the coexistence of liberties, we can be sure about the metaphysical—that is, nonempirical—status of a postulate that section C says "is incapable of further proof."[3] The following step then imposes itself. The legitimation of constraint is analytically implied in the conditions for the coexistence of lib-erties. This connection can be immediately perceived if we observe that the constraint consists principally in an obstacle opposed to what is itself an obstacle to liberty. Hence, we are not dealing with two moments: obligation following a law and the legitimacy of that constraint. If the agreement between liberties is to be recipro-cal, the legitimate exercise of this constraint must equally be so. This connection between the two moments is so close that the principle of possibility of an external constraint comes to occupy the place on the juridical plane of the place that the conscious-ness of obligation—of *Gesinnung*—occupies among the motives on the plane of morality taken in the strict sense. Hence, legal-ity, which in the *Groundwork* was nothing other than a counter-concept, becomes the regulative principle of the juridical order.

If we keep in mind both the breadth of the juridical field and the internal limits of juridical principles in the plural, there is no longer a place from which to accuse juridical philosophy of mor-alism. The paradigm that Nicholas Luhmann says is "lost" can be validly proclaimed to be "rediscovered," once "revisited" by Höffe! It is the paradigm of a juridical moral philosophy without moral-ism, and, paradoxically, a juridical moral philosophy without mo-rality. This gap between legality and morality confirms that the juridical categorical imperative belongs to the second metaphys-ics, using Höffe's vocabulary.

3. Ibid., 388.

As for the anthropological moment that stands in counter-point to the transcendental moment, even in Kant—despite the declared claim of the *Groundwork* to constitute a metaphysics of morals apart from any anthropological admixture—it is tacitly present in the recognition of the status of human beings as finite rational beings, and moreover as tending to prefer their inclinations over their duty. But it is openly admitted in the philosophy of justice in a roundabout way through the elementary situations that put practical reason to the test on the plane of the coexistence of liberties. Thus, it has to be granted without embarrassment that the anthropology does not contaminate the moral philosophy; it defines, as Höffe nicely puts it, the challenge without which the moral imperative would have no function. It leaves this moral imperative open to itself.

Höffe has prepared us for what ought not to be called a confession through his careful analysis of the maxims in his *Introduction à la philosophie pratique de Kant*. The rule of universalization applies only to already-elaborated projects of action, even if they are rooted in inclinations that function not only as the enemies of morality but as "matter" that needs to be given "moral" form. Juridical philosophy does not escape this. The doctrine of virtue has to face up to typical situations, such as a dissatisfaction with life over against the prohibition of suicide, personal distress over against the prohibition of false promises, another's distress over against the command to bear assistance, even laziness over against the command to cultivate one's talents. The doctrine of justice arises from challenges that proceed from social relations that threaten human coexistence, that is, from those situations where it is tempting, for example, to hurt others on the plane of exchanges and contracts or on the plane of "my" property.

This is what the second part of Höffe's work vigorously demonstrates in regard to the well-known "examples" that we are invited to classify at the third level of the categorical, that of juridical imperatives in the plural. They are no less categorical than those on the higher level, but their plurality provides the occasion for a particularly detailed and differentiated articulation of the transcendental and the anthropological. The anthropology itself takes on the form of a particular juridical anthropology, distinct from a general one required by the juridical imperative in the singular.

An "increasingly empirical dimension" infiltrates the formation of the maxims submitted to the judgment of justice. Juridical ethics cannot be separated from the adversaries found in social life. That people have an effect on one another, that every liberty of action has to come to terms with that of others, and that there is competition over more or less rare goods are a few of the features that clothe the *condition humana* in the juridical sphere.

We must not conclude from this necessary negotiation between the transcendental and the anthropological that the latter capitulates to the former. The transcendental conditions of agreement of one will with another "following a universal law of liberty" escape the empirical conditions. What we call "human rights" are the result of nothing other than this imperative of a universal compatibility applied to the liberty of action. What distinguishes them from the general formulation of the juridical imperative is the accent placed on the equal restriction and equal protection implied by this requirement for compatibility. In this respect, Höffe is right to emphasize that for Kant the idea of exchange takes precedence over that of distribution: justice is commutative before being—and in order to be—distributive.

In short, in the contemporary debate over the question of the grounds of juridical ethics, the Kantian project of a juridical ethics, owing to its integrative dimension, can claim that "systematic" theories, like that of Luhmann, either misunderstand or are mistaken in their claims. In the same vein, we may observe that Höffe's project puts brakes on the move to the pluralism without limits of postmodernism, as much as it takes on the multiple enterprises meant to "demoralize" the juridical. But it is in replying to utilitarianism that Kant has the most success, by assigning to it the role of a counterpoint to its own counterpoint, through its own recourse to anthropology.

In the third part of Höffe's book, readers are sure to find interesting his discussion of those contemporary thinkers who claim to draw on Kant even while they claim to go beyond him—Rawls, Apel, and Habermas.

The notion of counterpoint takes on a new sense here in a strategy whose target is no longer utilitarianism but those fellow travelers whose adversaries are the same ones as Kant's, allowing for the rich variations to be found in contemporary utilitarianism.

The strategy for such a family quarrel has to differ from that for an open battle against outsiders. Allowing for the differences we shall return to below, once the key difference that distinguishes the three thinkers mentioned has been acknowledged, two main arguments are to be found in the three chapters in question. On the one hand, all three are reproached for having misunderstood the exact tenor of the juridically categorical in Kant. On the other hand, Höffe works to show that the foundation substituted for that of Kant presupposes it, under the threat of giving in to the adversary. These two arguments are meant to add to the detailed labor of hierarchization and sorting things out by which Höffe seeks to establish a modest, yet intransient position for Kantianism.

These arguments are articulated in the clearest fashion against Rawls. By characterizing his own theory as "political, but not metaphysical," Rawls has misunderstood the meaning of Kant's practical metaphysics and, at the same time, the exact sense of the juridical categorical imperative. As for the principles of justice, Rawls's formulation is assuredly close to Kant's insofar as, thanks to the veil of ignorance, the same universal aim guides the discussion from the initial situation of fairness to the ultimate determination of principles. Yet we can call this universal aim into doubt inasmuch as the search for a maximal mean utility is what is at stake in the contract. Thus, according to Höffe, the demonstration is not really well differentiated from what we could call a calculation of this maximal mean utility. What is lacking is the universal categorical moment that could transform a rational prudential choice into a moral one. It seems to me that, for Höffe, in the final analysis it is the transfer of the discussion from the juridical-political to the economic sphere that is responsible for the finally undecidable character of Rawls's position between the categorical and the utilitarian. Nevertheless, we must not deny the nuanced aspect of Höffe's final evaluation.[4]

The discussion with Apel calls for subtlety. Who, today, has pleaded more vigorously than Apel in favor of a transcendental type of thinking? Who, other than Habermas, has better known how to negotiate between Continental traditions and Anglo-American modes of thought? Thus, Höffe can acknowledge with some sat-

---

4. Höffe, *Principles du droit*, 222.

isfaction the "profusion of points they hold in common." Yet does
the linguistic turn that Apel elevates to the rank of a paradigm
shift—from that of consciousness to that of language—better
permit the grounding of the imperative? I shall consider here only
the accusation of a monological foundation directed against Kant
in the name of a dialogical principle, a principle included in the
aim of an ideal communicative community and in the search for a
consensus reached through discussion. According to Höffe, communicability is virtually included in the Kantian rule about universalization, as, moreover, the requirement of publicity for every
critical exercise of the faculty of judgment underscores. But, above
all, communicability is at the center of the doctrine of justice, in
the requirement for compatibility among spheres of free action. In
another direction, one can doubt whether the notion of an ideal
consensus allows us really to distinguish between a common and
a universal will. Hence, Höffe can declare that Apel's alternative
itself falls under the Kantian criterion. Less unexpected is the in-
sinuation of a danger of hubris, attached to an enterprise in which
omniscience and omnipotence are to be conferred on a community
of communication, owing to the elimination of the problematic of
the conciliation between virtue and happiness, which is in truth
wholly different from the search for the categorical, which occupies the much decried Dialectic of the *Critique of Practical Reason:*
"the best possible will does not allow the communicative community to fulfill the task set out by Kant under the key word of the
dialectic of pure practical reason." Clearly, family quarrels do not
lack force or sting.

   We come, finally, to Habermas. Höffe had already argued
against him in his *Justice politique.* Therefore, we ought to see in
the pages devoted to Habermas in this new work just a segment
of an ongoing discussion. Over against Habermas, Höffe admits
being overwhelmed at first by the amount of empirical-pragmatic
data in Habermas's *magum opus,* on the theory of communicative
action. But does not the choice of this concept as the central axis
of discussion run the risk of losing sight of the categorical in the
profusion of heterogeneous references to the social sciences and to
the grounds of these sciences? Does not taking into account the
figures of social pathology tend to make us adjourn, if not abandon,
the problem of a final ground, which Apel, however, has returned

to the place of honor? Starting from these doubts, Höffe's critique is sinuous, even persnickety, expressing the uneasiness of a strictly critical mode of thought when faced with an enterprise that projects nothing less than a general theory of society. In an enterprise of this scope, the place left to Apel's pragmatic transcendental foundation can only become more and more modest. It is when Habermas concentrates on the ethics of discussion that Höffe sees himself confronted with a more limited argument, one where universalization receives at least the status of a "bridge principle." His two arguments addressed in turn to the members of the large family of rebel heirs then find a more delimited field of application. What is finally held against Habermas is, opposite to the critique addressed to Apel, an excess of modesty, by which I mean a transcendental modesty. How can one denounce a pragmatic contradiction in the skeptical adversaries of an ethics of discussion unless one professes openly and firmly the "categorical principles of justice"? Only on this condition can the transcendental moment claim to preserve its significance as a counterpoint at an equal distance from overevaluation and capitulation in the dialogue with the social sciences.

It is to this tenacious plea that Höffe's most recent work devotes, more than a thematic and methodological unity, a unity of tone.

The Fundamental Categories
in Max Weber's Sociology

It is not my goal to give an overall view of Max Weber's thought, as Pierre Bouretz does in *Les promesses du monde*.[1] My goal is more limited; it is to present an *explication de texte* applied to the opening sections of the first chapter of the first part of Weber's *Economy and Society*, entitled "Basic Sociological Terms," along with the first sections of chapter 3, "The Types of Legitimate Domination" ("Die Typen der Herrschaft"). I do not intend to undertake this reading, which has many implications, without making use of a guideline. As it turns out, we can draw here on a trustworthy text, based on Weber's own working notes as edited by Winckelmann.[2] My guideline in fact will have a focus that is both thematic and methodological. From the thematic point of view, what is at stake is the construction of the pair domination and legitimation (*Herrschaft* and *Legitimität*). We should already pause here over the question of how to translate *Herrschaft*. In both French and English, the translators have used "domination," in part recalling the Hegelian dialectic of the master and the slave in the *Phenomenology of Spirit*. From the methodological point of view, what is significant is to follow how Weber lays out his concepts. Here, I make no presupposition concerning the problems posed by Heinz Wismann concerning the rationalization of history on the grand scale. We shall concentrate, rather, on the working out of some

---

1. This lecture was originally presented at a conference on Weber held in Sofia, Bulgaria, in March 1999 and was first published in *Divinatio* (Sofia, 2000).

2. Weber, *Wirtschaft und Gesellschaft*.

of the basic concepts in a relatively brief portion of the text. This process rests on a strategy of argumentation that brings together two procedures. One is linear and aims at the progressive conceptual determination of the notion of domination, which works together with that of legitimation, or even in a triad if we add the role of belief (*Vorstellung*). The other consists in a typological distribution of the notions that joins the linear procedure to a many-sided structure. I want to demonstrate how this complex strategy is appropriate to the theme of domination.

Let us begin with the opening section of the first chapter. It unfolds in three steps. First comes the definition of the sociological project as a science that undertakes to understand through interpretation (*bedeutendes Verstehen*). We need to emphasize the pairing here of understanding and explanation:

> Sociology . . . is a science concerning itself with the interpretive understanding [*bedeutendes Verstehen*] of social action and thereby with a causal explanation of its course and consequences. (4)

Here is the difference from Dilthey, who opposes explanation and understanding to each other. Weber helps us to get out of the impasse created by this massive opposition. For him, the causal factor is included in the movement of interpretation. Indeed, it is because sociology is interpretive that it can produce a causal explanation. It is true that in what follows in the text interpretation is sometimes opposed to causality. But this is to a causality detached from its connection to *Deutung*, "meaning." Having said this, of what is there an interpretation? The answer is action (*Handlung*). (I prefer this term to the French translation's *activité* because it brings us closer to the usage of this term in an important current of contemporary history and sociology.) In this context, action is opposed to mere behavior, as a set of movements in space, whereas action makes sense for a human agent:

> We shall speak of "action" insofar as the acting individual attaches a subjective meaning to his behavior. (4)

The following decisive step is the one where the definition of the action includes the notion of meaning that this action has for the agent. But at the same time, and this is the third moment, action has also to make sense in relation to other subjects.

The notion of social action proceeds from this interaction of the subjective and the intersubjective:

> Action is "social" insofar as its subjective meaning takes account of the behavior of others and is thereby oriented in its course. (4)

The intersubjective element is thus present from the beginning, and sociology is interpretive insofar as its object implies a subjective meaning, on the one hand, and taking into account the motivations of others, on the other. The correlation between interpretive *Verstehen* and its specific object, meaningful action, is thus a strong one. I would sum up these three elements with the idea of a motivational model that is opposed, not to causality in general, but to a mechanical, deterministic idea of causality. Here, following Weber, we could take up a great number of details that help specify this concept of social action, in particular those having to do with the distinction between active and passive adhesion, which receives application in the typology of *Herrschaft:* not to act is still to act, as in behaviors that are acts of omission or of a withdrawal from the sphere of action. Among other important such determinations must be placed the temporal ones. They have to do with the orientation of social action, for example, in relation to an expected behavior on the part of others. Here is a feature that links up with Alfred Schutz's analysis of the orientation of action as directed toward contemporaries, predecessors, or successors. This introduces not only a historical dimension in general but more precisely a transgenerational one.

This first triad is followed by a pause that provides the first occasion to introduce the notion of an ideal type that we can see to be, in fact, already at work. This notion consists of a reflective concept applied to the notion of meaning as constitutive of the object under study, meaningful action. What is meaningful for agents is also what makes sense for the sociologist's reflection, that is, the possibility of constructing types. These are methodological constructs, to be sure, but not arbitrary ones. One can call into question the epistemological consistency of this concept and always propose alternative interpretations. Let us say therefore, as a first approximation, that it is a question of a means of identifying, inventorying, classifying forms of action and, at the same time, of a procedure that makes room for a typology. In this regard, we have to situate the ideal types, as ideal, both along the linear trajectory of the conceptual development and in terms of the expanding redistributions of the typologies. We have to start from the fact that what is real for Weber is always the individual. The ideal types must not be dissociated from what we can call his methodological individualism. We are always dealing with individuals who orient themselves in relation to other individuals, once the notion of social action implies intersubjectivity. In this regard, Weber is not so far from Husserl's thesis in his *Cartesian Meditations* regarding the "communalization of intersubjective relations."[3]

This is the moment in the text when the first typology appears on the linear trajectory—in fact, we find several more or less discordant typologies in the first fifteen sections, but the discordances matter less than the operation of proceeding by way of the use of such typologies. This first typology has to do with the notion of social action. It precedes that of the types of legitimation of domination:

> Social action, like all action, may be oriented in four ways. It may be:
>
> (1) *instrumentally rational* (*zweckrational*), that is, determined by expectations as to the behavior of objects in the environment and of other human beings; these expectations are used as "conditions" or "means" for the attainment of the actor's own rationally pursued and calculated ends;
>
> (2) *value-rational* (*wertrational*), that is, determined by a conscious belief in the value for its own sake of some ethical, aesthetic, religious, or other forms of behavior, independently of its prospects of success;
>
> (3) *affectual* (especially emotional), that is, determined by the actor's specific affects and feeling states;
>
> (4) *traditional*, that is, determined by ingrained habituation. (24–25)

Here four types are distinguished; in other places three are. Therefore, there is no conceptual rigidity but rather an operation, one that remains exploratory in nature. An instrument is put to the

3. Husserl, *Cartesian Meditations,* §56, "Constitution of Higher Levels of Intermonadic Community."

test, which will later lead to the systems of legitimation. But it is not by chance that the first one named is the one called *zweckrational,* to which later the bureaucratic type of system will correspond. The virtue of these typologies is that they put in place a strong correlation between the conceptual structure, on the epistemological level, and the connection between authority or domination and legitimation, on the thematic one. In fact, this first table is already, we may say, a table of legitimation (*Geltung*). What is interesting about this text, in its functioning, is not that it begins with legitimation but that it gets there by degrees.

We are not going to dwell on the intermediary concepts between this trilogy—orientation toward meaning, toward others, and the notion of social action—and the notion of domination. But three such intermediary concepts are proposed before the notion of *Herrschaft* comes onstage.

First, we have the notion of order. The German term *Ordnung* means more than a command. There will only be a command, an imperative, with *Herrschaft*. The more fundamental concept of order designates an organization or organism endowed with its own stability. The concept of *Ordnung* still awaits its complement, the predicate "legitimate." Order requires legitimation in order to be an order. And the section on *Ordnung* proposes a new typology that bears precisely on this legitimation. The concept of *Geltung,* which is progressively going to move to center stage, consists above all in a demand for recognition. The German *Geltung* turns on the active character of such a demand, what in English can be called a claim. Under the heading of *Ordnung* this demand for legitimacy falls under the concept of a guarantee: an order can be guaranteed (*garantiert*) by affects, by moving beyond an emotional order, or in a rational manner in terms of values or in virtue of faith in its validity, or in a religious manner or uniquely as a function of the expectation of certain specific external consequences, for example, in situations that bring some interest into play. Once again, the distribution in terms of types turns out to be extraordinarily shifting, to the benefit of engendering a concept by narrowing in on it, by a progressive determination. What is most important, however, remains that the problem of legitimacy should be introduced by that of order. In this sense we are not dealing with a view from on high, so to speak, but from below, from that of

social agents, to anticipate the comparison with other, more recent enterprises I shall return to in concluding. It is agents who
can grant a legitimate validity to an order: through tradition, affective belief, rational belief in values, or a positive disposition toward equality. Again, the discordances among typologies do not
really matter. We are dealing only with exploratory classifications
that all link up with one another.

The second intermediary concept is that of the difference between ways in which *Ordnung* functions, depending on whether
it is integrative or simply associative. Here we are truly on the
trajectory of legitimation. The difference is as follows. Either the
agents have a feeling of a shared sense of belonging, that is, they
form a *Gemeinschaft* (or one can even make use of a substantive
form, *Vergemeinschaftung*, "communalization"), or they consider
their reciprocal ties as a contractual relationship, the bond being
more external and not implying the personal commitment of the
agents to such a degree—*Gesellschaft*. Here we rejoin a classic distinction of German sociology at the time, one that unfortunately
has led to terrible consequences. It was not Weber's intention, but
Nazi sociologists magnified community over against association,
a bad use of Tönnies's famous dichotomy. In this regard, we can
state that Weber situates himself on the side of *Gesellschaft*, which
figures in the title of his book, rather than on that of *Gemeinschaft*.
In fact, the preference given to the associative relation comes from
the juridical tradition of the social contract found in Hobbes,
Rousseau, and Kant. We ought also to recall that all these concepts were meant to cover the economic, juridical, and political
planes, as can be seen from what follows in Weber's work. He
needed sufficiently powerful operative concepts to cover at least
these three fields, if not also that of religion. What counts, beyond
the formality of the contract, is the opposition between the bond
of *Gesellschaft* and that of *Gemeinschaft*, the former finally culminating in the administrative system. We will want to keep in mind
the idea that the combination of these two concepts turns out to
be more fruitful when it comes to producing the social bond, the
willingness to live together, as we see in Hannah Arendt.

Next comes the connecting concept of closure. It indicates
the degree of openness of a group or grouping (*Verband*). What
is at issue here is collective identity, insofar as this depends on the

existence of limits, territorial or other limits, which determine whether an individual belongs or not. I think here of Michael Walzer's *Spheres of Justice,* which begins precisely with a chapter entitled "Membership." It is a question here of rules that govern inclusion, and hence also exclusion, both equally significant for the constituting of the identity of a group. In this regard, the elaboration of the degree of openness of a group leads to the conceptual space of motivation.

Next, comes the third intermediary concept, that of hierarchy. It proceeds from a differentiation within closed groups between those who govern and those who are governed. "The leadership in an organization may claim a legitimate right to impose new rules" (50). Here we are at the threshold of the political concept, but the distinction between leading and being led operates at all three levels, the economic, the juridical, and the political. It is worth noting that the action of leading is named before the one who leads and before the act of commanding, which will be tied to the specificity of the concept of *Herrschaft.* The progressive determination of the major concepts thus advances in step with the problem of legitimation. In this regard, the Hegelian problematic of recognition is constantly in the background of the question of legitimacy. It is what is anticipated through the eventual challenging of every position of leadership as regards the position of subordination. At the same time we can see the outlines unfolding of the conjunction between the problematic of legitimation and that of violence. No ruling power is established solely through formal rules. It is also instituted through the imposition of constraints. The threat of the use of force remains on the horizon of the problem of authority. Weber makes a long pause here and asks whether there can exist societies exempt from such constraining rules. It is not plausible, he says, that any form of government can satisfy everybody. There are differences of interest, of age, and so on. And the assumption that the minority should submit to the majority reintroduces the idea of coercion. We might think that it is only within a unanimous group that constraint would be absent. In reality, such a group may be the most coercive of all. The law of unanimity is more dangerous than is that of majority rule, which alone allows the minority to be identified and thereby for its rights to be defined. To use George Orwell's rhetoric, we could say that in 1793 all the French were equal except for those who were more equal than others, those who were sent to the guillotine. The strength of Weber's argument in favor of majority rule lies here:

> In our terminology, an order is always "imposed" to the extent that it does not originate from a voluntary personal agreement of all the individuals concerned. The concept of imposition hence includes "majority rule," in that the minority must submit. For that reason there have been long periods when the legitimacy of majority rule has either not been recognized at all, or been held doubtful. (51)

The underlying concept of recognition appears central here. But we also see that even a voluntary agreement implies some imposition.

I can state my point now. I have followed this conceptual development: social action, the alternative of integration or association, whether a group is closed or open, and finally hierarchy, which includes in turn a structure of authority. It is only at this moment that Weber introduces *Herrschaft* as a separate concept, that is—and this is important—the relation of giving and obeying orders. Some translations, Parsons's in particular, translate *Herrschaft* by "authority," others by "imperative control." I will use "domination," for the reason, already mentioned, among others, of its proximity to the Hegelian problematic. I quote:

> "Domination" [*Herrschaft*] is the probability that a command with a given specific content will be obeyed by a given group of persons. (53)

Therefore, at the center of things are the ideas of commanding and obedience. *Herrschaft* is defined by the expectation that others will obey. The system of power must therefore possess a certain credibility that allows it to count on the obedience of its members. But the question of physical constraint remains constantly paired with that of legitimation, of *Geltung*. We must insist on this point, for people have too often isolated the next text I am going to cite, where Weber seems to tie the definition of the state not to its end but to its means, as Lenin will do in *The State and Revolution:*

> It is not possible to define a political organization, including the state, in terms of the end to which its action is devoted. . . . Thus it is possible to define the "political" character of an organization only in terms of the *means* peculiar to it, the use of force. This

means is, however, in the above sense specific, and is indispensable to its character. It is even, under certain circumstances, elevated into an end in itself. (55)

But if we restore the context, the important predicate remains "legitimate." On the previous page, we read:

A compulsory political organization with continuous operations [*politischer Anstaltsbetrieb*] will be called a "state" insofar as its administrative staff successfully upholds the claim to the *monopoly* of the *legitimate* use of physical force in the enforcement of its order. (54)

Everything that follows will verify that the problematic of *Herrschaft* is, from one end to the other, one of legitimation in relation to the threat of the use of violence. This is so to such an extent that we have a system with four terms: domination, legitimacy, violence, and belief.

We should pause again at this point to consider the use made here of certain ideal types, as we did earlier. Someone may object to this recourse to concepts that are at least transhistorical, if not ahistorical. Do they hold for pre-Columbian, Asiatic, or other societies? We can make the following provisional reply. For a perspective that would remain historicist, it would be simply impossible to speak of a different organization than our own if we could not identify it on the basis of analogical concepts, capable of making sense in our linguistic universe of what explains itself to itself in terms of another cultural field. If we were to assume a state of total indifference, as an ideology of difference entails, we could not even name differences, beyond the assertion that they would become perfectly indifferent. We may state a different criticism. Do these concepts, beyond their ahistorical character, also carry a dissimulated critical value? The Frankfurt School will rush into this gap and confer a value of denunciation on these ideal types that involves precisely the violence and legitimation pair.

But let us leave this question hanging for the time being and turn to the third important chapter, entitled "Legitimität der Geltung." There, legitimation figures as something sought, demanded, claimed. The central thesis is that all power asks for adhesion and that this demand claims to be legitimate and in this sense appeals to our belief. At the beginning of this chapter, Weber offers a recapitulation of the concepts necessary to the conceptual structure of this appeal for legitimacy. These are the ones we have already considered: *Ordnung*, an order; the distinction between communalization and socialization; openness versus closedness; the threat of the use of violence. Next comes his examination of the claim to legitimacy. What is most interesting and perhaps finally astonishing in this text—which below will lead us to shift the notion of an ideal type beyond its simple classificatory function—is that the belief by means of which agents respond to the claim of legitimacy is presented as a supplement, a category to which Jacques Derrida has devoted much attention. But a supplement to what? To known forms of motivation: "custom, personal advantage, purely affectual or ideal motives of solidarity, do not form a sufficiently reliable basis for a given domination. In addition there is normally a further element, the belief in *legitimacy*" (213). This belief in legitimacy indicates something extra, and this is what has to hold our attention. In one sense, the whole typology we are about to consider has to do with this something extra. A few lines after the text just cited, we read: "Experience shows that in no instance does domination voluntarily limit itself to the appeal to material or affectual or ideal motives as a basis for its continuance." Three guarantees of social action are enumerated here. "In addition [*Zumal*] every such system attempts to establish and to cultivate the belief in its legitimacy." It is experience, we are told, that demonstrates this—as though we could not derive this factor from the basic categories that had been elaborated with such precision. Belief in legitimacy is a supplement that has to be treated as a pure and simple fact resulting from experience. Perhaps this fact is destined to remain enigmatic. Belief adds something, which allows the claim to be heard, taken up, even by those who exercise this *Geltung*, this demand. As we can see, we have to deal here with the problematic of recognition. It makes me think of an apt text of Gadamer's where he says that all obedience to authority rests on the recognition of superiority (*Überlegenheit*). If I stop believing in the superiority of an authority, it simply returns to a kind of violence. Elsewhere I considered whether we might not find something here like the Marxist notion of *Mehrwert*, "surplus value," but as extended beyond its economic meaning, which makes surplus value consist in a levy forced on labor, used to engender the accumulation of capital.[4] Marx himself sees there is something enigmatic about this mechanism and suspects there may be something like a residue of theology in it, as we see in the well-known chapter on the "fetishism of merchandise" in the first volume of *Capital*. In the same way, because power functions only when something extra is attached to known motivations, we touch here on the root of the phenomenon of ideology, as seeking a surplus value to values that itself always threatens to be lacking. In this regard, Louis Althusser makes an important contribution with his theory of symbolic institutions of domination.

It is on the basis of this enigma that Weber unfolds his well-known triad of types of legitimate domination:

> There are three pure types of legitimate domination. The validity of the claims to legitimacy may be based on:
>
> 1. Rational grounds—resting on a belief in the legality of enacted rules and the right of those elevated to authority under such rules to issue commands (legal authority).
>
> 2. Traditional grounds—resting on an established belief in the sanctity of immemorial traditions and the legitimacy of those exercising authority under them (traditional authority); or finally,
>
> 3. Charismatic grounds—resting on devotion to exceptional sanctity, heroism or exemplary character of an individual person, and of the normative pattern or order revealed or ordained by him (charismatic authority). (215)

The order of presentation is important here. It is one of a descending order of clarity and of increasing opacity. Perhaps this feature has something to do in the end with the functioning of the ideal types, insofar as these are assigned to the potential rationality of their referent. If we follow the descending order, which is not historical, there is no reason to think that, historically, things happened in the reverse order: from the charismatic to the traditional to the rational. Actually, there is a whole aspect of Weber's sociology that could be suspected of being motivated by considerations having to do with the philosophy of history, if not the theology of history, or of an inverted theology of history. But let us stick to the framework of the typology. We see then that it is important

4. See Ricoeur, *Lectures on Ideology and Utopia*.

for this typology to be organized in terms of degrees of decreasing rationality. What is most conceivable is motivation resting on the belief in legality. With the charismatic, after the traditional, we touch on what presents itself as most opaque. Indeed, Weber's lengthiest developments are devoted to authority resting on belief in the legality of rules and the right to give orders. Five criteria are proposed, of which we shall take up just the first one:

> any given legal norm may be established by agreement or by imposition, on grounds of expediency or value-rationality or both, with a claim to obedience at least on the part of the members of the organization. (217)

What is taken into account here is uniquely the formal structure of belief. The presentation of the other criteria proceeds in terms of a decreasing order of such rationality, starting from the most depersonalized aspects and moving in the direction of the most personalized aspects of organization, inasmuch as belief in the formalization remains at the same time belief in the quality of the one who makes this claim. Hence we can ask whether, in each actual system of domination, there does not subsist in a residual way the signs of the charismatic in the traditional and of the traditional in the legal. If we were simply to underscore the conjunction between what is called administrative direction, which characterizes the bureaucratic system overall, we could say that on the typological plane it represents the extreme point of rationality based on legality. However, we can ask here whether the typology here is really devoid of evaluation, if it is really *wertfrei?* We may suspect that a prejudice in favor of rationality is at work that is most clearly expressed in the functioning of authority. It is true that Weber does not conceal the importance of questions about the person and the charisma that adhere to what he calls control. But the question continues to pose itself whether every trace of charisma or traditionality has disappeared from the power of control exercised by existing bureaucratic systems. In any case, this control by nonspecialists is possible only in a quite limited manner over those experts who most often end up winning their way with a minister who lacks their expertise even while in principle being their superior. This text is quite remarkable.

The question of who controls the bureaucratic apparatus sums up the whole question of the relation between the expert and the politician. The hypothesis that I would form from reading this typology is that the ideal type of legality remains a form of domination to the degree that we can discern in it something of the other two structures of claiming legitimacy, legality tending to dissimulate the residues of traditional domination and charismatic motivation. Thus, we find ourselves on the terrain of Norbert Elias, for whom the confiscation of the threat of force, the use of violence, permits the establishment of a symbolic order that will have hidden its violence beneath its symbolization. We find something similar in Pierre Bourdieu. But, for Max Weber, we remain on the plane of a purely abstract and neutral typology. For him, there is no shadow of suspicion being exercised, as is the case for the Frankfurt School. To be prudent, let us say, at least, that no power functions on a unique, isolated basis and that every real system of power undoubtedly implies legal, traditional, and charismatic elements in varying proportions, with the legal type functioning only on the basis of what subsists in it of the traditional and charismatic types.

Let us now turn quickly to the definition of the traditional and charismatic types, which are well known. Domination is qualified as traditional when its legitimacy is claimed and acknowledged in virtue of the *heilig* character attached to the very age of ancient power. The opaque character of the traditional in relation to the rational is indicated by this term: sacred. I will pass over many of the details concerning how this functions. I will emphasize only the descending, decreasing character of rationality across the whole classification. Let us end therefore with the definition of the process of legitimation of charismatic domination. It rests on an extraordinary yielding to sacrality, to the strength of heroes, to the exemplary character of a person or order of things revealed or created by this sacrality.

To illumine this passage, I propose a reference to the moment in Hegel's *Philosophy of Right* where rationality, bound to the idea of constitution (*Verwaltung*), opens onto the figure of the prince, which is not bound to the monarchy but rather constitutes the blind spot of every structure of power, that is, the capacity to make decisions, which in any system of power always remains subjective to some degree.[5] We can suspect that the phenomenon of personalizing power is at work here. It is discussed in terms similar to those Hegel uses by Eric Weil in his *Philosophie politique,* where he says that "the state is the organization of a historical community. Organized as a state, the community is capable of making decisions."[6] Does not this capacity to make decisions always have something to do with what is traditional, even charismatic? The whole problematic then has something to do with that of credibility from one end to the other. Let us therefore cite a final text from Max Weber: "It is recognition on the part of those subject to authority which is decisive for the validity of charisma" (242). It is remarkable that it is in the discussion of charisma that we should find something said about recognition. But perhaps this is what constitutes the problematic that governs the whole realm of *Geltung,* as involving someone's claim to exercise authority, to give an order.

To conclude, I would like to return to our guideline, the relation between a thematic and a methodological interest, as it relates to the unfolding of the conceptual construction. We must ask ourselves here about the appropriateness of this strategy of argumentation in relation to the problematic of domination, along with its legitimacy and its creditability. Does not the linear construction, on the one hand, and branching, on the other, stand in an intimate and deep relation to the very theme of domination and legitimation? And are not the hidden stakes here the mastering by sociological rationality of the residual irrationality attached to the very phenomenon of the exercising of power? We have noted the order of decreasing rationality in the typology of legitimation. Is not this order in return one of increasing opacity, in the face of what appeared to us to be a supplement, the *Zumal* of belief, within which the very enigma of recognition takes refuge? Does the work of rationalization not work, if I may put it this way, in an opposite way, or as a countereffort, to the increasing opacity of the concepts considered, up to this ultimate residue of belief?

Confronted with these questions, what aid do we find in reading other sociologists who are less committed to a top-down reading focused on the phenomenon of authority (even if a bottom-up

5. Hegel, *Philosophy of Right,* §273.
6. Weil, *Philosophie politique,* §31.

one, starting from the charismatic phenomenon, subsists in the interstices of Weber's typology)? Among such top-down readings we find the work of Norbert Elias, devoted to the way in which the state system imposes itself in an imperious manner thanks to the monopolization of physical violence as camouflaged symbolic violence. What is important then is the correlation between the progress in civility at the level of systems of power and intellectual, practical, and affective self-control at the level of individual functioning.

We should next bring into play a crisscrossing of such top-down and bottom-up readings. We would then encounter strategies of negotiation and appropriation, whereby a decisive power of initiative is restored to social agents. I am thinking here of the work on microhistory done by the Italian historians Carlo Ginzburg and Giovanni Levi and of some work in the sociology of action, such as that by Luc Boltanski and Laurent Thévenot.[7] We learn from them that agents pursue the legitimation of their action in a plurality of cities or worlds, which call for a typology of a new type, no longer in terms of a model of obedience to authority but in terms of types of argument for legitimacy exercised by social agents themselves, when acting in the city of renown, or that of inspiration, or those of commercial exchange, of industry, of citizenship. In Walzer we find the same plurality of orders of legitimation and an equal interest granted to strategies of negotiation and compromise, irreducible to the mere relation of domination to obedience. We could even expand the space of the constituting of the social bond and the search for collective identity further by exploring with Michel de Certeau and Bernard Lepetit the many strategies for appropriating norms used by social agents. All these works have in common a concern for the constitution of the social bond, thanks to a great variety of procedures of appropriation and identification.

Have we thereby moved completely beyond Max Weber and his theory of legitimate domination? I do not think so. We have simply situated his analyses in a social space traversed by a multitude of strategies appropriate in each instance to transactions

---

7. Ginzburg, *The Cheese and the Worms*; Levi, *Le pouvoir au village*; Boltanski and Thévenot, *De la justification*.

of different kinds. Perhaps we would even rediscover, with these different trajectories, Weber's other contributions to the exploration of the formation of the social and political bond, as in his "Politics as a Vocation."[8] What we might have to give up in the process is the axiological neutrality so proudly claimed by the theory of fundamental sociological categories presented in *Economy and Society*.

8. Weber, "Politics as a Vocation," in *The Vocation Lectures*, 32–94.

Bouretz on Weber

Pierre Bouretz has given me the great pleasure of sharing with his readers what I see as the strengths and original features of his book *Les promesses du monde*.[1] Many excellent works have dealt with Max Weber's contribution to the epistemology of the social sciences, whether it be a question of the relation between explanation and understanding in the mixed notion of "interpretive understanding," or of methodological individualism, which authorizes a reduction of collective entities to constructs derived from human interactions. Others have placed the accent on the ethics related to this epistemology, under the title of "axiological neutrality." Bouretz has taken the option of subordinating Weber's two important innovations to the question that seems to him to underlie all others, that of the disenchantment of the world. Weber is thus placed in company with such great political thinkers as Hobbes, Machiavelli, Kant, Hegel, and Marx. And having chosen this perspective, Bouretz has undertaken to verify his central hypothesis by transporting it successively into the three fields of economics, politics, and the law. From the convergences and correlations between the results obtained in these three areas, he expects them to provide the philosophical equivalent, the only one possible, of what would amount to verification and refutation in descriptive political science. To strengthen this proof, he confronts the leading interpretations, in French and other languages, of Weberian sociology or of the philosophy that underlies

---

1. This chapter was originally published as the preface to Bouretz's *Les promesses du monde*.

this great oeuvre. The place he occupies in this critical band is thereby clearly delimited. While adopting the broad lines of the "skeptical" diagnostic that Weber brings to bear on modern rationality, Bouretz vigorously resists the "nihilistic" fascination suggested by Weber's neo-Nietzscheism. We can speak of *resistance* in that what is philosophically at stake in this whole book consists in localizing the moments where the Weberian analysis of modernity sacrifices the capacity of rationality to still be an instrument of liberation today to a kind of speculative discouragement—whence the pathetic tone of a scrupulous, analytic work, which reveals a thinker personally struck by the theme of the disenchantment of the world and seeking good reasons not to despair about reason. It is not by chance if, in the epilogue, a sort of last word is left to an unexpected visitor: Walter Benjamin, for whom the key word in the philosophy of history was *Rettung*, "salvation." Pierre Bouretz thus seems to say to us: if Weber was correct in his description, how can we say that he was in error axiologically? This is what Thomas Nagel would call a "mortal question."

If the thesis about the disenchantment of the world is the true key to Weber's works, it means that we have to enter into them not through the *Essais sur la théorie de la science,* as they were brought together for us in 1965 by Julien Freund, but by way of the writings devoted to the sociology of religion. The roots of disenchantment are to be found within the religious sphere as motivating action. The very idea stands out against the background of an enchanted world, that of magic and ritual, in which human beings live harmoniously. It was Jewish prophetism, in breaking with this enchanted world, that introduced both the promise of rationality and the distant sources of disenchantment. This is a double disenchantment insofar as to the loss of the enchanted garden gets added the loss of the new reasons for life attached to the rationalization of ethical life through the command to be moral. This will be a constant theme for Weber: that as soon as rationality triumphs, it turns against itself. Pierre Bouretz situates this moment with precision. It is contemporary with the birth of the great ancient Near Eastern theodicies. These ask, how is the imperfection of the world to be endured if this world is the work of a unique, all-powerful, and good god? The disappointment that results from asking this question opens an alternative: either to flee the world or worldly asceticism. It was the second branch of this alternative that triumphed with English Puritanism. The importance of this moment cannot be overestimated. It was, as we know from reading Weber's *Protestant Ethic and the Spirit of Capitalism,* an axial time, if we may borrow this phrase from Karl Jaspers, one where the dominant motive of the modern economy was articulated in terms of a strong religious motivation, one that bore all the subsequent ambivalence to be found attached to the theme of the rationalization of the world. The confrontation with Marx's materialistic explanation thus ceases to be the principal motive of controversy. It was the simultaneous positing of the Protestant ethic and of an economic motivation, along the trajectory of rationalization and disenchantment, that gives the strongest meaning to the conjoining of the religious and the economic. But, already at this stage, we can ask if it is true that Weber's consideration of the figures of the religious to the point of their confluence with the economic problematic does not allow for an alternative reading. From the perspective that will finally be that of Pierre Bouretz, that of a resistance to the nihilism implied by the thesis of the rationalization of the world's turning against itself, one can ask whether Weber did not systematically avoid the question of the univocity of his overall interpretation of the religious phenomenon, and whether he usurped the qualifications of the scientist's axiological neutrality to the benefit of a highly problematic overall interpretation, one that places the disenchantment of the world thesis at the same level as Hegel's cunning of reason. Was theodicy really the most important question attached to Jewish prophetism? Was the concern to find a guarantee and a reassurance against the risk of damnation the exclusive motivation behind Christianity, and more specifically behind Puritanism? What happens to salvation by grace, and a faith with no guarantee, in relation to the perhaps overemphasized theme of predestination? It would be interesting to know if in his work, which Bouretz several times says is ambivalent, Weber ever encountered the problem of the equivocity in the interpretation of cultural phenomena on the grand scale.

On the side of economics, we could pose symmetrical questions. They would concern the other term in the pair that Weber brings together when he attaches the rational motive that generates the capitalist enterprise, the accumulation of capital under the aegis of the entrepreneurial spirit, to the religious motive of invest-ing religious faith in a terrestrial vocation. Is this motive the sole generating focal point of economic rationality? What about the virtues attached to exchange and commerce and to the connec-tion Montesquieu caught sight of between these virtues and what he called "English liberty"? The recurring question about pluri-vocity can thus be posed about both terms of the equation: the Protestant ethic and the spirit of capitalism.

Turning back from the royal gate of the sociology of religions toward the servants' entrance of the epistemology of the social sciences, we can ask if things are really as clear on this episte-mological plane as they might have seemed to be in the era of Raymond Aron and Henri Irénée Marrou. How are we to hold together the *wertfrei* posture, claimed by Weber, with having to make recourse to the meanings experienced by social actors in the identification of the object of the social sciences? To be sure, one can give an impartial account of what seemed to be laden with meaning for these actors. But is the same impartiality tenable once these meanings reveal themselves to be what Charles Taylor, in his *Sources of the Self,* calls "strong evaluations"? It is a question of such strong evaluations when the meanings in question have to do with the whole historical process of the rationalization of the world. It is also such strong evaluations that are at issue in the eco-nomic world of work, wealth, and enjoyment. Even more so, they are at issue in the political register, under the figure of the large-scale motives for obedience, which contribute to the legitima-tion of domination. When Bouretz, *in fine,* reproaches Weber for having misunderstood the full range of meanings still caught up in the process of disenchantment—petrifaction, dehumanization, mortification—we can ask whether interpretive sociology itself, given its epistemological stance, is safe from this presumed dis-enchantment, which would be a presupposition as well as a result. We might try to hold that such disenchantment only touches—if we can put it this way—the meaning of meaning, the reflexive sense of meaning, not the direct meaning of behavior. Neverthe-less, the question will remain concerning how well Weber's epis-temology really succeeds in immunizing itself by means of such axiological neutrality against the bite of nihilism. Thus, having overly isolated the essays on the theory of science from the rest of

Weber's works, perhaps today it is also necessary to protect them from the nihilistic contamination engendered by the rest of his work through a systematically critical reading.[2]

A new series of questions is posed by the degree of convergence between what are called here "ways of disenchantment"—that is, the economic, political, and juridical spheres. In truth, these ways of rationalization remain quite disparate. We have already seen that this is the case for the problems posed by the "spirit of capitalism." The political realm poses quite specific problems, once we admit the prevalence of the problematic of domination. It is clear that for Weber the moment of violence is first, last, and always. We find it at one extreme as the generating matrix of power, in the middle as a force appropriated by the state, and it reappears again at the other end of political history as a kind of arbitrary decision. As for legitimation, it lies only in the motives for obedience. But it never rises to the rank of Hegelian recognition, as ensured in the final analysis by the constitution, in the *Philosophy of Right*. But this problematic never appears, it would seem, in Weber. With Habermas, we may regret that from one end to the other the analysis of "rationality in terms of ends"—that is, of instrumental reason—should cover over the "rationality of values," which alone could have given rise to a distinct problematic of legitimation. The result is that the rationalization of power and the turning of this into its contrary are concentrated on the bureaucratic phenomenon alone.[3] In this way, the bureaucratic phenomenon is directly grafted to the "logic of objectifying constraint," hence to domination, and not to the rationalizing aspects of legitimacy, which we would expect to see identified with the resources of liberation offered by the state ruled by law. Hence, Bouretz is correct when he places his analysis of the bureaucratic phenomenon under the heading of the "disenchanted rationalism of the modern universe, including the economy, politics, and the law."

So the convergence of the three orders of phenomena considered consists less in some intelligible character than in an unfathomable

2. It is striking that, in the typology of motives for obedience (*wert-rational* and so forth), the adjective "rational" should be privileged when it is the very process of rationalization that is the seat of disenchantment.

3. Cf., for example, the discussion in chapter 3 of Weber's *Economy and Society* entitled "Legal Authority with a Bureaucratic Administrative Staff" (217–26).

enigma, namely, that it is in the same instance and, we might say, the same instant that rationalization both reaches its high point and begins to turn into its contrary. I have already noted this strange superimposition in the analysis of Puritanism, which marked the extreme rationalization of worldly asceticism and the beginnings of its turning into something else. No interpretation of this phenomenon is proposed, which is called sometimes a paradox, sometimes an enigma, sometimes a reversal, which in the beginning I said constitutes something strictly symmetrical to the Hegelian cunning of reason. What then does this exact superimposition of rationalization and a loss of meaning signify? Is it a question of a phenomenon of inertia in virtue of which a process, once begun in history, outlives its initial motivation and produces perverse effects beyond the control of its original justification? One can understand why Bouretz comes back in a number of places to Weber's "shadows," to his "secret" or "silence" regarding the overall sense of his enterprise.

These perplexities concerning the interpretation of Weber's work under the heading of the disenchantment of the world have their repercussion in the work of reconstruction through which Bouretz undertakes to remove the "nihilistic" threat contained in the skeptical diagnostic that Weber brings to the course of modernity. The question is: at what moment along the long sequence of Weber's analytic propositions will Bouretz set up his line of resistance? It seems to me that what I shall call his arguments for such resistance can be assigned to three different levels.

On the first one, he resists univocity in his reading of the very process of rationalization that is supposed to turn against itself. In this regard, he is close to Leo Strauss when he criticizes an analysis that reinforces the phenomenon being described with complacency, even complicity. If this is the case, our reservations have to reach back as far as the *wertfrei* posture adopted on the plane of the social sciences. Above, I already asked to what point this axiological neutrality was sheltered from the contamination of the nihilistic turn of Weber's work. I also invoked this question of a plurivocity of interpretation in regard to the Puritan phenomenon as well as the political phenomenon of domination and that of the law-governed state. The question remains open: to what point must we withdraw in order to open up such plurivocity? This question seems essential to me, if we want to resist the dazzling effect created by Weber's metaphors: the "iron cage," the "battle of the gods," the "last man," enchantment and disenchantment. On a second level, the question posed is that of how to save a noninstrumental reason, a rationality based on values. This is the Habermasian side of Bouretz's book. But to what point does Bouretz really assume for himself Habermas's moral cognitivism and his foundational enterprise that extends to the level of a consensus based on the principles of an ethics of discussion? This is the same plane where his recourse to Rawls, at least to Rawls's *Theory of Justice*, seeks to justify itself. Whether it is a question of Habermas or Rawls, or even of Popper or Hayek, the question is whether this plea for a noninstrumental reason is compatible with the skeptical diagnostic that Bouretz seems to take for granted. Does the dividing line pass between skepticism and nihilism or between the arguments that give rise to skepticism? It seems to me that Habermas and Rawls distance themselves from Weber in their starting points more than Bouretz appears to allow.

Finally, on a third level, what is at stake is nothing less than the possibility of reconstructing the categories of thought and action, at the very level where we find situated the opening propositions of *Economy and Society*. This is where the arguments borrowed from Hegel about *Sittlichkeit* (where a problematic of objectification without reification of relations of interaction is at stake) are concentrated, as are the correlation between the closing sections of Husserl's fifth Cartesian Meditation and Weber's social categories, and the different borrowings from Hannah Arendt (common sense, public space, the will to live together). The borrowings from the later Rawls, of an "overlapping consensus" and "reasonable disagreements," and from Ronald Dworkin, with his narrative version of the production of the rules of justice against a mid-range ethical-political horizon, also belong to this third level. Finally—and above all—it is on this level that Bouretz takes on directly the pathos of what is at issue, in an epilogue, which does not really amount to a conclusion. The tone of riposte is given by the surprise guest I mentioned above: Walter Benjamin. It is really Paul Klee's "angel of history" who is called upon, through the voice of Pierre Bouretz, to an awakening "beyond the twentieth century."

Antoine Garapon's
Le Gardien des Promesses

Antoine Garapon's book appears at an opportune moment, when the contradiction has become glaring between the increasing grip that the legal system exercises on collective life in France and the crisis of delegitimation that confronts every institution exercising some form of authority in a democratic country.[1] The major thesis of his book is that legal system and democracy have to be criticized and amended together. In this sense this book written by a judge is meant to be a political one.

The junction between the point of view of the law and that of democracy already begins with the basic diagnosis presented. Along with Philippe Raynaud, who speaks of "democracy seized by the law," Garapon refuses to see in the extreme "juridicization of public and private life" a simple contamination stemming from the procedural spirit of the United States. It is within democratic society itself that he sees the source of this pathological phenomenon. It is within the very structure of our democracy that we have to see the reason for the ending of those immunities that placed many important people and the Jacobin state itself beyond the reach of the legal system. It is within the political arena that the weakening of the national law has been produced, eaten away as much from above, by the higher courts, as from below, by the multiplicity and diversity of places where juridical decisions are made. Therefore, we have to connect transformations in the role of the judge with the transformation within our democracy itself.

1. This chapter was first published as the preface to Garapon's *Le gardien des promesses*, 9–16.

And this is why we have to turn to the reasons for the delegitimation of the state to explain what first presents itself as an inflation of the legal system. This is a delegitimation that has itself to be traced back to the focal point of the democratic imagination, that innermost site of the citizen's conscience where the *authority* of the political institution is recognized and acknowledged.

Garapon devotes the first half of his book to justifying this diagnosis that ties together the fate of the judiciary and the political in what may appear to a first, superficial glance as a mere reversal of places, one where the judiciary alone would be the arrogant agent—the "small-time judge" becoming the unique symbol of this usurpation. However, if there is something paradoxical about judicial activism, it is because it has to do with "juridical democracy" considered as a whole.

This concern to link together the fate of the judiciary and the political explains why our author does not welcome what rightly can be called "judicial activism" without any express reservation. Apart from any corporate sense of satisfaction, any professional glorification, it is the changes linked to this inflationary phenomenon that are first emphasized—whether it be judges setting themselves up as a new clerisy or star performers supported by the media who set themselves up as guardians of public virtue, reawakening in this way the "old inquisitional demon always present to the Latin imagination." It is only at this level that the comparisons between the American and French systems make sense, in that they allow us to distinguish the different ways in which the same changes have been occurring in both systems. In this regard, Tocqueville remains, at the end of this book, the perspicacious analyst of the divergent ways assumed by the overall phenomenon of the "juridicization" of political life. Concerning our own country, Garapon has these painful words to offer:

> Thus we have the ambiguous promise of modern justice: lower court judges will rid us of the crooked politicians and the highest court judges of politics in general.

It would not be possible to go further in the double diagnosis of the decline of the political and the rise in power of the juridical without saying what it is that constitutes the hard core of the juridical, and hence what it is toward which the whole system is veering. The key idea of this book is therefore the characterization of the "juridical subbasement of justice" as a stepping away from, or more precisely as a conquest of, the just distance by which we understand bit by bit both what can be accomplished in court and what it means to be a citizen. One major reason for broaching this theme of distance near the beginning of the book is that the illusion of a direct democracy, which supports and even creates all the pieces of a system focused on the media, is the major temptation that conjointly threatens both the juridical and the political. Thus, we can see that the new clerisy of judges, under the pressure of the media, is haunted by the old dream of redemptive justice at the same time that representative democracy is short-circuited by the dream of direct democracy. At the same time, and again under the pressure of the media, the legal system is dislodged from its protected space, deprived of both its distance in time from the facts and its professional distance—and political deliberation is rendered superfluous by the bludgeon of publicity that functions like a tribune and by the hoax of polls that reduce elections to the final poll. Readers may be surprised by the virulence of this attack on the perverse effects of the media. But once one has understood that it is the same threat that affects the position of the third party in the juridical relation and the institutional mediation of the political relation, one will not be surprised to see Garapon join up with Claude Lefort in his denunciation of the invisible ideology of the media.

In this way, we are ready for more, beyond the severe judgment of this two-sided diagnosis that accounts for the originality of the first part of the book. To put a stop to the unilateral trial of the justice system that one might be tempted to pursue on the pretext of its having invaded every sphere of public and private life, we must first turn to the side of democracy itself to seek the flaw. Moreover, it is in what Tocqueville praised as the "equality of conditions" that we have to search for the beginning of all these changes. The equality of conditions can occur only at the price of ancient hierarchies, those natural traditions that assigned each person his or her place and limited the occasions for conflict. What must then be invented, artificially created, fabricated (all terms used by Garapon) is *authority*. And it is because we have not been able to do this that our society has handed itself over to the judges. The demand for justice comes from a politics in distress, when "the law becomes the last common moral system in a society." Sentences with the same tone pile up as we move through the book: "Democracy tolerates no other magistracy than that of the judge"; "a common norm with no common mores . . ." Below we shall have to ask whether this severe diagnosis still allows for any therapy that may apply to both our legal system and our democracy. Can we ever really get to responsible individuals who would be citizens from those scattered individuals who are a perverse effect of the equality of conditions?

Garapon pursues his descent into the hell of a thoroughly confused democracy in an intrepid manner, a hell where contracts are meant to compensate for the loss of a common world, where the judiciary can no longer say in whose name it exercises its control, where prisons take over the function of asylums for our most fragile subjects, where norms are internalized given the lack of recognized external rules. All these symptoms confirm what François Ewald says: "The less certain the law, the more society is forced to become juridical." But if the legal system must serve to reintroduce mediations that are lacking elsewhere, what will authorize the required prudence of individuals when the lawbreaker's presumed responsibility becomes the long-term objective of the enterprise of educating subjects in the new version of the providential state that poorly sets itself in place on the ruins of what went before?

Here we touch the cause of the vicious circle that outlines both the decline in democratic practice and the advance of judicial inventions. What is uncovered here is the subject himself in his double capacity as subject to the jurisdiction of a court and as a citizen. The real paradox that the present situation presents, one that is both political and judicial, is that responsibility is the postulate of both every defense of democracy (and, as a backlash to this, of every attempt to curb the growth of appeals for a judicial solution) *and* the sought-after goal of every attempt at reconstructing the social bond. In his later chapters, devoted to a diagnosis regarding society as both juridicized and depoliticized, Garapon offers a summary of contemporary expressions of the fragility that has invaded the scene. In fact, it is as though the democratic crisis and juridical swelling give rise to each other because they both stem from a third source: new figures of fragility. Thus, the argument between law and politics gives way to a disturbing triangular relation: "depoliticization, juridicization, fragility." Still more seriously, the judicial system is pushed to first place by failing political institutions and confronted with an impossible task: to assume the responsibility that the tutelary forms of justice which take the place of repression paradoxically reawake, even bring back to life.

It is from the point of view of this paradox of a tutelization of the subject, and under the heading of the impossible task that this tutelary function gives rise to, halfway between constraint and good advice, that we can situate all the pathologies that this book draws together before risking a proposal for a reconstituting of the citizen and all those who fall under the jurisdiction of the legal system.

Everyone talks about the impasses of individualism. But the jurist has his own way of speaking about it. Refusing to lose sight of the judge as a third party in conflicts, he sees in an emotional identification with victims the most telling symptom of the erasure of a position of impartiality; an emotional identification of oneself with the victims has its counterpart in the demonizing of the guilty parties. At the limit lies lynching, the direct act that reveals the failure of all symbolic distance and that marks the return in force of the old sacrificial ideology. The rise of a logic of victimization can thus be seen as a hindrance to the attempt by the legal system to put in place that tutelary function which, as we shall see below, is inseparable from exactly those precise conditions that make up the democratization of society. Because of this, I shall be careful not to give in to simple condemnation in describing the substituted identity functions assumed today by an initiatory juvenile delinquency or by other forms of desocialized violence. Instead, I shall limit myself to linking these social evils to the overall paradoxes that structure this book—fear of the aggressor, identification with the victim, and demonizing of the guilty party all bear witness to the erasure of the third-party position occupied by the judge. "Consensus grows on the basis of suffering and not on the basis of shared values." Hence from one end to another it is a question of a depoliticization of the subject, as either victim or accuser, even as someone who admits he is subject to the legal system. It is this triangle of plaintiff, accused, and judge that has broken into pieces.

This new fragility, it is true, is on a scale hitherto unheard of and stems from more than just the political sphere. Yet it needs to be thought about politically. It is to the lack of communal references that we have to attach both the loss of creditability of political structures and the inflation in judicial interventions, which appear then as effects of the phenomena of marginalization so characteristic of the new sense of criminality. This is why, at the end of part 1, we encounter not a triumphant but rather a perplexed judge, one charged with rehabilitating a political system for which he should really serve only as the guarantee.

The question then arises whether still more procedures will really be able to compensate for the weakness in the sense of the normative, as much in the judicial as in the political dimension. This is the question that dominates the second part of the book. The conjoined therapies applied to the judiciary and the political will be creditable only if the judiciary refuses the overevaluation perfidiously conferred upon it, and if it returns to its minimal function, which is at the same time its optimal position, namely, its job to say what is the law: not to punish, not to compensate, but to produce the word that names the crime and that thereby puts the victim and the criminal in their just places thanks to a work of language which extends from the qualifying of the crime to the pronouncement of the sentence at the end of a real argument carried out in words. Justice will assist democracy, which itself is a speech act, an act of discourse, by modestly, yet firmly fulfilling its "obligation toward language, the institution behind every institution." "Judgment signifies a repatriation to the human world, that is, to one of language." Even prior to its function of authorizing legitimate violence, justice is a way of speaking, and the judgment is a public form of speaking. Everything else follows from this: purgation of the past, the continuity of the person, and also, and above all, the affirmation of the continuity of public space. Let us be clear about this. If the judgment is an act of public speaking, all its effects, including detention, which is a kind of exclusion, have to unfold in public space, whether it be a question of riders to penalties or human, family, or labor relations, and so on. This plea is a public one. It signifies that, even when deprived of liberty, the prisoner remains a citizen and that the purpose of any deprivation of liberty is the recovery of all those juridical capacities that make anyone a full citizen. In this sense, a promise is made to the community to restore a citizen to it.

How then will authority constitute a "moment drawn from the democratic contractual relation" if a simple-minded "authority based on discussion and an authority always open to discussion" get substituted for a nondebatable authority? And how will the permanent discussion about legitimacy give rise to authority if the ethics of discussion rests only on the prestige of procedures of argumentation? It this were the only issue, the expectation that the judge could "legitimate political action, uphold the subject, organize the social bond, oversee symbolic constructions, and cultivate the truth" would lead only to those illusions regarding judicial activity denounced in the opening chapter of this book. This is why I find myself more comfortable with some of Garapon's other formulations, such as: "Authority ensures the tie to the origins, the power to project about the future. . . . Authority is the foundation, the power of innovation." "Rules guard power, authority guards the rule." "Power is what can act and authority is what authorizes the act." What procedural constraints would ever reach the heights of this ambition? I believe that the origin of authority is elusive, that it is inherited from prior convictions, the critique of which ensures turn by turn their decay, replacement, and renewal. Otherwise, the position of the judge as a neutral third party will become that of an absolute third party more powerless than any tyrant. The judge, Garapon says, "must not substitute himself for some absolute third party whose loss democracy continues to mourn." Well yes, but what would mourning be that does not internalize in some way or another a lost love object in order to elevate it to the rank of a structurally operative symbol?

In fact, all the remainder of the second part of the book rests upon an initial gesture toward reconstruction concerning which we are told, at the beginning of this new navigation, that it will seek to "retrace the path of the institution by starting from those which began it."

But if it is by so insisting on the tie to be preserved between justice and public speech that every attempt at rebuilding has to begin, and if it is the very instituting of this tie that is the aim of this reflection—that is, the tie between the citizen and the person before the court—the difficulty then is how to continue along this pathway without stumbling over the obstacle that the delegitimizing of the foundational function of authority constitutes, for both the legal system and democracy, as much regarding the position of the third party on the juridical level as regarding the institution of mediations on the political one. We are told that both the exercise of public speech and the exercise of power lack legitimation. As a result, can the substitution of the legal system for politics as the final court of appeal, as the last institution, constitute anything other than an illusion as regards this lack that affects the proposed substitute as much as it does the political paradigm? The disappearance of a common world turns out to be the most entrenched thesis of this book, as much in its therapeutic as in its diagnostic part. For substitution turns out not to be healing but rather eventually a means of aggravating what is wrong: "The position of the legal system is paradoxical. It reacts to a threat of disintegration that it however tends to promote." The most troubling, even most disarming chapter title of this book is "Necessary and Impossible Authority." Here Garapon seems unreservedly to accept Gauchet's theses:

A society that has left behind the kind of regime marked by constraints taken as self-evident, stemming from a community that always would precede its individuals, such a so-called emancipated society has more need of authority than did the one that preceded it.

Indeed, the formula "necessary and impossible authority" itself comes from Gauchet, who speaks of "a complement that has become a lack for us—in short, both an indispensable and impossible relay." I must say that I do not really see a solution to this paradox in the proposed recourse to Montesquieu, who speaks of, "not the absence of a teacher, but the acceptance of equals as teachers." That an equal should be taken as a teacher still presupposes that his fragile expertise be recognized as superior and worthy of being obeyed. Rather than abandoning myself to the Sisyphean task of re-creating a permanent symbolic structure, I would look instead for an escape from this paradox on the side of what Rawls speaks of as "well-considered convictions," of "tolerance in a pluralistic society," of an "overlapping consensus," of "reasonable disagreements," all expressions that presuppose the revivifying of cultural heritages that are today fragmented but still motivating in the final analysis. I would also refer with Charles Taylor, in his *Sources of the Self*, to the possible synergy of large-scale but not yet exhausted heritages, from Judeo-Christianity, Enlightenment rationalism, and the German and English Romanticism of the nineteenth century, interpreted in terms of their unkept promises. Without such multiple and mutually criticized heritages, I do not see how we can get beyond the empty notion of a "foundational symbolism." Perhaps we have not yet finished with such symbolic resources imprinted with the triple seal of anteriority, exteriority, and superiority. The Terror of the French Revolution and of those totalitarian systems that claimed to begin again from zero to create a new man may be said to demonstrate this by default. We find something similar in Garapon when he affirms without any apparent reticence that the court when it says what is just is also legitimated in positing itself as an institution that gives us identity thanks precisely to its symbolic dimension.

Professing this symbolic dimension plays the role of a new beginning for what follows in the book, one I would say based on conviction. The legal system is called on to fill this function of being a unifying institution by making legal argument and its occurrence, accepted with no mental reservations, the visible place within whose limits a ceremony in words sets up the just distance between all those subject to the court's decision. Yet the perplexed meditation referred to earlier returns in a nagging way on the occasion of this courageous plea presented in favor of the ritual aspect of the trial process. How can we today, following all that is said about a "necessary and impossible authority," call for a symbolic deployment that would repeat the founding experience? It is right that Garapon here refers to the world of the Bible, Greek reason, Roman law, Justinian, Saint Louis, Charlemagne, and Napoleon. But what reconciliation with the murdered father allows authority to base itself on something anterior to itself, unlike the case of power, concerning which Hannah Arendt tells us that it exists only so long as a community's will to live together does?

The rest of the book, however, rests on this premise: authority is the necessary force for changing things. Foundation, repetition. It looks as though Garapon makes procedure carry the whole weight of this relation between foundation and repetition. "The framework is thus what takes the place of tradition for modern people." "Recourse to the moment of foundation, unavailable to us by definition, is all the more necessary and vital in that our pluralism is so large scale." Can the idea of a foundational future do away with that of a founding event? And do we not expect too much of the symbolic function in asking it to play the role of an "authority by default"?

The following pages on the spectacle presented within the courtroom, of the repetition of the transgression and its being absorbed under the rubric of a mediating language, are quite remarkable. It is a good idea to link together tightly the apology for this setting that stands apart and the theme of the formation of a subject of rights beyond any individual psychology, that is, a subject whose capacities are immediately tied to the quality of being a citizen. The person who can appear before a court is a citizen—a subject with rights in a state governed by a rule of law. Everything rests here on the primacy of the symbolic function, hence on a common language, over psychological individuals identified by their suffering and their desires. One leitmotif recurs at this point:

> the challenge that the preservation of authority presents for a de-sacralized society and a disoriented individual, that is, the management of both the legitimate use of force and the symbolic dimension.

What is said next about the compromise between the use of sanctions and the role of reintegrating someone into society through imprisonment follows directly from this thesis of a just distance within a continuous public space, guaranteeing thereby the continuity of the subject of rights. In this regard, a purely psychiatric, hence therapeutic, approach to sanctions paradoxically remains akin to a sacrificial vision that sets the victim radically apart from the group. There are secret connections between expiation and therapy. Garapon does not overlook the sluggishness, the resistance, the prejudices, the fears that delay the conquest of an idea combining sanction and reintegration, at the expense of one combining sanction and punishment. At this price the residual violence of punishment can be a part of a just institution. But the reformer's job is to think, to make sense of a reform that does not give in to either Foucault's skepticism or the public's obsession with safety. A faith in public language is from beginning to end the mobilizing conviction of a thoughtful reform effort. To allow a subject to make commitments is to stay within the circle of public language common to both those at liberty and those in detention. Beyond the culture of vengeance and the utopia of a world without penalties, there is a place of an "intelligent penalty," where the idea of sanction would be conceived of as more than merely a penalty, following its etymological sense as combining both approbation and reprobation. Hence, in order not to succumb to a new type of reformist utopia, Garapon draws on his own experience and that of his peers for precise recommendations whose professional character is manifest.

But I do not want to end this introduction, which really consists of a few notes taken in reading this book, without acknowledging the side of this book dealing with the defense of democracy. We have seen how much Garapon's diagnosis of judicial activism is dependent on an erasure of politics. The transition toward a militant stance on both fronts is ensured by the idea of the kinship and the solidarity between the third-person position of the legal system, leading to a just distance between the parties in court, and the mediating role of the representative institutions of the state governed by a rule of law. It is this latter aspect of reconstruction that is affirmed in the last pages of the book. The danger of a new form of utopia based on the judicial system, which would only add to the condemned forms of judicial activism, can be dealt with only if at the same time we reopen the question of political representation. If we want to get back to the idea of a place of justice for those who come before our courts, political representation needs to be deprofessionalized as much as possible. A "new act of judging" requires a context that is political in nature, that is, an advance in democratic association and participation. That the key to judicial institutions is in the hands of politicians is all the more inevitable in that the judiciary, in our country, is not a distinct power separate from the executive and legislative branches but rather an authority. It is important, therefore, that Garapon guards himself against every sort of incantatory invocation regarding the independence of the judicial system as well as any return to the temptation of thinking in terms of redemption. In the final analysis, it is the same power of judging that makes both the judge and the citizen.

The Fundamental and the Historical

Notes on Charles Taylor's *Sources of the Self*

I want to explore the resources that may be found in Charles Taylor's *Sources of the Self* for resolving a major difficulty that seems to me to be one result of the composition of this work, one that may extend beyond this difficulty to its very substance. This difficulty has to do with the contrast between the first part, devoted to what are taken to be the "inescapable frameworks" of moral experience, and the remainder of the book, which essentially consists of a genealogy of modernity, as the book's subtitle—*The Making of the Modern Identity*—suggests. The question has to do with the apparently epistemological hiatus that results from the competition between the fundamental and the historical in the constitution of moral ipseity.

I

Part 1 is based upon a major correlation that is fundamental to the book, namely, the correlation between what we may call the universals that make up ethics and those that make up ipseity.

Let us examine more closely how this correlation is established.

Let us begin first on the side of the figures of the "good." I just spoke of universals that make up ethics. At the beginning of the book Taylor objects that the inescapable frameworks that will be in question do not stem from the level of the formal universality of an ethics of obligation (Kant) or that of a transcendental pragmatics of communication (Habermas), but, in an Aristotelian or neo-Aristotelian vein, from the primordial constitution of the aim of a good life. Hence, to do justice to this work, we must acknowledge that it starts from an *epoche* applied precisely to these types of deontological universality and transcendental pragmatics. Yet it is also true that, already at this primordial level, moral experience is assumed to present a structure that justifies the expression "inescapable frameworks." We may speak in this regard of a concrete universality, leaving for later discussion whether this is an ahistorical structure, and so would be difficult to connect to the genealogy of modernity, or a transhistorical one, where it would be precisely a question of discerning those features compatible with the genealogical approach that prevails in the later part of the book. The problem of inescapable frameworks comes from the question of how we recognize the ethical (or moral, the distinction does not matter here) character of any question, argument, or conviction. In this sense, it has to do with how we can reveal something like the existential structures of moral existence in either a transhistorical or an ahistorical sense of universality. In this regard, we might propose the following paradox: It is in terms of a moral philosophy attentive to those habitual dispositions most rooted in life, or, if I can put it this way, attentive to those ways of leading one's life following such an orientation—it is in such a philosophy that the question becomes most urgent of how to give a stable status to the least ethically qualified aspects of a theory, ones that are nevertheless capable of ensuring the transition between natural or biological life and the good life of human ethical existence. It is these intermediate ethical qualities between living and living well that are taken to be inevitable, unavoidable, or indispensable (possible French translations of the English "inescapable"). It is concerning these qualities that we can ask, in the final analysis, whether they are ahistorical or transhistorical, in a sense that we still need to spell out.

The first inevitable, unavoidable, indispensable dimension is designated by the phrase "strong evaluation." "Evaluation" implies polarization and discrimination (good/bad, better/worse, honorable/shameful, praiseworthy/condemnable, admirable/abominable). This polarization gives a moral stamp to desires, inclinations, brute reactions. Moreover, by making the term "evaluation" more precise with the adjective "strong," Taylor emphasizes the depth, the force, and the universality of such an evaluation. Its depth: in relation to the rapid changes in desires and reactions, dispositions have a more durable character than do mere emotions. Its force: its motivating capacity in opposition to objective conclusions that do not imply any personal or communal commitment. Its universality: its claim of being shared, its communicability in principle; hence, in any controversy, ethical agents not only hold to their convictions but offer them for approbation by other people. To take this recourse to strong evaluations to be inescapable is to affirm that the moral significance conferred in this way on life itself is not something added to it as a projection, a point that gets strongly affirmed in the discussion of all the forms of "naturalism" on the plane of moral theories. In this regard, the thesis of a neutrality of both life and human action already stems from the theorizing that the *epoche* referred to earlier places in suspension. Such a thesis comes down to an unjustified transfer of models taken from scientific thought. What is more, this transfer is equivalent to a misreading of the specificity of action and human life. The ethical response to a situation is something other than a de facto reaction. Other discussions on other fronts—that of the "state of nature" presupposed by Enlightenment philosophers, that of the post-Nietzscheanism illustrated by the Weberian theme of the disenchantment of the world—strengthen this thesis that the idea of a strong evaluation is supposed to resist the erosion of every cultural heritage, whether ancient or modern.

The second characteristic of strong evaluations—discrimination—brings into play new components of what, to make things plain, I am calling here a concrete universal. Discrimination implies hierarchization. We could say that with this feature the avowal regarding a good life already penetrates the sphere of moral obligation, with its features of universality and impartiality. It is true that the Socratic call for an "examined life" engenders a critical moment, a crisis of evaluation in exemplary fashion. But is this to say that this critical moment is already to be placed outside the field of originary moral experience? There is strong pressure to invoke the extrinsic occurrence of an act of judgment, which, in turn, would impose the passage from a teleological point of view to a deontological one. Without denying the force of this demand, it must rather be said that the critique of evaluative terms can take place only within what is itself an evaluative language. Justification is constitutive of what amounts to the force of an evaluation, and reasons of a higher order remain homogeneous with strong evaluations. Socratic examination seeks to say what it is that allows us to say that we reckon that one thing is more valuable than another. In any case, the consideration of this moment of discrimination accentuates the transhistorical or ahistorical character of the very notion of an evaluation. And with the notion of hierarchy comes to light the notion that Charles Taylor calls *hypergoods*, that is, goods of a higher rank that articulate and thereby delimit the morality of a group, a culture, in each instance defining a different system of priorities. The treatises on virtue of the ancient world—and even those of the early modern period—both express the plurality of ultimate bases of evaluation for a given culture and the concern to give an order to this plurality. It is in this way that justice gets raised in many conceptions of morality to a higher rank. Still, however much we must insist on the variability of the contents by which we define these hypergoods, to the same extent we have to affirm that no moral experience worthy of the name escapes this kind of structuring that gives a hierarchical profile to every moral life.

A last step brings us to the borders—if not the margins—of the phenomenology of moral experience. We have to add to the ideas of strong evaluation, hierarchization, and articulation the idea of a mobilizing force, issuing from those "moral sources" that stem from the "inescapable framework" of moral life. Consideration of these moral sources is born from the question concerning what it is that pushes us to act, what it is that led one French philosopher (Fouillée) to speak of a moral idea as an *idée-force*, an idea that empowers us to do what is right and to be good. Platonic *eros* and Christian *agape* have played this role. Even the most formal conceptions and the most procedural forms of ethics do not escape such consideration. Kant reserves a whole chapter of the *Critique of Practical Reason* for the idea of respect as just such a motive, without worrying about attaching the counterpart that is the passivity of a humiliated, as well as elevated, feeling to the idea of a reason that can move our feelings. This polarity between a motivating force and a receptive passivity does seem to constitute the most originary ground of morality. It takes on various forms: the avowal of the antecedence of a law in relation to our present choices, to which corresponds a humble feeling of recognition; an authority attached to the superiority of ideals which merit sacrificing goods judged to be inferior to such ideals; and so on. In various ways, the articulation, the ordering, of such higher goods has to be a condition of such adhesion and entailment. Ought we not here more forcefully than at the two preceding levels underscore the profoundly conflictual character of these basic figures of the moral life? We could do so, following in the wake of Nietzsche's "genealogy of morals." As I shall say below, the modern self is one lacerated by such challenges, such suspicions, such demystifications. Hence, it seems difficult to plead for the idea of a moral source belonging to a pretheoretical level of moral life. Yet if we do refer to Platonic eros, Christian agape, Enlightenment reason, Romantic genius, Nietzschean transvaluation, or even the disenchantment of the world, there can be no question of moral distress unless the idea of some ultimate motivation is an integral part of the inescapable framework of moral life, as are such strong evaluations.

We cannot move beyond the first part of *Sources of the Self* without having looked at the major correlation presented in the title of this first part: "Identity and the Good." The universals of ipseity correspond to the concrete universals of ethics. Thus, this analysis brings us back to Socrates' famous saying about the examined life. It gets placed expressly at the point of articulation linking visions of the self and those of the good. Our answers to the question "Who am I?" are structured by our answers to the question "How ought I to live?"—a more basic question than "What ought I to do?"

Regarding this point of view, we may repeat what was already said about strong evaluations, articulations in terms of higher-order goods, and finally about moral sources: in short, about everything that has to do with the side of moral predicates taken at their pretheoretical or prepredicative stage, as we could say using phenomenological language.

To the idea of a strong evaluation corresponds that of a way of maintaining oneself, of holding on to oneself over time (here I stand!). It is worth noting that these expressions underscore not only the temporal dimension of our adhesion to strong evaluations but their spatial dimension as well. We can speak in this sense of an "orientation" in some moral space (an aspect to which one is particularly sensible when one feels disoriented or, as we say today, without any point of reference). We must therefore distinguish this moral space from Euclidean geometrical space, following the model of the distinction between *ipse* and *idem* temporality, and speak of a space of selfhood or of ipseity. The spatial metaphor (which may contain a more originary sense of space itself) easily moves back and forth between an evaluating self and the goods to be judged. We could even speak of the "map" on which are indicated those ethical points of reference that govern our orientation and from which we take our angles of perspective. Nor will we forget notions like wandering, departure (Abraham), or a return home (Ulysses). Even in an age of disenchantment, the absence of points of reference still refers to the "space of qualitative distinctions it incorporates" (30). One inescapable characteristic of the human ability to act is "to exist in a space of questions about strongly valued goods" (31). This is what a naturalistic conception of life and action as neutral territory, hence as lacking orientation, suppresses by the unwarranted reduction of the idea of moral space to the status of a merely rhetorical metaphor.

This equivalence between the question of *who* I am and that of *where* I stand in moral space returns when we pass from the idea of a strong evaluation to that of its articulation, with its double character of hierarchization and of a heterogeneity of second-order goods, and finally to that of moral sources. The connection between the two sides of the spatial metaphor takes place through the intermediary of the idea of a space of interlocution, of webs of interlocution. On the side of moral space, the idea of articulation presents a manifest character of spatialization. It is a question of specifying not only how different goods relate to one another but also what distance there is between them. Another way of situating ourselves within moral space results from this reflective labor. What we have then to conceive of is the idea of a double orientation in narrative space and in moral space.

With the ideas of heterogeneity and hierarchization of higher goods, and above all with the idea of moral sources, a more dramatic aspect of the correlation between the idea of the self and that of the good comes to light, namely, that of an increasing conflict which symmetrically affects both our strong evaluations and our identity. It seems to be one of the most basic features of moral experience that we cannot aim at the good, at fulfillment, at plentitude, as a partial, fragmentary horizon, without facing the test of this constitutive conflict.

The grandeur and fragility of the moral life lie first in the recognition of those qualitative evaluations of a higher rank, which above I called hypergoods. It seems to be part of the inescapable structure of moral life that the goods of a higher rank serve as the point of view from which we think, judge, and adopt goods of lesser importance. And our moral personality is structured in correlation with this articulation of moral space. Taylor is undoubtedly correct when he writes: "hypergoods are generally a source of conflict" (64).

Before giving a few concrete examples of such conflictual places in our moral space, under the heading of the historicity of the construction of the modern self, I must say that this conflict reaches its peak with the elevation of the idea of "moral sources" to the rank of strong motivations. Let us recall that if the idea of articulation emphasizes the ordering function exercised by certain ideas of a higher rank, that of moral sources emphasizes, as I have said, the mobilizing side of the energy of moral concepts considered as idea-forces. It is at this level that conflict affects the sense of moral identity more strongly, if that is possible, than that of articulation. The place in which a moral idea is welcomed as a moral source is the self. But this self is placed in a position of passivity by what makes it capable of adhering to such idea-forces. What gives the power to act, following the injunction of some good of a higher rank, has receptivity to such a moral injunction as its correlate. In this way, the considered goods can be said to be constitutive not only in regard to subordinate goods but in regard to the self enjoined by them.

II

The time has come to oppose the historicity that characterizes "The Making of the Modern Identity" to this inescapable structure constitutive of the correlation between the notion of the good and that of the self.

It is essential to emphasize at the beginning of this discussion that the kind of "genealogy of morals" that constitutes this work has as its horizon, not to say *telos,* the identification of a malaise, a predicament, characteristic of the self in the modern era. The concluding chapter in fact carries the title "The Conflicts of Modernity." Which is to say that the enterprise in no way is that of a neutral history of mentalities, but, if I may put it this way, is an emplotment of our cultural history. The reconstruction of the path leading from the Greeks to us is governed by three large-scale structural themes that, as I shall show below, serve as a bridge between what I spoke of above in my introductory remarks as the fundamental and the historical. An initial discussion is structured in terms of the theme of interiority or, better, of "inwardness"; a second, in terms of the "affirmation of ordinary life"; and finally a third, in terms of the "way of nature." Let us begin by following the first axis.

If the idea of reflexivity can be stated formally without any reference to history, this is not the case with the sense of interiority, whose rise, development, and decline we can trace. That the self is the correlate of a moral space still stems from the inescapable structure of all moral experience. But the distinction between inside and outside has a history, one that is typically Western. Plato, from whom we must begin, places the moral source in the domain of what is taken to be a hegemonic type of thought; within the framework of a topography of the soul, the *logos* appears as the site of certain moral sources. At the same time, a higher conception of reason is connected with a cosmic order of truth, of the "highest good," which makes the Good above us accessible only through a turning within ourselves.

The "inner" person, according to Augustine, shares features in common with Plato's rational soul, but on the basis of an identification between God and the Good and between the inward regard and the memory of God. Christian agape gives strength to the self in the first person, a discovery that makes Augustine the real inventor of radical reflexivity.

With Descartes, the "disengagement of reason" gives a new turn to such inwardness, which at the same time receives as its correlate a mechanical, disenchanted universe open to instrumental control. Nevertheless, the neo-Stoic coloration of Cartesian "generosity" still preserves something of the ancient ethics of honor. Next, with Locke, appears a "punctual self," totally freed of all supervision by external authority, at the same time that the progress in the instrumentalizing of the control of external reality announces the affirmation of procedural reason. The moral ideal of self-mastery therefore has a history apart from which any discussion of personal identity, of responsibility for oneself, and of the emergence of contractual theories in political philosophy would be incomprehensible.

With the affirmation of "ordinary life," the superiority of the contemplative over practical life—that is, a certain hierarchization of goods of a higher order issuing as much from Platonism as from Christian monasticism—is called into question. The Reformation contributed to this with its idea of "vocation" apart from the ascetic life, whose apogee is to be found among English Puritans (see, for example, Michael Walzer's *The Revolution of the Saints*). Following this we find the appearance of deism as a "rationalized Christianity." This revolution at the level of the religious sources of morality is crucial for understanding the modern malaise. Charles Taylor strongly emphasizes that deism, with its faith in a providential order, by which it is to be distinguished from the subsequent atheism of some Enlightenment thinkers, is genuinely religious. As for the self, it is enriched in many ways by an investigation into moral sentiments (with Shaftesbury and Hutchinson, who laid the basis for modern English morality). A culture of an "inward nature" is born, opposed to all externally imposed authority, and oriented toward a positive evaluation of natural inclination toward benevolence in harmony with a providential universe.

The decisive stage in this rapid history of the construction of the modern self and its torments is the great bifurcation between the atheistic rationalism of the French Lumières and the rise of philosophical Romanticism, particularly in Germany. Thus, the last two hundred pages of Taylor's book are devoted to laying out a picture of "fractured horizons," where three resources clash: the recourse to what is both a transcendent and an inner divine source, the self-affirmation of a reason which posits itself as sovereign, and the borrowing from the creative energies of a nature that is vaster than human existence. Only the latter two currents can be called modern. But as a result there are two models of modernity—and the conflict is in no way abolished between these two models, so long as the Augustinian base persists in spite of secularization. In this regard, Taylor proposes an interesting interpretation of secularization that does not reduce, for him, to the progress of the sciences and the development of a commercial economy but that consists in the birth of new alternatives on the most radical plane of moral sources. Autonomous reason as productive of meaning and the voice of nature each occupy a place, within moral space, comparable to that formerly occupied by Christian agape, which nourished the Augustinian inward human existence. Theism, rationalism, and Romanticism clash in us, engendering the modern "predicament." For Taylor, these three claims to an ultimate foundation make one another fragile, even if their half-hearted borrowings from each other deepen the wounds to our contemporary moral consciousness. In this regard, what is perhaps most striking about the portrait he paints of the modern self is its conflicts, considered to be just as strong between disengaged reason and the creativity of nature as between the two branches of modernity and the unexhausted heritage of Hellenism and Judeo-Christianity.

III

Now is the time to confront what we can call the synchronic aspect of the first part of this book with the diachronic perspective of the three long chapters whose story I have just sketched. We have to acknowledge that Taylor himself does not discuss the problem posed by juxtaposing the two styles that he gives priority to in turn. Although one of his chapters is entitled "A Digression on Historical Explanation," it deals with something other than the relation between what I am calling here the fundamental and the historical. What Taylor is preoccupied with is above all the more or less vertical relation between the level of ethical conceptions and that of the economic, social, and political phenomena characterizing a given era. His discussion is interesting, to be sure, in that it takes on the accusation of idealism, which comes not only from Marxist authors. His idea of a circular relation among all the components of the overall historical phenomenon is certainly valuable, as is the idea that it is in terms of practices that the ideals of ethical conceptions get integrated into the general current of history. Yet, even if this latter suggestion does touch on the question of what gives force to certain ideas at a certain moment, and if it is correct to say that the question posed calls for an "interpretive," rather than a causal, answer, these remarks do not allow us to account for the diachronic development of moral ideas. What we find in this brief chapter is still the idea of a vertical relation, of the infra-superstructure type, whereas our problem has to do with the relation between the verticality of the universals that together structure the good and the self and the longitudinal course of the development of moral ideas, a relation testified to by regularly recurring expressions, such as "birth," "mutation," "displacement," "surpassing," and "decline." But it is precisely these connections that underlie the historicity that principally affects the higher-order goods and the notions that play the role of moral sources. The problem posed here clearly has to do with periodization in terms of long stretches, such as that which opposes ancients and moderns, and eventually postmoderns, as existing in two different epochs. On this large scale, the problem is still posed in terms that are too broad to give rise to fine-scale analyses. Furthermore, the changes that occurred on this level are themselves the result of more subtle transformations on a level closer to the shorter-term periodizations that subdivide the three large rubrics called "inwardness," "affirmation of ordinary life," and "the voice of nature," not to mention the supplementary one of "subtler languages."

If we want to make sense of the dialectical relation between the fundamental and the historical, we have to pay particular attention to the interplay of retrospection and anticipation that governs the interpretive strategy of the historical sections of *Sources of the Self.*

Let us consider again the first rubric. The term "inwardness" is already interesting in itself inasmuch as it deals with a notion constructed by the interpreter in order to account for the "rise," the "development," of what Taylor calls "a certain meaning," or perhaps a "family of senses" (111), placed under the heading of "inwardness."

A similar comment is called for by the notion of a "moral topography," which serves in a way as the subtitle to this chapter. It allows exploration of the successive forms through which the opposition of internal and external passes, as well as of the places where Augustine, Descartes, and Locke situate the principle of interiority. Taylor says of this localization that it "is not a universal one, which human beings recognize as a matter of course" (111). Another remark: We can ask if the series reviewed is not constructed beginning from its ending, which still is located in the eighteenth century, and if this end in turn does not draw its meaning from the final interpretation of modernity in terms of a predicament. In this sense, chapter 11, entitled "Inner Nature," which concludes this long section, can be understood, not so much as a recapitulation of the development considered, as an anticipation of the subsequent evolution directed toward the emergence of a plainly autonomous subject (particularly on the occasion of the breakthrough of a political philosophy based on atomistic premises). A secret, uncriticized teleology thus seems to govern the "meaning" of the whole "family of meanings" placed under the heading "inwardness."

The title of the following section—"Affirmation of Ordinary Life"—is no less a construct than the preceding one. If the role played by the Reformation, in particular under the impetus of English Puritanism, allows us to say that the affirmation of ordinary life finds its origin in Judeo-Christian spirituality, and we can also therefore speak of the Calvinist theology of a profane "vocation" as a continuation of Stoicism by other means, it is nonetheless in terms of a "transvaluation of values" that the earlier hierarchy brought about by Francis Bacon is characterized. The result is that the emergence of the theme of the instrumental control of nature is overdetermined. The interplay between retrospection and anticipation continues from chapter to chapter. Thus, for example, we find Locke at the point where the future divides. As much as Taylor is careful to distinguish Locke's deism, as well as the culture of feelings associated with this deism, from the unbelief of the English and French radical Enlightenment of the eighteenth century, so too he takes care to see in Locke's deism not only the premises of an entirely secularized reason but also those of the worship of nature. Below, we shall have to speak of what justifies this back-and-forth movement in the very dynamic of change over time.

The interpreter's strategy changes very little in the long section titled "The Voice of Nature." He first emphasizes what we could call the acquisition of modernity, that is, first of all, individualism in the three forms of autonomy, introspection, and personal commitment, with their political corollaries, including the formulating of subjective rights, the value given to productive work and the family, and, finally, the new relationship to nature. All this makes up a new meaning of the "good life." Yet the strong evaluations that we can take as common to this whole era are limited to what we can call "life goods." The aim at a good life begins to diverge once we move to the level of "constitutive goods," another name for the moral sources in part 1. It is precisely in regard to the idea of nature that a bifurcation appears, one that will become an abyss following the period of Romanticism. It is also at this stage that Taylor's main thesis takes shape, namely, that the modern soul is the site of a competition among several legitimating and motivating forces. With the passing of deism and its providentialism came an atheism that left room for two rival claims about so-called natural reason and a living nature. The emergence of these two forces at the rank of moral sources that generate constitutive goods—hence at the rank where Christian spirituality had reigned almost single-handedly—constitutes the actual explanation of the phenomenon of secularization. It was not, let me repeat, the rise of scientific thought or the growth of the market economy that constituted the decisive factor, but the fact that new moral sources became available: "This is the cultural shift we have to understand" (313). However, if theism as a moral source becomes problematic, secularized thought does not present a unique alternative to it. It consists of an empire divided against itself. In the eighteenth century what defines our contemporary situation began to emerge, namely, the opposition between two "fronts," that of reason as master of itself and of all order external to itself, and that of capacities of expression reaching out to the depths of a vaster, more powerful nature than ourselves. An overview here becomes the interpreter's dominant strategy. He shifts back and forth systematically between the contemporary predicament and a detailed deciphering of the changes that have occurred over the course of more than two centuries. In turn, this strategy is used to support the book's major thesis, according to which "all positions are problematized by the fact that they exist in a field of alternatives" (317). Faith, reason, and nature clash at the summit of the hierarchies of constitutive goods. Cautiously, and I would say half-heartedly, Taylor suggests that "the three directions can be seen as rivals, but also as complementary" (318). I shall not follow Taylor in his review of the development of Enlightenment rationalism and Romanticism, to which he attaches equal importance, no doubt because he wants to maintain an equal pressure among the forces affecting the three-dimensional space outlined by the latest three forces motivating our moral energies. Instead, I want to conclude by saying something about the style of historicity at work in this historical hermeneutics.

IV

The question underlying the strategy of retrospection and anticipation that we have found to be at work in the long historical section of this book is in what sense that strategy finds justification in the style of historicity characterizing the basic constitution of inescapable frameworks. Let me first say, in negative terms, that it is not a question in the remainder of the book of a linear history, in which one moral conception replaces another, nor of a Hegelian type of dialectic, where what is surpassed would be retained, as the expression "historical supersessions" might suggest. The temporality of this history is of a quite singular kind. What we could call the perenniality of traces is what ensures the conjunction between the historical character of moral conceptions and the transhistorical character of ethical universals. My own distinction between sameness and ipseity may find a new application here. No position remains identical to itself in the sense of sameness, except perhaps in that a position is our access to the problematic realm to which the most venerable sources get condemned when confronted with competition from new motivating sources. But the fate of ipseity, which I have illustrated elsewhere by the example of the kept promise, gets expressed in a wholly different way here. In the moral order, the past leaves not only inert traces, or residues, but also dormant energies, unexplored sources which we might assimilate to something like unkept promises, those which ground memory, as Paul Valéry put it, in speaking about the future of the past. This dormant character of as-yet-unfolded potentialities is what allows for resumptions, rebirths, reawakenings, through which the new gets connected with the old. In a more general way, this sui generis temporal constitution justifies what we can call deliberate anachronisms, as used by the historian of moral ideas. It is always after the fact that one discerns in the past what did not reach maturity in its own time. In this respect, the counterpart to the ideas of trace, debt, and unemployed potentialities would have to be sought on the side of events in thinking through which one tries to make sense of the mutations that in their turn make possible such resumptions, those retrievals that are so abundant in the history of ethical ideas.

In this way we rediscover the better known theme of the dialectic of innovation and tradition. We find a more dramatic and, we could say, more exalted expression of this exchange between the present of resumption and the past as freed of its shackles in Walter Benjamin. In his conception of narration and of history, Benjamin assigns a salvific (*Rettung*) or redemptive (*Erlösung*) function to memory from the perspective of Jewish messianism. This function is particularly urgent when it is a question of saving the victims of political history from oblivion. Someone may object that we encounter nothing so dramatic in the history of ideas. But this is not always true. The decline of some moral conceptions sometimes presents a comparable spectacle of ruin. Forgetting in the spiritual order takes forms that extend from an almost-biological decay, or running out of breath, to violent rejection, in passing through negligence and discrediting. Enlightenment thinkers in particular, in their most radical form, stand in such a relation to historical Christianity, and even to deism and the culture of benevolent feelings. In moral history we do find breaks and not just peaceful reinterpretations, although we must say that in this extreme case it becomes almost impossible to recognize the inescapable framework of a moral phenomenology. But it is also the task of the historian of ideas to attenuate the allegation of such a radical break between ancients and moderns, which in large part is not only exaggerated but not well founded, resulting in the refusal of the sense of debt that is surely part of the message of a certain modernity. Perhaps soon we shall have to say the same thing about the neo-Nietzschean claims of postmodernity.

To take into account every case of such figures, we could express these complex temporal relations by turning to the neighboring vocabulary of the uncanny and the familiar, of contemporaneity and noncontemporaneity, or even of proximity and distance. In privileging this metaphor of distance, we can take the erasure, the loss of its power of persuasion, of this or that moral source as an increase in distance, and the phenomenon of resumption (for example, of Stoicism in the sixteenth century) as one of "de-distanciation." In truth, the whole course of Taylor's book can be understood as a vast exercise in such de-distanciation, where the sense of distance is constantly presupposed in order to overcome it.

We are now prepared to reply to the question we posed in beginning: what is it that holds together the fundamental of the first part and the historicity that prevails in the longest part of this book? We can ask if the fundamental of the first part does not include within itself its own style of historicity, which is consonant with that of the large-scale genealogy of modernity. If it is true that, on the side of the historical, it is the overlapping of the contemporary and the noncontemporary in the same modern consciousness that ensures the epochal character of its moral experience, must we not also say that this style of historicity is made possible in turn by the very structures that were named "inescapable frameworks"? If we consider the notion of strong evaluations or that of hypergoods or, even more so, that of moral sources, we can say that conflict is a constitutional part, if I may put it this way, of the fundamental and can itself be taken as inescapable. We can now resolve our question. These inescapable structures are not ahistorical but transhistorical. Strong evaluations claim to be shared; therefore, they require a communicability in principle. But, for this very reason, they are also contestable. Their discrimination, which we saw was inevitable, opens the way to controversy. To put this, rather than that, "higher up" requires giving reasons. The question "How ought we to live?" opens a field of conflict as soon as our choices call for justification. As we have already noted: the Socratic call for an "examined life" brings criticism, a crisis of evaluation, into play in exemplary fashion. The heterogeneity of hypergoods also opens the way to controversy, for how are we to place what is fundamentally heterogeneous into a unique hierarchy? I remark in passing that it is this spectacle of competition among goods of a higher order, and even among whole systems of priority, that has from Kant to Rawls and Habermas motivated replacing the idea of the good, judged to be conflictual, with the reputedly more irenic ideas of what is valid, just, or obligatory, at the price of reducing morality to procedural rules. But in so doing, we have only displaced the tragic moment of moral life by shifting it to the point of articulation between the formal universal and moral judgment in some actual situation. It would be better to admit that this specific form of the tragic, bound to the heterogeneity of goods of a higher rank, is constitutive of the most originary form of ethical life, and hence that this cannot be conceived other than as an "examined life." What are we to conclude then about this unsurpassable conflict of moral sources, which Taylor does not hesitate to place, in spite of everything, among the components of inescapable frameworks? At this level, the tie between conflict and historicity is blindingly obvious. In fact, Taylor would not have ended the first part of his book with the theme of the "sources of moral life" unless he had in view, from the beginning, the predicament of the self in modernity. In this sense, the strategy of anticipation and retrospection, which we have seen at work in the historical segments of the book, governs its overall structure, the historicity of the ethical field being projected in anticipation into the a priori constitutive of the self. We may even risk saying that it is the historicity belonging to the construction of the modern self that is anticipated in the transhistorical structure of moral experience, originarily indicated as having an epochal character. It is possible for us to revive in imagination and in sympathy all the epochs of morality because our conscience suffers in equal measure from the noncontemporaneous character of contemporaneity and the contemporary character of noncontemporaneity. In this sense the first part of the book can be considered the result, as much as the presupposition, of this wholly original cumulative character of moral life.

III. Exercises

The Difference between the Normal and the Pathological as a Source of Respect

The goal of the reflections I propose to present is to begin to lay the basis for the respect—and, beyond such respect, for the friendship—we owe to the physically and mentally handicapped, as well as to all others struck by infirmities. I want to do this through an argument drawing on the very notion of the pathological. In this way, I mean to shake up the all too easy and lax way in which we often simply juxtapose too vague a notion of respect for every human person without distinction and a notion of the pathological understood as merely a deficit in relation to some presumed ideal of normality. Thus, my aim is to begin the process of fitting a more differentiated notion of respect to a notion of the pathological characterized by more positive values. I want to insist on this idea of beginning to fit these two notions together, for what in the long term is at issue is the idea of a more targeted respect derived from a revised understanding of the pathological, where this latter is now recognized as structurally worthy of respect.

I shall begin from the pole of the pathological and shall propose some reflections inspired by the philosophy of biology presented by Georges Canguilhem in his book *The Normal and the Pathological* and further developed in his later work *La connaissance de la vie*.[1]

Like Canguilhem, I shall give these reflections centered on the normal and the pathological a preface devoted to some more general concepts relating to the relationship between "the living creature

---

1. The page numbers given in the text following quotations from Canguilhem refer to his *La connaissance de la vie*.

and its milieu." In this way, I shall mark out a larger circle within which I shall place the narrower circle of the normal and the pathological. The idea I want to hold on to in doing this is that the living creature, as distinct from a physical machine, stands in a dialectical relation with its milieu, one of working things through and sorting them out. This idea represents a major advance in relation to the theory so long dominant in the behavioral sciences according to which the living creature is said to respond to external stimuli, which in a way have the priority of initiative: the milieu acts and the living creature responds. This, of course, is the behaviorist hypothesis, most fully developed by Tolman to its highest degree of sophistication. We may multiply the intermediary variables between stimulus and response—by introducing affective dispositions, motor explorations, and so on—but these are just ways of filling the black box that finally constitutes the organism itself and its capacity to structure things.

The attack on this theory has been twofold, both methodological and experimental. On the methodological plane, what is called into question is the initial defining of the milieu by the experimenter. The milieu, in this hypothesis, is the world as seen by the scientist, that is, one constructed solely in terms of physics and chemistry. Worse: what counts as a stimulus is manipulated by the experimenter, who, so to speak, extorts the patient's response. The proposed change in method goes in the opposite direction. The organism is allowed to orient itself freely to its setting—this is the ethologist's attitude—and one observes how the organism itself *defines* its milieu through selecting what are to count as significant signals; in other words, one observes (the experimental aspect) how the organism structures its relation to its milieu through a kind of double-entry registering of what is significant and what is not. This reversal in method and technique is indicated by the vocabulary utilized: the term "milieu" is replaced by "environment," "ambient milieu," or "lifeworld" (*Umwelt*).[2]

As a next step, I want to draw again from Canguilhem's analyses the important idea of a "vital value." As he puts it, "the animal's environment is nothing other than a milieu centered in

---

2. See Canguilhem's discussion of the importance of Uexküll's work in *La connaissance de la vie*, 144.

relation to a subject with a 'vital value' which essentially is what makes the living creature. We have to conceive at the root of this organization of the animal's environment a subjectivity analogous to the one we are led to consider to be at the root of the human environment" (145). This idea of a vital value is correlative with the idea of an interaction between the living creature and its milieu, an interaction where "the living creature brings its own norms to the evaluation of situations, whereby it dominates its milieu and accommodates itself to it" (146). Canguilhem adds—and this additional comment will serve as a transition for us: "This relationship does not consist essentially as one might believe in a struggle or opposition—that has to do with the pathological state" (146).

Let us now turn to the pathological-normal relation.

What sort of interaction with the milieu do we have to consider here?

I would like to proceed by developing one other suggestion from Canguilhem, still from *La connaissance de la vie*, where he writes: "Human life may have a biological sense, a social sense, and an existential sense" (155). What it is important to emphasize here is that it is a question not of successive stages but rather of an intertwining of simultaneous values, ones that we can distinguish only for the sake of our argument.

What does the pathological signify on the level of the biological? Or to put it in a more radical form: how is it possible that there should be anything pathological on the level of life itself?

To answer this question we have to return to the fundamental difference that distinguishes the biological from the physical order. In this latter order, a singular event (the fall of an apple) strictly obeys, as we put it, a law. In fact, the physical law is not a rule that can be broken. The apple does not "obey" the physical law. It is only with life that individuality includes the possibility of irregularity, of deviation, of abnormality. But in relation to what? Here it is no longer the undramatic relation between the type and the individual that is in play. The legality belonging to life is of a different order. But in relation to what then can we speak of deviation? The answer here has to be ambiguous. And this ambiguity will not disappear when we pass from one level to another. Two readings of "normal" propose themselves: we can identify the norm with a statistical average. The criterion then is one of frequency, deviation being deviation in relation to this average. But we can also understand a norm as an ideal, in a sense that itself has numerous senses: for example, success, well-being, satisfaction, happiness. From this ambiguity in the idea of the norm comes an ambiguity attached to the idea of health. Here it is important to take into account the fact that, as Canguilhem puts it, the object of medical science is at the same time an obstacle to life. This new ambiguity stems from the ambiguity attached to the idea of the norm as taken sometimes as the average, sometimes the ideal. In both cases, health characterizes individuals in their relation to the norm. This relation is ineluctably precarious (where I am taking the word "precarious" in an ontological sense, reserving "ambiguous" for the epistemological level). Life presents itself as an adventure in which we do not know what is a test or trial and what a failure. It is easy to see why: the value of life is not an observable fact. Life is always evaluated and this evaluation is always relative. To use the categories of Kurt Goldstein, still following Canguilhem, health presents itself as a limited capacity to deal with threats, dangers, and dysfunctions, including illnesses or handicaps. "To live, already, for the animal, and even more so for the human being, is not just to vegetate or to preserve oneself. It is to confront the demands of new milieux, in the form of reactions or undertakings dictated by such new situations" (165).

In this way, we arrive at the notion of disease on the biological level. In every case it is an individual who is sick. In the physical world there is no disease and, therefore, neither medicine nor physicians. There is no occasion to take care of or to heal, that is, to traverse the interval between disease and being cured. But neither is there an absolute definition of disease when we come to the biological level. At most we can say with Kurt Goldstein that "the norms of pathological life are those that henceforth oblige the organism to live in a 'shrunken' milieu, one that is qualitatively different in its structure from the previous life setting" (167).

Let us pause for a moment to consider this expression: a "shrunken" milieu.

Here two readings of the pathological join up with our two readings of the norm. Read negatively, the pathological signifies a deficit or deficiency. Read positively it signifies another, an *other* organization, one that has its own laws. Yes, another structure in the relationship between the living creature and its milieu. It is on the basis of this structure that at the end of our reflections we shall have to articulate the respect due to this other way of being-in-the-world, with its own values. These latter only unfold themselves at the third, existential level. But they have a biological basis in the idea of an adjustment to a "shrunken" milieu, with both its positive and its negative connotations.

Before leaving the biological level, I want to emphasize one other factor that tends to cover over any positive evaluation of any living organism's relation to its milieu. This has to do with what I will call the insolent aspect of health, which tends to turn the norm in the sense of an average toward the norm in the sense of an ideal. This idea of insolence is important. It consists essentially in our glorifying our own "good health," including the sense of power that makes us say, "I can do this, I can do that." Illness, it follows, can be defined only in terms of some impotence: what I cannot do, what I can no longer do. (Growing old may provide a favorable case for calling into question this insolence, which ancient and medieval moral thinkers called *concupiscencia essendi*, misplaced pride in existing.) Now certainly, health is not just an illusion. "What characterizes it," says Canguilhem, "is the capacity to tolerate variations from the norms, which are apparently guaranteed but always in fact necessarily precarious, on which the situations of any milieu confer a misleading value of being definitive values" (165). I want to emphasize the expression "misleading value." It is from this illusion that the negative evaluation of the pathological as univocal comes. In one sense, the very existence of medicine, as a social institution parallel to that of the tribunal, confirms this "vital depreciation of illness" (167). The project of—or, rather, the demand for—healing presupposes this depreciation. To feel ill, to say that one is sick, to behave as one who is sick, is to ratify this negative evaluation, this depreciation. And what might bring us to our senses? The feeling of incertitude that goes with our mortality: "Every success is threatened since individuals die, and even species die. Successes are retarded failures, failures aborted successes" (160). This is the episodic lesson of illness—the chronic lesson, if I may dare to put it this way, of growing old.

I hope you will forgive me for having lingered for such a long time on the biological level. So many things come into play on the social and, even more, on the existential levels; both are planes on which a new set of criteria for the normal and therefore also for the pathological come into play. A social normality of what to do gets substituted for the biological normality of living one's life. What is now normal is behavior capable of satisfying the social criteria for life together with others. Here is where the comparison of one living being with another intervenes in a forceful manner. For example, what fascinates us is what is permitted to others but forbidden to us. Something held to be pathological arising out of such a comparison can then come to occupy the foreground. In an individualistic society that emphasizes the capacity for autonomy, of being able to direct one's own life, any incapacity that reduces one to a state of tutelage in the double form of assistance and being controlled will be taken to be a handicap. Health, too, then is socially normed, as is sickness, as is the demand for care and the expectation that goes along with this demand. The criterion of being healed is that of gaining or recovering the power to be able to live like others, of being able to act like others. A displacement is produced in this way from the internal norm of the living being to the external social norm, as it is codified by others. And from this comes the social stigma par excellence, exclusion, which has no defined biological model but is terribly pertinent socially. Society would like to ignore, hide, even eliminate its handicapped. But why? Because they constitute a silent menace, a disturbing reminder of our fragility, our precariousness, our mortality. They constitute an unbearable *memento mori*. So we hide away pathological deviants, just as we hide away those deviants being punished. Medical deviants and penal deviants are both pathological deviants. What is fundamentally threatened by the spectacle of deviance is the very same insolence of life I spoke of earlier, ratified, consolidated, and turned into confidence and assurance by social success. Inferiority and depreciation are thus socially normed. Here even psychiatry, as a branch of medicine, is always threatened in the sense that it may fall into playing the role of an "objective sign of this universal, subjective reaction of distancing, that is, of the vital depreciation of illness" (167). The biological difference thus finds itself dramatically consolidated by social distinctions.

The psychiatric hospital runs the risk of reinforcing this threat of being excluded from society. The institutional structure operates

in a tacit and almost invisible way during the medical colloquy between two people. It is true that each sick patient is a unique being;
it is not true that each disease is: a case is not unique. Codified protocols for treatment in a way graft the case to be treated to medical
knowledge and practice, with worldwide ramifications concerning
the diagnosis, treatment, and prognosis. The competence exercised
hic et nunc by the physician faced with some disease brings into
play professional knowledge that, as communicated, learned, and
applied, inserts the whole medical institution into the intimate relation between the patient and his or her physician. This is not all.
The institutional structure in turn is connected to a whole complex
of administrative, juridical, and penal structures that relate to the
politics of health and that are characteristic of the law-governed
state under whose jurisdiction the medical profession operates. At
this level, the very concept of health receives a distinct significa-
tion. The being to which it applies is not precisely the individual
person but rather a statistical reality stemming from the notion of
a population, a notion that public health shares with demography.

This twofold intrusion of the institution into the medical act,
in the form of professional knowledge and a political framework,
has a noteworthy impact at the psychiatric level. Medical knowledge is the least commonly shared thing in the situation of mental handicaps. The physician is the only one who knows in the
strong sense of this term. But, above all, psychiatry gives rise to
a unique type of institution when it comes to social exclusion, an
institution that is most easily measured by the yardstick of the
dominant prejudices of a society and that gives these prejudices a
particularly visible form. To be sure, psychiatric hospitals want to
be hospitals like other hospitals. And in this regard, the education
of the public has made immense progress over the last half of the
twentieth century in presenting mental illness as one more disease
among other diseases. Psychiatric hospitalization has more and
more come to be seen as just one more form of hospitalization.

It remains the case, however, that the psychiatric clinic, for
many reasons, has remained an opaque mediator between the physician and his or her patient. This opacity affects the contract regarding the provision of care and its bilateral structure. For illness
in general, we have, on the one side, someone suffering and asking
for help and, on the other, someone who offers competence and

treatment. The meeting point is that of a diagnosis and a proposed treatment. It is this situation that is profoundly blurred in the case of mental illness. It is not just the affective, empathetic bond that is affected, but also the exercising of the very deontology that ensures the equity of the act of offering care. We need only to recall the three rules that govern the medical consultation to see this: the sharing of a medical secret; the right of the patient to know the truth about his or her case based on the physician's diagnosis, proposed treatment, and the likely outcome; and, above all, the right to informed consent. When one of the partners in this contract presents himself or herself as handicapped, be it on the emotional and relational level or on the mental and verbal one, the responsibility of the medical party is much heavier. How can one avoid abusing this responsibility by the, so to speak, monopoly offered, it would seem, by the actual situation? How are we to reach, beyond the disease, the patient's still-possible resources of the will to live, of initiative, of evaluation, of decision? In other words, how can we make up for the deficiency of the other person, the patient, without denying or excluding him or her? To pose such questions is already to indicate a willingness not to allow the act of social exclusion to penetrate to the heart of the medical consultation.

Yet it is here that the separation, tacitly assumed by average public opinion as regards anyone handicapped in terms of social life, gets reinforced a second time on the institutional level. The act of social exclusion takes on institutional form in multiple ways, first of all in an almost invisible fashion at every stage of medical intervention, then in a visible and terribly disturbing way with those fantasies that, perpetuating a horrible history, continue to inscribe themselves into everyday reality through public attitudes that make us flee pathological deviants just as we flee criminals. What holds in general for every illness applies with particular force to psychiatric deviance. Michel Foucault wrote both the history of madness and that of the prison. He recounts the slow conquest of providing care over the use of physical and mental violence. But the confusion between treatment and punishment continues to exist in the collective subconscious. The "madman" continues to frighten us and to bring about the rejection that the hospital is supposed to carry out under another name. The psychiatric hospital and the prison, for the collective imagination, are not part of the city. Symbolically, they exist outside the city walls. Why should this be the case? Where the does the force of exclusion draw its strength? Foucault suggests that the conquest of autonomous reason in the modern age had as its counterpart the exclusion of the irrational as the inhuman par excellence. In a similar sense, I would say that the more we charge the individual, solitary subject with responsibilities, the more this burden becomes unbearable for everyone. The line of exclusion then no longer runs between purportedly healthy subjects and the handicapped; it runs through each person's conscience. The threat of madness, along with the fear of social retribution, replaces the fear of hell. Exclusion stems from our very own inwardness; immanence, in replacing transcendence, turns out to be even more cruel. The mad person is my infinitely close double.

These are the prejudices, in the strong sense of this word, that public education has not been able to stop struggling against. How can medical practice eradicate them if, at the level of ordinary social practice, the sense of community has collapsed, leaving each individual confronted with his or her solitude?

We arrive in this way at the existential level of the evaluation of life. At this level, the norm is no longer defined statistically as an average but is defined as a singular project, what Sartre called an existential project. Individuals define themselves through their referring to themselves as a function of their horizon of action with its personal criteria of actualization and evaluation.

What is at stake here is one's recognition of oneself in terms of one's personal identity. In truth, this latter is the object of an indefinite, "interminable" quest, as Freud said with regard to some psychoanalytic cases. We should therefore speak of identification rather than of identity or even, with Peter Homans, in his *Ability to Mourn*, of "individuation" and "reappropriation." In fact, personal identity cannot be simply a project that one simply makes up; it requires a work of memory, thanks to which the subject gathers him- or herself together and attempts to construct a life story that is both intelligible and acceptable, one that is both intellectually readable and emotionally supportable. In turn, this work of memory implies a work of mourning applied to lost objects of one's desire and also to abandoned ideals and symbols. There is no coherence to the narrative of a life without the integration of loss. It is a double labor of memory and mourning that grafts together the sense of self-esteem—of *Selbstgefühl*—which confers a moral dimension on self-recognition. It is this *Selbstgefühl*, Freud tells us, that loses itself in melancholy, the loss of the object leading to the loss of self. But melancholy is not simply a psychic disturbance. It is a threat inscribed in each of us, once we begin to consent to sadness, to fatigue, to discouragement. Its name then is despair, the "sickness unto death" described by Kierkegaard. The contrary to this consent to sadness is that moral sentiment or, better, that spiritual attitude Paul Tillich called "the courage to be." The courage to be unites in one braid the work of memory, the work of mourning, and self-esteem. At the same time, it builds a bridge between the recovery of the past in self-recognition and the anticipation of the future in the project and, more specifically, in promise making.

It is this courage to be that is effectively attacked in mental illness under all the different figures that perturb our *Selbstgefühl*, following the complex nosography of the psychotic and the neurotic. But what is important to us at this level of our reflection is not this typology of disasters but the way in which the medical relationship is affected by these different troubles touching self-esteem and the way in which the medical art may reply to this extreme threat.

Here we need to introduce a new component that has so far escaped our analysis: self-esteem does not reduce to a simple relation of oneself to oneself alone. This feeling also includes within itself a claim addressed to others. It includes an expectation of approbation coming from these others. In this sense, self-esteem is both a reflexive and a relational phenomenon, where the notion of dignity reunites the two faces of such recognition.

It is at the level of this nexus between self-recognition and recognition by others that the process of exclusion we discussed at the level of social evaluation pursues its ravages, this time right up to the core of our self-esteem. This destructive effect is made possible structurally by the fact that disease tends to function as a kind of self-exclusion. What on the biological level appeared to us as falling back into a "shrunken" world, and then on the social level as exclusion sanctioned by institutions of many different or-ders, reappears on the existential level as the denial of dignity, as the denial of recognition. Here we touch on what may seem to be the most delicate point of the medical relationship: the other—the other than the ill person—who is the physician finds him- or herself given the charge to compensate for the deficit in the pa-tient's self-esteem and courage by a kind of shared esteem, what we could call a supplementary or supplementing esteem.

This supplementing esteem will be based on the recognition of positive values attached to any disease, not only as regards the pa-tient who is ill but also in his or her relation to others. In this way we rediscover on the existential level the interpretation of pathol-ogy proposed on the biological level. Disease, we said, is something other than a deficiency, a lack, a negative quantity. It is another way of being in the world. It is in this sense that the patient has dignity, is an object of respect. The value of the disease and of the patient remains even within the shadows of madness.

It is this ethical message properly speaking that I want to draw from all these long developments devoted to the relation between the normal and the pathological. It is important for the suppos-edly healthy individual to discern in the handicapped individual those resources of conviviality, of sympathy, of living with and suffering with that are bound expressly to the fact of being ill or handicapped. Yes, it is up to those who are well to welcome this proposition regarding the meaning of illness and to allow it to aid them in bearing their own precariousness, their own vulnerabil-ity, their own mortality.

The Three Levels of Medical Judgment

This essay places its accent on the therapeutic (or clinical) aspect of bioethics as distinct from that branch directed at research. In truth, both branches include a practical dimension, meant to serve either knowledge and science or treatment and healing. In this sense, both raise ethical questions in that both these branches have to do with deliberate interventions in the processes of life, whether human or nonhuman life. What seems to characterize the therapeutic (clinical) approach is that it gives rise to acts of judgment that take place on different levels. The first of these levels can be called "prudential" (the term "prudential" being the Latin version of the Greek *phronesis*). The faculty of judgment (to use Kantian terminology) is applied to singular situations in which an individual patient is placed in an interpersonal relation with an individual physician. The judgments offered on this occasion exemplify a practical wisdom whose nature is more or less intuitive and a result of training and practice. The second level can be called "deontological" inasmuch as its judgments have a normative function that transcends the singularity of the relation between a patient and a physician in different ways, as is apparent in the codes of medical ethics used in different countries. At a third level, bioethics deals with judgments of a reflective type applied to the attempt to legitimate the prudential and deontological judgments of the first two levels.

I want to present for discussion the following theses. First, it is from the prudential dimension of medical ethics that bioethics in the broadest sense borrows its properly ethical significance. Second, although based on prudential judgments, the judgments formulated at the deontological level exercise a great variety of irreducible critical functions that begin with the simple universalizing of the prudential maxims of the first level and that, among other things, deal with external or internal conflicts having to do with the sphere of clinical intervention and hence with the limits of every kind imposed on the norms of medical deontology in spite of their categorical nature. Third, at the reflective level moral judgment refers to one or more ethical traditions themselves rooted in a philosophical anthropology. It is at this level that notions such as health and happiness are called into question and where ethical reflection touches on problems as radical as those having to do with life and death.

The Agreement regarding Trust

Why is it necessary to begin from the prudential level? Here is the place to recall the nature of the situations to which the virtue of prudence gets applied. Its domain is that of decisions taken in singular situations. Even though science, according to Aristotle, has to do with the general, *techne* has to do with the particular. This is eminently true in the situation where the medical profession intervenes, namely, that of human suffering. Suffering, along with enjoyment, is the ultimate refuge of singularity. It is also, we could say in passing, the reason for the distinction within bioethics between the branch oriented toward the clinical and that oriented toward biomedical research, taking into account the ways in which they overlap, which I shall speak of below. It is true that suffering is not just the concern of the practice of medicine. It affects and upsets one's relation to oneself as the bearer of a variety of abilities and also many of our relations with others, in our family, at work, or with respect to a wide variety of institutions, but medicine is one of those practices based on a social relation for which suffering is the basic motivation and whose *telos* is the hope of finding help and perhaps healing. In other words, medicine is the one practice that has physical and mental health as its defining goal. At the end of this chapter, I shall return to the variety of meanings attached to this notion of health. At its beginning, though, I shall take as given our ordinary expectations, however controversial they may be, connected to the notion of health as a form of well-being and happiness. At the base of prudential judgments, therefore, we find the relational structure of the medical act: the desire to be released from the burden of suffering and the hope for healing constitute the prime motivation for the social relation that makes medicine a practice of a particular kind whose origins as an institution are lost to the depths of time.

Having said this, we can go directly to the heart of what is at issue. What, we shall ask, is the ethical core of this singular encounter? It is the agreement governing trust that commits both parties, both the patient and the physician. At this prudential level, we do not yet speak of a contract or of medical secrecy, but of an agreement regarding caregiving based on trust. And this agreement concludes a particular process. In the beginning, a moat and even a noteworthy dissymmetry separate the two protagonists. On the one side is someone who knows what to do; on the other, someone who is suffering. This moat gets filled, and the initial conditions become more equal, through a series of steps beginning from each side of the relationship. The patient—this patient—"brings to language" his suffering in speaking of it as a complaint that includes what will become a descriptive element (a symptom) and a narrative one (an individual entangled in these details). In turn, the complaint becomes more precise as a request: a request for . . . (healing and, who knows, health and, why not, in the background, immortality) and a request to . . . (addressed as an appeal to some physician). To this request gets grafted the *promise* to carry out the protocol of the proposed treatment, once the request is accepted.

At the other pole, in passing through the successive stages of accepting a client, formulating a diagnosis, and finally offering a prescription, the physician makes up the other half of the path leading to that equalization of conditions through which Tocqueville defined the spirit of democracy. These are the canonical phases of the establishing of the caregiving agreement, which in binding together two people overcomes the initial dissymmetry of their encounter. The reliability of this agreement still has to be tested on both sides by the physician's commitment to "follow" his patient and by the patient's "conducting" himself as the agent of his treatment. In this way, the caregiving agreement becomes a type of *covenant* sealed between two people against a common enemy, the disease in question. This agreement owes its moral character to the tacit promise shared by the two protagonists faithfully to fulfill their respective commitments. This tacit promise is constitutive of the prudential status of the moral judgment implied in the speech act of making a promise.

We cannot overemphasize the fragility of this agreement from its start. The contrary of trust is distrust or suspicion. And this contrary accompanies every phase in the establishing of this agreement. Trust is threatened, on the patient's side, by an impure mixture of distrust regarding the presumed abuse of power on the part of every member of the medical profession and the suspicion that the physician will not be up to the patient's extravagant expectations regarding his care. Every patient asks for too much (I have already alluded to our desire for immortality) and distrusts the excess of power on the part of the one in whom he also places an excessive trust. As for the physician, the limits placed on his commitment, beyond any negligence or presumed indifference, will appear later when we speak of the intrusion of the biomedical sciences, which tend to objectify and reify the human body, and of the problems having to do with public-health policies, which focus more on the collective than on the individual aspect of the general phenomenon of health. This fragility in the agreement of trust is one of the reasons for the transition from the prudential to the deontological plane of moral judgment.

Nevertheless, I want to say that in spite of its intimate character, the caregiving agreement does not lack resources regarding its generalization, ones that justify the very term "prudence" or "practical wisdom" attached to this level of medical judgment. I have spoken of this kind of judgment as intuitive because it proceeds from training and practice. Yet to speak of the level of moral commitment bound to the caregiving agreement as prudential does not mean for all that to hand it over to the vagaries of benevolence. Like every art that is practiced case by case, medical practice (precisely thanks to such training and practice) engenders what we can call precepts—without yet speaking of norms—that set a prudential judgment on the way to becoming a deontological judgment.

I take as the first of these precepts the practical wisdom exercised on the medical level of recognizing the singular character of the situation of providing care and, especially, of regarding the patient as an individual. This singularity implies that one person cannot be substituted for another, which excludes, among other things, the reproduction of one and the same individual through cloning. The diversity of human beings means that it is not the species that one heals but in each case a unique example of this species. The second precept underscores the indivisibility of each person. It is not multiple organs that one treats, but a whole illness, if we can put it that way. This precept is opposed to the fragmentation imposed by the variety of illnesses and their locations in the body, as well as the corresponding specializations of knowledge and skills meant to deal with them. My second precept is equally opposed to another kind of cleavage between the biological, the psychological, and the social. A third precept adds to the ideas of nonsubstitutability and indivisibility that of self-esteem, which is already a more reflexive form. This precept speaks of more than the respect due to another person. It aims at balancing the unilateral character of respect, running from one person to another, by one's recognition of one's own value. Esteem has to do with oneself. Yet in the situation of caregiving, particularly when someone is hospitalized, there is a tendency to encourage the sick person to regress to dependent forms of behavior and for the caregivers to act in ways that are offensive and humiliating to the dignity of the patient.

The occasion of such a falling back to forms of dependence strengthens the pernicious mixture of excessive demands and a latent distrust that corrupts the agreement governing caregiving. In this way, another kind of fragility is emphasized, one already referred to above. The caregiving agreement ideally implies a correspondence between the two partners in this agreement. But the regression to a situation of dependence, once one enters the phase of serious treatments and situations that may be lethal, tends insidiously to reestablish the situation of inequality that was supposed to be set aside by the caregiving agreement. It is essentially the feeling of personal esteem threatened by the situation of being dependent that prevails in hospitals. The patient's dignity is threatened not only at the level of language but by all the concessions having to do with the familiarity, the triviality, and the vulgarity of everyday relations between the medical personnel and hospitalized patients. The only way to fight against such offensive kinds of behavior is to return to the exigency at the base of the caregiving, that is, to the associating of the patient with the carrying out of his treatment or, in other words, to the agreement that makes the physician and the patient allies in a common struggle against disease and suffering. I want to emphasize again that I am placing this concept of self-esteem at the prudential level, reserving the concept of respect for the deontological level. In self-esteem a human being approves his existence and expresses a need to know that his existence is approved by others. Self-esteem thus involves a touch of *amour-propre*, of personal pride about being oneself—this is the ethical basis for what we today call human dignity.

The Medical Contract

Why must we now shift from the prudential to the deontological level, and why must we do so in terms of the framework of a bioethics oriented toward the clinical and the therapeutic setting? The answer involves a number of reasons linked to the multiple functions of the deontological judgment.

The first such function is to universalize the precepts arising from the caregiving agreement that binds the patient and the physician. Whereas I spoke of prudential precepts using a vocabulary close to that of ancient Greek comments applied to the virtues connected with professions, techniques, and practices, it is in a vocabulary more marked by Kantian moral philosophy that I shall speak of norms considered in terms of their universalizing function in relation to those precepts that Kant placed under the category of maxims of action, which have yet to undergo the test of universalization capable of elevating them to the rank of imperatives. If the agreement to trust each other and the promise to keep this agreement constitute the ethical core of the relation that binds the physician and the patient, it is the elevation of this agreement to the rank of a norm that constitutes the deontological moment of judgment. It is essentially the universal character of the norm that is affirmed. It binds every physician to every patient, hence everyone entering into the caregiving agreement. Still more fundamentally, it is no accident that the norm bears the form of a prohibition, that of not breaking medical secrecy. At the prudential level, what was still only a precept of confidentiality preserved the features of an affinity linking two people in an elective manner. In this sense, the precept could still be assigned to the virtue of friendship. As a prohibition, the norm excludes the third person, placing the individual commitment under the rule of justice and no longer under the precepts of friendship. The caregiving agreement, which was in question at the prudential level, can now be expressed in the vocabulary of a contractual relation. Certainly there are exceptions that have to be considered (I shall speak of them below), but they themselves follow a rule: no exceptions unless there is a rule allowing an exception to the rule. In this way, the professional secret can be "opposed" to every colleague who is not a part of the treatment, to judicial authorities who may expect or be tempted to require testimony from medical personnel, to curious employers seeking medical information regarding potential employees, to polltakers interested in personal data, to the bureaucrats in the insurance industry or the social security office not entitled by law to have access to medical files. The deontological character of the judgment governing medical practice is confirmed by the obligation laid on the members of the medical profession in general to offer aid not only to their patients but to any sick or wounded person they may come upon in a life-threatening situation. At this level of generality, the duties applying to the medical profession tend to become confused with the categorical imperative to help any person in danger.

The second function of deontological judgment is one of connection. Insofar as the norm governing medical secrecy is part of a professional code, it has to be related to all the other norms governing the medical corps in some given political body. This kind of deontological code works like a subsystem within the vaster domain of medical ethics. For example, section 1 of the *French Code of Medical Deontology* sets out the general obligations of every physician in relation to those rules governing every profession, which confers a social status on these rules. In this sense, one article of the French code specifies that medicine is not a form of commerce. Why? Because the patient, as a person, is not a form of merchandise, even though further along something has to be said concerning the financial cost of providing care, something that stems from the contractual relation and brings into play the social dimension of medicine. The articles that set out the physician's freedom to prescribe and the patient's to choose a physician are to be placed under the same heading of universality within the framework of a profession. These articles not only characterize a certain kind of medicine, that of a free market, but also reaffirm the basic distinction between the medical contract and every other form of contract governing the exchange of salable goods. But the connective function of the deontological judgment does not end with these rules setting up the medical corps as a social and professional body. Within this clearly delimited subsystem, the rights and duties of every member of the medical corps are coordinated with those of patients. For example, to the norms defining medical secrecy correspond norms governing the rights of patients to be informed about the state of their health. In this way, the fact of a shared truth is meant to balance that of the medical secrecy that applies only to the physician. On one side, secrecy; on the other, truth. When stated in deontological terms, the prohibition against breaking professional secrecy cannot be "opposed" to the patient. In this way, the two norms constituting the unity of the contract, which lies at the center of this deontology, are brought together, in the same way that reciprocal trust constitutes the main prudential presupposition of the caregiving agreement. Here, too, restrictions had to be included in the code, taking into account the capacity of the sick person to understand, accept, internalize, and, if I may put it this way, to share information with the attending physician. Discovering the truth, especially if it means a death warrant, is equivalent to an initiatory trial, with its traumatic episodes affecting self-understanding and one's relations with other people. It is the horizon of life as a whole that gets narrowed down. The clearly stated connection in the medical code between professional secrecy and the right to the truth allows us to attribute one very particular function of the architecture of deontological judgment to such deontological codes, namely, that of serving as a turning point between the deontological and prudential levels of medical judgment and its ethics. It is by making the place held by each norm in the deontological code part of its overall meaning that the professional code exercises its connective function within the deontological field as a whole.

A third function of the deontological level is to arbitrate among a multiplicity of conflicts that arise on the frontiers of medical practice based on a "humanistic" orientation. In truth, arbitrating among such conflicts has always constituted the critical part of every deontology. Here we move beyond the letter of such codes, which, as read, if they do not dissimulate those conflicts we are going to consider, at least tend to formulate only certain compromises, stemming from arguments carried out at different levels of the medical corps, public opinion, and the political powers that be. What is written in the code is often a solution that conceals the problem.

Yet conflicts do arise on two fronts today where the orientation of medical practice that I have spoken of as "humanistic" finds itself more and more threatened.

The first such front is the one where medical ethics oriented toward the clinic—the only ethics I am considering—runs up against medical ethics oriented toward research. These two branches taken together make up what we today call bioethics, which also includes a legal dimension, strongly emphasized in the English-speaking world, which has in turn given rise to the formation of the relatively recent concept of biolaw. I will leave aside the dimension of those controversies internal to research ethics as well as those relating to some higher legal body. Yet, despite their different orientations—improve caregiving and/or advance science—the clinic and the research laboratory do share a common frontier along which conflicts unavoidably occur. Progress in medicine depends largely on progress in the biological and medical sciences. The ultimate reason is that the human body is both a personal being and the observable object of scientific investigation as a part of nature. It is principally on the occasion of those types of exploration of the human body where experimentation intervenes that conflicts can arise, in that the self-conscious, voluntary participation of the patients is in question. In this regard, the development of medical research has increased the pressure of objectifying techniques on medicine practiced as an art. Here is where the rule of "informed consent" comes into play. This rule implies that the patient not only must be informed that he is a participant in an experiment but that he must give his consent to such participation, even when the experiment is devoted solely to research. We all know the innumerable obstacles opposed to fully respecting this norm. Compromise solutions swing back and forth between an honest attempt to place limits on medical power (a concept quite clearly missing from the codes) and more or less admitted precautions taken by the medical corps to protect itself against legal actions taken by its patients-turned-adversaries, in cases of presumed concealed abuses or, more frequently, in the face of failures that angry patients (all too ready to confuse the duty to provide care, that is, means, with a duty to heal, that is, to produce results) take to be the result of malpractice. The ravages produced in the United States by the legal ardor of conflicting parties is well known, ravages whose effect is to replace the agreement based on trust, the life-giving heart of prudential ethics, by one based on distrust.

Yet not everything is undercut, or perverted, by the compromises imposed by unsurpassable conflictual situations. What ought we to say, for example, about the limit case, arising in medical research, of the double-blind test, where both the patient and the researcher are kept uninformed? What happens then to the idea of informed consent? At this point, the role of arbitration in medical deontology takes on the features not only of jurisprudence but of casuistry as well.

The second front follows the uncertain dividing line between concern for the personal well-being of the patient—the presumed cornerstone of free access to medical care—and taking public health into account. A latent conflict tends to oppose the concern for the person and his or her dignity and that for health as a social phenomenon. This is the type of conflict that a code, like the *French Code of Medical Deontology*, tends, if not to dissimulate, at least to minimize.[1] For example, article 2 states that "the physician, serving the individual and public health, exercises his mission respecting human life, the person, and his dignity." This article is a model of compromise. The accent, to be sure, is on the person and his dignity, but human life can also be understood in

1. See my preface to René, *Code français de déontologie médicale*, 9–25.

the broader sense of populations, even of the human species as a whole. Taking public health into account affects all the rules considered earlier, and first of all that of medical secrecy. There is a question, for example, whether a physician has the duty to require his patient to inform his sexual partner that he is infected with HIV (which certainly affects the practice of keeping diagnoses private), even if a systematic investigation of everyone possibly involved need not be undertaken. Here, obviously, is where the law has to intervene and bioethics becomes a part of legal ethics. It is up to the legislative bodies of a society (parliament in some countries, the higher courts in others) to prescribe the duties of each person and to define any exceptions to the rule. Yet the duty of telling the patient the truth is no less mishandled once numerous third parties are implicated in his or her treatment. In the case of hospitalization, the sick person tends to relate to the hospital itself as an institution, at the price of an uncontrollable loss of responsibility. The need to consider public health also affects the third pillar of normative ethics, along with medical privacy and the right to the truth, namely, informed consent. I have already alluded to the increasing difficulty in giving a concrete content to this latter notion, which is a particular problem when research teams or institutions situated at the other side of the planet are in charge of the investigatory protocols for or trials of new treatments.

In the final analysis, this conflict along the front with pubic health is not surprising. We could even rewrite the medical contract in terms of a series of paradoxes. First paradox: the human person is not a thing, and yet his body is a part of observable physical nature. Second paradox: the person is not merchandise, nor is medicine a form of commerce, but medicine has a price and costs society money. Final paradox (which overlaps the first two): suffering is private, but health is public. We ought not therefore to be surprised if this conflict along the front with public health continues to grow, given the ever higher cost of medical research and given the highly sophisticated exploration of the human body and the development of new surgical procedures, all of which is further aggravated by the prolongation of human life, not to speak of the unreasonable expectations of public opinion that demands too much from the medical corps while at the same time fearing its abuses of power. In short, the gulf can only continue to grow between the demand for an unlimited individual liberty and the preservation of equality in the public distribution of care under the heading of a rule of solidarity.

THE UNSAID OF THE CODES

I come now to what in my introduction I called the reflective function of deontological judgment. A new cycle of considerations follow from this function, considerations which have less to do with norms capable of being inscribed in a code of medical deontology than with the legitimation of that deontology itself as a codification of norms. In this sense, one might be tempted to denounce the unspoken aspect of every attempt at codification. Instead, let us begin from what was said concerning the potential conflict implied by the duality of interests that the medical art is supposed to serve: the interest of the person and that of society. A conflict between different philosophies underlies this, which brings to light what we could call the whole history of solicitude. Thus, prudential judgment preserves the best of Greek reflection on the virtues attached to specific practices. To say what a physician is, is to define the kinds of excellence, the "virtues," that make a *good* physician. The Hippocratic oath continues to bind today's medical doctor. And it is the phronesis of the authors of Greek tragedy and Aristotle's ethics that is perpetuated in the Latin and medieval conception of prudence. Next, it is to Christianity and to Augustine that we owe the sense of the nonsubstitutable person. And the Enlightenment takes up this same theme in its discourse about autonomy. Furthermore, how are we not to make a place for the history of casuistry coming from the Talmudic tradition, even before the subtlety of the Jesuits? We need only to think of our sophisticated debates about the embryo as a "potential person" or the limit situations in which treatment of terminal illnesses oscillates between heroic treatment, passive or active euthanasia, and assisted suicide!

This condensed history of moral ideas summed up in lapidary and sometimes ambiguous formulas in our codes does not end there. The pressure exercised by biomedical science and the neurosciences proceeds from a rationalistic, even materialistic approach whose pedigree leads back to Bacon, Hobbes, Diderot, and d'Alembert. And how are we to ignore the influence, particularly perceptible in the English-speaking world, of different forms of utilitarianism exemplified by the maximization of QUALYS (quality-adjusted life years)? We come to the point where medical ethics is grounded in bioethics along with its legal dimension. In fact, the compromises aimed at damping down the conflicts mentioned earlier along the two frontiers of the biomedical sciences and the socialization of health in the name of solidarity themselves express compromises, no longer between norms but between moral sources, in the sense that Charles Taylor uses this term in his *Sources of the Self.* And we should not reproach deontological codes for not speaking about these moral sources. Certainly, these sources are not silent, but it is no longer in the field of deontology that they express themselves. The unsaid, emphasized here, is all the more entrenched.

What is at issue, in the final resort, is the very notion of health, whether private or public. But this is not separable from what we think about—or try not to think about—the relations between life and death, birth and suffering, sexuality and identity, oneself and the other. Here a new threshold is crossed where deontology is grafted to a philosophical anthropology, which cannot escape the pluralism of convictions in democratic societies. If our codes can nevertheless, without stating their sources, give credit to a spirit of compromise, it is because democratic societies themselves come about, on the moral plane, only on the basis of what John Rawls calls an "overlapping consensus," which he completes with the concept of "reasonable disagreements."

I would like to conclude this chapter with two remarks. The first one has to do with the three-level architecture of medical ethics and the path I have proposed from one level to another. It turns out that, without deliberately having set out to do so, I have come back to the fundamental structure of moral judgment that I presented in the "little ethics" of my *Oneself as Another.* This discovery is not fortuitous inasmuch as medical ethics fits into the general ethics of living well and life together. But here I have covered the three levels (teleological, deontological, and prudential) of this ethics in reverse order. Nor is this reverse order unexpected. What specifies medical ethics within the domain of a general ethics is the initial circumstance that leads to the way in which medical ethics gets structured, namely, human suffering. The fact of suffering and the wish to be delivered from it motivate the basic medical act, with its therapy and its basic ethics, that is, the caregiving agreement and the confidentiality that this implies. This is why, starting from the third level of the ethics in *Oneself as Another*, which I define as that of practical wisdom, I went from this level to the normative or deontological one characterized here by the three rules of medical secrecy, the patient's right to the truth, and informed consent. And the difficulties associated with this deontological level of medical ethics lead to the reflective moment that brings ethics to its teleological level. What I rediscover there is the basic structure of all ethics, as I defined it in *Oneself as Another*, using the following canonical formulation: the wish to live well, with and for others, in just institutions. The perplexities I referred to earlier concerning the meaning attached to the idea of health are to be inscribed precisely within the framework of a reflection on the wish to live well. Health is one mode of living well within this limit that suffering gives to moral reflection. Furthermore, the caregiving agreement leads, through the deontological phase of judgment, to the triadic structure of ethics at the teleological level. If the wish for health is the figure that clothes the wish to live well under the constraint of suffering, the caregiving agreement and the confidentiality it requires imply a relation to other people, in the figure of the attending physician, and within a basic institution, the medical profession. In this way this chapter proposes another traversal of the three stages of my fundamental ethic.

My second remark has to do with the specific fragility of medical ethics. This fragility is expressed in different but convergent terms at the three levels of medical ethics. On the prudential plane, this fragility is expressed by the dialectic of trust and distrust that renders fragile the caregiving agreement and its precept of confidentiality. A comparable fragility, at the turning point between the prudential and the deontological judgment, affects the three precepts that concluded the first phase of our investigation. Whether it be a question of the nonsubstitutability of persons, their individuality (or, as I would put it, their integral nature), or, finally, self-esteem, each of these requirements designates a cumulative vulnerability of medical judgment at the prudential level. It is a fragility of another kind that medical ethics is exposed to on the deontological plane. It was expressed earlier by the double threat that weighs on the "humanistic" practice of the medical contract, whether it be a question of the inevitable objectifying of the human body resulting from the interference between the therapeutic project and the epistemic project tied up with biomedical research, or whether it be a question of the tensions between the solicitude addressed to the sick person as a person and the protection of public health. The arbitration function we recognized in the medical judgment in its deontological phase finds itself in this way fundamentally motivated by the types of fragility belonging to this normative level of judgment. But it is quite clearly on the reflective plane of moral judgment that the most intractable kinds of fragility belonging to medical ethics are revealed. What connection can we make between the request for health and the wish to live well? How can we integrate suffering and the acceptance of mortality into the idea that we have of happiness? How does a society integrate into its conception of the common good the heterogeneous strata deposited in contemporary culture by the sedimented history of solicitude? The ultimate fragility of medical ethics results from the consensual yet conflictual structure of the "sources" of common morality. The compromises I have placed under the heading of the two notions of an overlapping consensus and reasonable disagreements constitute the only replies democratic societies have when confronted by the heterogeneity of the sources of their common morality.

Decision Making in Medical
and Judicial Judgments

Medical ethics has too often been treated as a closed domain. I think it is better understood by being related to other activities involving judgments and the making of decisions. Here I propose a parallel between two typical situations from the point of view of decision making, namely, the medical and the judicial cases. As a first approximation, in both cases it is a question of moving from a knowledge base constituted by norms and theoretical knowledge to a concrete decision in some situation—the medical prescription on the one side, the judicial sentence on the other. In both cases, it is a matter of putting a singular, unique decision, relative to an individual person, under a general rule and, in return, of applying a rule to a case. This back and forth movement between the rule and the case takes place in each instance through a comparable act, a judgment—the medical judgment in a therapeutic project, the judicial one in a project whose stake is to say something regarding justice. Here is how we are going to proceed. I shall present in turn the dynamic of the medical judgment and the judicial judgment and then propose a few reflections in concluding concerning the increase in intelligibility that can be expected for each of these cases of acts of judgment from having placed them in parallel to each other.

Let me recall what constitutes the heart of medical ethics, the establishment of a caregiving agreement. This is an act between two people, one of whom is suffering, who presents his complaint and requests help from an expert in matters of health, and the other of whom knows, knows how, and offers his assistance. Between these two people an agreement is concluded based on trust: the patient believes that the physician can help him and wants, if not to cure him, at least to provide care for him. The physician counts on the patient's being able to act as the agent of his own treatment. The act that establishes this agreement is confirmed in the prescription that below will find a symmetrical form, if not its equivalent, in the sentence pronounced by a criminal court.

It would be impossible to overemphasize the singular character of the caregiving agreement concluded between two unique individuals: this physician and this patient, and the prescription which opens a singular history, that of the treatment of this patient confided to this physician. Yet, however singular this agreement may be in each case, it can be placed under a number of different rules. In a table with three columns, I would place in the central one the ethical rules that overall constitute the deontological code governing each medical act. Below, I shall say what I would place in the other two columns.

In considering the deontological code, we need to recall some of its basic rules before showing how they pass from the general to the particular, and what model of application this process corresponds to. It is in terms of this structure that we shall seek the equivalent in the juridical order.

The first norm is the one that gives the form of a right to the agreement about confidentiality sealed by the act of prescription. This norm is named the medical secret. It governs the relation between every physician and every patient, with exceptions that themselves call for a rule. Later we shall see what is equivalent to this on the judicial plane.

The second norm is the right of the patient to know the truth. If professional secrecy is an obligation for the physician, the access of the patient to the truth of his or her case constitutes a right for that patient. This right also has its limits, which stem less from a right in the strict sense of a law than from prudence, in the sense of the ancient virtue of *prudentia*, a synonym for "practical wisdom." The truth does not strike someone like a blow. Its revelation ought to be proportioned to the patient's capacity to receive and accept it. This norm too will find an echo in the courtroom.

The third norm is informed consent. In a way, this norm is situated at the turning point between the two preceding ones.

It presupposes knowing the truth and sanctions the rule about secrecy in associating the patient with the risks that go with his treatment, in this way making the patient a partner in a common struggle against his illness. In a moment, we shall also look at the juridical counterpart of this norm.

So we have the central column of our table of rules and general norms. The two columns that frame this central column also include systems of rules presiding over the concrete act of medical judgment.

The first system has to do with the laboratory rather than the consulting room or the hospital. It deals with the knowledge coming from the biological and the medical sciences. This knowledge guides medical know-how, which has its own methods of diagnosis, prescription, and treatment. Yet the major advances in this art have been due to scientific progress, whose primary motive is not to reduce suffering but rather to know more about the human organism. Curiosity is the primary motive, not solicitude or compassion. The threat therefore is that the center of gravity will shift from know-how to *knowing that*, from the care of a person to being able to control a laboratory object. Hence, we can already speak of the equilibrium to be sought between knowing that and knowing how, between the biological and medical sciences and therapeutic practice, as a question of equity or fairness. The setting at a distance I shall speak of later has to be preserved between them. Today the danger has to do with placing the therapeutic act completely under the control of the biological and medical sciences reduced simply to techniques to be applied. The development of medical science has increased the pressure of such scientific knowledge on therapeutic practice. The medical act can even be colonized from within, for example, in scientific and medical consultations during a surgical operation or on the occasion of treatments with possibly serious side effects. Science advances more quickly, often by far, than do actual diagnoses at the patient's bedside. Thus, we need to recall that the birthplace of medicine is human suffering and that its first act consists in giving help to a person in danger. This is even the norm of all norms that obligates physicians to provide care to any sick person met along the way outside the closed precinct of their consulting rooms.

Every human being has the right to receive care, whatever his social condition, race, ethnicity, religion, customs, or beliefs. This norm of every norm makes the medical act the axis of the central column, one of whose side columns we have been considering.

Over the third column, which is symmetrical to the first one, a heading is written in large letters: public health. If suffering is private, as is the request for care and the desire for healing, diseases are both private and public affairs. Epidemics, often spread by forms of air pollution, are only the most visible part of this double inscription of disease as being both public and private. The level of health of a whole population is a statistical phenomenon of interest to public officials and citizens. To this is added the financial cost of medicine for a political body whose resources remain governed by a law of scarcity. Health, as seen by an individual, may not have a "price" in terms of value, but seen from the point of view of society, it has a "cost" in monetary terms. Public health therefore becomes a political problem, once the risks are shared, in the name of solidarity. A politics of health policy thus becomes a necessity and an obligation for the authorities in charge of a state. In this way, medicine, even in a free-market economy, finds itself situated at the intersection of two potentially conflicting demands which, for example, the *French Code of Medical Deontology* juxtaposes and whose opposition it tends to minimize if not dissimulate. In its article 2, it stipulates: "The physician, in serving the individual and public health, exercises his mission in respecting human life, the person, and his dignity." The accent is certainly on the person, but the daily practice of medicine, especially in hospital settings, finds itself submitted to criteria, restrictions, rules, and imperatives that were produced by the administrative offices of the ministry of public health. For these offices a person is one fragment of the population. And it cannot be otherwise, inasmuch as it is the fate of every human organism that is of interest in one way or another to the whole community. Each accident of individual health constitutes a risk for the whole population. The first imperative for a political policy regarding public health is to decide in what manner this risk can and must be shared. Here, too, the scale can tip toward the side of the concept and practice of public health at the expense of concern for unique, irreplaceable individuals who cannot be substituted for one another. Fairness here is a way of doing justice, as we say, to the initial concept of solicitude for suffering, the ultimate object of any medical act.

So we have the framework for the concrete medical act, where the caregiving agreement leads to a concrete decision, the prescription. Here judgment links one level to another. On the one side, we have the set of rules made up of deontological norms, scientific knowledge concerning the human organism and its dysfunctions, and the general orientation of the politics of public health; on the other, the concrete medical act, the caregiving agreement leading to a concrete decision, the medical prescription. But we have not yet said anything about the process of decision making that leads from one level to another, from rules and norms to a concrete decision. It is this process that is illumined by an analysis that we can also apply to the process of decision making in the judicial order.

At first sight, the differences between these two domains are more visible than the resemblances. The original situation from which the medical act stems is suffering and the request for care. The situation from which juridical operation proceeds is one of conflict. And from this initial opposition follows a similar opposition of the same amplitude at the end of these two processes. On the side of medicine, we have a caregiving agreement that unites the physician and his patient in a single struggle; on the judicial side, a sentence that separates the protagonists, designating one as guilty, the other as the victim.

Having said this, however, there are pertinent resemblances having to do with the span that stretches between the initial situation and the final decision. This is where the decision is made that leads from a normative level to the concrete level of resolving an initial state of uncertainty. In both cases, one proceeds from a general rule to a decision having to do with a unique concrete situation. The general rule on the medical side, as we have seen, is made up of scientific knowledge, the professional know-how inseparable from the principles of medical deontology, and the principal orientation of the political policy regarding public health. What about the parallel on the judicial side? There, too, we can separate into three columns the rules and norms of a general character. In the central one we can place the written codes, the state of jurisprudence, and the procedural rules that govern the trial process. This set is once again flanked by two other systems of general rules. In parallel to scientific knowledge, we can place the legal theory of juridical theorists, principally to be found among university professors. These latter claim to exercise an evaluative judgment applicable to every judicial decision, including those of appellate courts and the supreme court, in the name of a doctrine that has to be accountable only to itself. In the other column, in parallel with the political policy of public health, we have to place the penal policy of the ministry of justice, as one component of the general policy of the government. Between these two will occur the process of decision making in a concrete situation. We then shall have, on one side, in light of the diagnosis, the medical prescription, and on the other, at the end of the argument in words that makes up the trial process, the verdict and the sentence. We could push the parallel beyond this point of no return constituted by the prescription and the sentencing: then we would have on the penal side the carrying out of the sentence, whose parallel on the medical side would be the carrying out of the treatment.

Yet it is between the normative level and that where the decision is made that we find the closest parallel between the medical and the judicial act. In this in-between area we find the space for arguments and interpretations that confirms the resemblances between these two domains. It is here that our comprehension of the phenomenon of the medical decision gains the most from a comparison with the parallel phenomenon in the judicial domain. It is easy to understand why: the operations I have spoken of as arguments and interpretations are most explicit here. As a result they have been widely discussed and carefully studied.[1] The judicial process leading to a decision, apportioned to a number of different protagonists, has been spelled out in detail, and reflected upon, in terms of a complex dialectic of judgment. In turn, this notion of judgment, considered at first in its juridical sense, receives its full scope from being transferred into a nonjuridical domain. To judge is most often to place a singular case under a rule. This is what Kant called a determinative judgment, when we know the rule better than we do its application. But it also can mean seeking a rule for the case when we know the case better than the rule. This is what Kant called a reflective judgment.

1. See Ricoeur, "Interpretation and/or Argumentation," in *The Just*, 109–26.

This operation is far from being a mechanical, linear, automatic process. Practical syllogisms are mixed with the work of the imagination as it plays with variations on the meaning of the rule or the case. Here we are dealing with a mixture of argumentation and interpretation, where the former designates the logical side of the process, as deduction or induction, and the latter places the accent on invention, originality, creativity. This mixture can well be called *application:* to apply a rule to a case or to find a rule for a case—in both instances this amounts to producing a meaning.

We can see this better in the judicial order because there the phases are more clearly distinguished and the roles divided among more than one actor. For example, it is necessary to interpret the law in order to decide which one the case falls under. But it is also necessary to interpret the case, principally through the use of narrative, in order to be able to give a ruling regarding the fit between the description of the case and the angle from which the law is interpreted.

The same thing applies in decision making in the medical order. Every case is particular in relation to medical knowledge and general medical know-how. Here too it is necessary to interpret in an appropriate manner the available medical knowledge, through an intelligent use of the ability to classify the disease in question, that is, in terms of a typology of diseases, but this also requires describing, in an appropriate fashion, on the narrative plane, if I can put it this way, the symptoms of the case, which come from the personal history of the patient. In this way, the decision made on the medical plane too is situated at the crossroads between an argument and an interpretation wholly comparable to those procedures used in making the judicial decision.

We can push the parallel in these processes of forming a judgment to the moment where the decision is made and occurs like an event. Thus, we can see that the medical prescription and the judicial sentence present the same formal features.

First, despite the fact that one of them—the judicial sentence—separates the protagonists, while the other—the medical prescription—unites them, both the judge and the physician are constrained to judge, usually within a limited time frame. Neither the physician nor the judge can avoid this obligation, unless they declare themselves incompetent to deal with the case before them.

The second common feature is that in both examples the making of a decision constitutes an event irreducible to the process it concludes. The decision properly speaking cuts off the prior hesitation and puts an end to it. A risk is taken, the verdict pronounced. From a subjective point of view this irreducibility of this moment that is an event is expressed on the judicial plane by the reserve that is an inner conviction which transcends all applied knowledge. And the physician can invoke a similar conviction with the same force as does the judge should his decision be questioned.

A third formal feature completes and mitigates the last one: neither the judge nor the physician is absolutely alone in this important moment. They are accompanied as long as possible and as far as possible by what we can call an advisory body. If, on the juridical side, it looks dispersed owing to the distribution of roles among the presiding judge, the prosecuting and defense attorneys, and other representatives of the parties involved, it looks much narrower at the patient's bedside. In this regard, I want especially to emphasize the necessity to flatten the medical hierarchy, from the head physician to the nurses, in situations having to do with the end of life and the care of the dying.

The kinship thus established between our two classes of judgment at the level of the medical prescription and the penal (or civil) sentence spreads out to include other components of medical and judicial judgments at the level of the formation of the judgments. We can return here to the three basic rules of medical deontology in light of comparable rules on the judicial side.

The elevating of the singular relation of confidentiality to the deontological rank of the medical secret makes the caregiving contract an act of justice of the same rank as oaths, covenants, and treaties that bind together the contracting parties in the juridical order. What we can call a "just distance" gets established between the contracting parties in the caregiving agreement, halfway between indifference, condescension, even disregard, but in any case suspicion, on the one side, and an emotional fusion in which two identities are lost, on the other. Not too close, not too far away. In this sense the caregiving agreement, too, separates those who ought not to merge into each other, as in some overwhelming passion.

As for the right of the patient to the truth, it gets expressed in terms of a right, insofar as it belongs to the deontological level of the medical judgment. This applies to every patient and every physician. And this is why it can be claimed even to the point of being brought before the courts.

The juridical aspect of informed consent is still more evident than the two preceding norms, inasmuch as it is the source for legal processes more and more frequently today in both the United States and Europe. We can understand why this right is directly appealed to. The caregiving agreement is not univocally one of simple trust; it potentially includes an element of suspicion, the patient, rightly or wrongly, fearing that the physician has abused his power (the expression "medical power" is not an abusive one!) thanks to his greater knowledge and know-how and because of the situation of dependence into which illness plunges the patient, especially in hospital settings. In return, the physician can fear that the patient, confusing the obligation to help with that of providing the desired result, will expect—even demand—something that the physician cannot provide, in the last analysis, immortality. In this way, informed consent constitutes a kind of guarantee and assurance that the two parties involved—the physician no doubt more than the patient—guard against failure and against the charge of having failed.

I do not want to end without having considered one instance where the relationship between medical ethics and that of the judiciary finds itself inverted. What is it that remains implicit in the process of decision making on the judicial plane? It is that the judicial process finds its origin in conflict and its framework in the trial process. Antagonism is what makes visible every dimension of this process. But can we not say in return that the medical judgment illumines a dimension of the judicial one that remains in the shadows? The sentencing, I have said, brings an end to the trial in the law court. This is true. Something is ended; a word of justice has been spoken. But another history begins for the condemned person, that of the penalty, especially if the condemned person is sent to prison. A new question thus is posed: that of the final purpose of the sentence. Is it only meant to punish, to compensate for harm done, for an offense, to give satisfaction to the victim? To protect the public order? Is it not also meant to rehabilitate the condemned, to bring them eventually back from prison to liberty, that is, to reestablish them as having their full rights? If this is indeed the case, the question of the long-term purpose of justice arises. If the short-term purpose is to settle a conflict, is not the long-term one to reestablish the social bond, to put an end to conflict, to establish peace? If so, the medical judgment clarifies the judicial one. The whole juridical apparatus appears as one vast enterprise meant to take care of social ills, even while respecting the different roles of the physician and the judge.

Justice and Vengeance

My intention here is to reflect upon the paradox connected to the irresistible resurgence of the spirit of vengeance at the cost of the sense of justice, whose goal is precisely to overcome vengeance. This regression begins when partisans call for reprisal and vengeance to benefit themselves. This is the initial claim that never gets completely eradicated. Why?

Let us begin by following the trajectory of justice beyond this initial point of confusion. The first stage in the emergence of justice beyond vengeance coincides with the feeling of indignation, which finds its least sophisticated expression in the simple cry: "It's not fair!" It is not difficult to recall typical situations of this preserved in our memories of childhood, when we uttered this cry: unequal shares between brothers and sisters, disproportionate punishments (or rewards), and, perhaps most of all, unkept promises. These typical situations anticipate the basic division into social justice, penal justice, and civil justice governing exchanges, agreements, and contracts.

What does this sense of indignation lack in order to satisfy the moral demand of a veritable sense of justice? Essentially, it lacks a distance between the protagonists in the social game—a distance between the alleged harm done and the hasty reprisal, a distance between the imposition of an initial suffering by the offender and that of a supplementary one applied as punishment. More fundamentally, what indignation lacks is a clear break between the initial tie between vengeance and justice. In fact, it is this same distance that already undercuts the claim by advocates of immediate reprisal that they themselves should directly carry out justice. No one is authorized to do justice for himself. This is why we speak of a rule of justice. And it is in order to obtain such a distance that a third person, a third party, is required between the offender and his victim, between the crime and its punishment—a third person as the guarantee of a just distance between the two actions and the two agents.

The establishing of this distance requires the transition between justice as a virtue and justice as an institution.

That justice is a virtue is unquestionable. From Socrates, Plato, and Aristotle to Kant and Hegel, moral philosophy has always underscored the connection between justice and equality, the well-known Greek *isotēs*. Yet by "equality," we must not too quickly introduce a reference to those goods that get distributed among rival agents. This model of distributive justice presupposes a more radical form of equality, an equality in the value of every agent. The formula for this basic kind of equality is: your life is as important, as significant, as valuable as my own. The minimal expression of this recognition would consist in taking into account in every circumstance the intentions, interests, beliefs, and requirements of others. Justice as a virtue implies this recurrent reference to another person. In this sense, justice is not one virtue among many, along with courage, temperance, generosity, friendship, and prudence. It does share with all these virtues the rational status of aiming at an equilibrium between an excess and a default. But, above all, justice has to do with that side of all these other virtues which is directed toward others, inasmuch as these virtues take into account the existence, needs, and requirements of someone else.

It is within this broad framework that the question of a just distance can now be posed. And it is this demand, this search for a just distance, that calls in turn for the mediation of an institution capable of incarnating the third person. In this new context, the term "mediation" no longer signifies simply moderation in a single agent; it signifies arbitration among competing claims issuing from people who oppose one another. Our problem thus will be to know in what measure this role of arbitration by a third party contributes to the break in the tie between justice and vengeance. This question is all the more legitimate in that vengeance, too, is oriented toward another person. For this reason, the confrontation between justice and vengeance has first of all to do with the fact that justice is directed toward others, and in this way connected to all the other virtues as well.

Now what are we to understand by the institution of justice in terms of a third party? Under this term "institution" it is not only one specific entity that must be taken into account but a whole chain of institutions, which present a hierarchical structure. Let us proceed from the summit to the base of this set of institutions.

The decisive break, as regards the use of private violence, is ensured by the emergence of a political entity—*politeia, res publica, commonwealth, state, Staat*. If you accept, with Max Weber, that the state is characterized by *Herrschaft*, "domination," that is, by its capacity to impose its will on subordinate individuals or communities, then the claim to the monopoly on the use of legitimate violence can be taken as the direct corollary of the ruling power of the state. The interruption of the course of violence begins with this expropriation by social agents, depriving victims of the right to carry out direct justice, to do justice by themselves, to reply using reprisals. In this sense, justice cannot be entirely identified with the suppression of violence; rather, violence is displaced from the private sphere to the advantage of the political entity. Nevertheless, we cannot stop with this much too simple consideration. You will have observed that Weber himself had to correct his definition of the state in terms of domination by adding the adjective "legitimate" to what he says about violence: the use of legitimate violence. Adding this precise detail leads to a further consideration having to do with the whole scope of the notion of an institution, as this is required by the very notion of a law-governed state, that is, one governed by rules, a constitutional state. This is the case for modern democratic states governed by an implicit political philosophy that we can designate by the phrase "political liberalism." This notion of a state governed by rules brings us to the enigma of the ultimate source of legitimation of the state per se. It is not my intention to deal with this enigma itself. It suffices here that this enigma—whatever the appropriate answer to it may be—draws our attention to what can be taken as the second component of the institution as a kind of third party, namely, the establishment of a *corpus* of written laws, at the heart of our cultural heritage. The emergence of such a body of written laws constitutes a very significant event in the general history of culture, which can be easily illustrated by the institutions of the ancient Near East, the Hebrews, Greece, and Rome. The transition of the whole system of rules and norms from an oral to a written status is both the result of the emergence of the state as a political entity and the most distinct support for its ambition to be legitimate. A noteworthy circular relation is established in this way between state and written law, whether the latter has to do with constitutional, penal, or civil law.

A third candidate for the role of a third party is represented by the judicial institution itself, with its tribunals and courtrooms, whose task is to pronounce the word of justice in a concrete situation. But this responsibility and this task cannot be separated from the right of coercion, thanks to which public authority has the capacity to impose a decision regarding justice. Later we shall return to this connection between justice and force, emphasized in a famous saying of Pascal's. Here we need to linger for a moment over the specific use of language and discourse through which the tribunal constitutes the appropriate setting for justice. To speak, to pronounce, the word of justice in a singular situation of conflict is the primordial function and task of the judicial institution within the walls of the tribunal.

Next, in light of the carrying out of this task, a fourth component of the institution of justice must be introduced. I am thinking of the judge as an actual person clothed with the right and the power to state the word of justice we have just spoken of. Judges are human beings like ourselves, ordinary citizens; human beings, not gods or angels. But they are raised above us in virtue of the specific rules that create them, with the goal of stating the word of justice which it is the function of the judicial system overall to elaborate. Judges, we can say, give flesh to justice. They are the mouthpiece of justice.

We have now reached the point where all these components of the institution of justice can be brought together, namely, the trial process, the ceremony carried out in language at the end of which the word of justice can be pronounced, must be pronounced. Within this ceremonial framework unfolds a complex language game, one governed by rules of procedure that ensure the required fairness of the whole process. This game consists essentially in an exchange of arguments between the representatives of the plaintiff and the adverse party. With regard to the problematic of violence and justice, the primary function of the trial process is to transfer conflicts from the plane of violence to that of language and discourse. The trial process elevates the art of verbal confrontation to its peak with the help of rhetorical procedures based on the use of probable arguments. In this sense, the art of argumentation can be taken as one branch of what we can call a transcendental pragmatics of language, inasmuch as the whole trial process rests on the presumption of the validity of the norms applied in a given situation. From a logical point of view, it is a question of "application"—in other words, of the movement from the norm to the case in question. This is a complex operation that combines in a remarkable way argumentation as a deductive procedure and interpretation as an exercise of the productive imagination. Allow me to say something more about this connection between argumentation and interpretation. The argumentation is meant to descend from the claimed validity of the admitted rules and norms to that of the specific case. But this transfer of validity cannot be reduced to a mechanical operation. It implies interpretation in two complementary ways. On the one hand, a choice has to be made among the available laws and more precisely between the prior interpretations of those laws accumulated over the long history of jurisprudence. This choice is governed by a presumption of affinity, let us say of "fit," between the laws selected and the case under consideration. On the other hand, the case itself has to be described in an appropriate fashion as a function of the norm at issue in the given case. This description is a test of what in fact constitutes a narrative interpretation of the case considered. But we know that several "stories" can be constructed regarding the same course of events. Therefore, the legal and the narrative interpretations have to be combined in the process of reaching a decision. I shall not say more about this domain of a logic of application as a combination of argument and interpretation. The preceding brief overview will suffice for our present investigation, whose orientation is more ethical than logical. Let it suffice to say that it is within the framework of this process of application that the institutional attempt to overcome violence through discourse unfolds. In my opinion, it is beyond doubt that the procedural rules of the trial process by themselves alone constitute an advance in justice over the spirit of vengeance. They do so insofar as the trial process furnishes an appropriate discursive framework for the peaceful arbitration of conflicts. It is the indisputable merit of the establishment of such procedural rules to allow the trial process as a distinct institution to transfer conflicts from the sphere of violence to that of language and discourse.

But this primacy conferred on discourse in dealing with interpersonal and social conflicts is not exhaustive. A residual degree of violence remains.

Why? Because violence continues to be affirmed at the two extremes of the whole process starting from the establishment of the state as a political entity up to the establishment of that specific body, the legal system. On the one side, the state, as already said, always claims for itself the monopoly on legitimate violence. From a historical point of view, this claim is rooted in the founding events, usually of a violent nature, presiding over the birth of the state. This violence, let us call it foundational violence, which can still be observed at the heart of liberal states, finds its ultimate expression in the threat to make use of violence against the presumed enemies of the democratic order. And it is this violence, in the final analysis, that endows each decision regarding justice with the right to impose itself. The right to exercise coercion, which constitutes an essential distinction between morality and legality, has no other origin. But let us return to the decision regarding justice at the other extremity of the trial process. Up to now I have not said a word about the sentence as itself a decision. I have confined myself to emphasizing the equal contribution of argumentation and interpretation in the process of applying a legal norm to a single case. I have still to take into account the ultimate stage, the act of pronouncing sentence. In fact, this act has two faces. On the one side, it brings to an end a verbal confrontation, and in this sense it is a concluding act. On the other hand, it constitutes the starting point for a new process and a new history, at least for one of the parties, namely, the imposing of the sentence as a form of punishment. Let us consider these two sides of the judicial decision in turn, since it belongs to the sentencing as the concluding act of the process to engender a subsequent process, the punishment, the infliction of this punishment with its own history.

JUSTICE AND VENGEANCE 229

As a decision, the sentence is a distinct act that transcends the whole process of decision making. It adds something to this process. In the first place, the court is obligated by its rules to decide the case within a limited time span. Second, it is expected that the sentence will put an end to an earlier state of uncertainty. Third, the court is required to speak the word of justice that establishes the just distance between the parties in the conflict. Finally, and above all, such a decision exercises power over liberty and, still in some countries, over life and death. A part of our liberty is placed in the hands of the justice system, inasmuch as its fate is transferred, as I have said, from the sphere of private violence to that of language and discourse. But at the point of imposing the sentence, this part of justice is at the same time a word of force and, hence, in a certain measure, one of violence. In this way, the sentence becomes the starting point of a new process, namely, the carrying out of the sentence, which in the case of criminal trials consists in the administration of some form of punishment. Even in civil court when the sentence leads to a fine or compensation and even more so when it involves the suppression of liberty, the simple imposition of some penalty implies the addition of a supplementary suffering to the earlier suffering imposed on the victim by a criminal act.

As I have said, a new history begins, in particular for those of our fellow citizens put in prison, for the detainees. In this sense, the imposition of a penal sentence consists in a kind of legal violence that repeats, at the end of a whole process, the primary violence from which the state of law stems at some greater or lesser distance in time. At the same time, a new dimension is added to our quest to lower the level of violence in a democratic society. The problem is not resolved by the certitude we may have that the punishment is fair, proportional to the offense, that it has taken the degree of responsibility of the accused into account, whatever this affirmation of responsibility may signify. A fair penalty remains a punishment, a kind of suffering. In this sense, the punishment as a type of penalty reopens the way to the spirit of vengeance, in spite of the fact that it came about through a mediation that took time and involved the whole trial process, because the trial process in no way completely suppressed or abolished this spirit of vengeance. We are reminded of the sad fact that the whole society is tested by and, if I may put it this way, judged by its way of dealing with the problem of depriving people of their liberty, which has replaced corporal punishment behind the walls of our prisons. We are confronted with the absence of a practical alternative to such a loss of liberty through imprisonment. Admitting this is equivalent to admitting a collective failure on the part of our society. It is a fact that we have no viable project for the total abolition of imprisonment. What remains is the duty to preserve for those detainees the possibility of their reinscription into the community of free citizens, the project of a recovery of their full citizenship. The task is to restore to the prisoner his capacity to become again a full citizen at the end of his term, to put an end to the physical and symbolic exclusion which is imprisonment. From this perspective, the prison has to be taken as part of the city, as an institution internal to and not external to the city. In this sense, we must speak of a continuity of public space. To that end, all those measures that do not contribute to the defense and protection of society need to be gradually suppressed; I mean those restrictive measures having to do with health, work, education, leisure, and visitation. The discussion concerning the length of imprisonment compatible with the defense of society and the rehabilitation of the prisoner stems from the same concern. Apart from such projects, punishment remains in the grip of the spirit of vengeance, which the spirit of justice has the project of overcoming. Under the guidance of a concept of rehabilitation, concrete measures need to be explored that are an integral part of a pragmatic enterprise open to public discussion in a democratic society. But the purpose of this enterprise falls under the moral responsibility of the political body as a whole. Perhaps we can agree with the following affirmative propositions. Punishment has two ends, a short-term one, which is the protection of society as regards a threat to public order, and a long-term one, which is the restoration of social peace. Every measure of rehabilitation, in our penal system, is meant to serve this ultimate end.

It is not my purpose to discuss the legitimacy and the feasibility of this or that measure currently submitted to public discussion. My task is only to evaluate correctly what is at stake in this discussion, namely, the practical treatment of the basic paradox we confronted at the beginning of this essay, the resurgence of

JUSTICE AND VENGEANCE 231

the spirit of vengeance at each stage of the long process through which our sense of justice attempts to overcome its initial rootedness in violence, in vengeance as violence. That there is no speculative solution available to this paradox, but only a pragmatic solution, is the only, modest conclusion that this brief essay can reach.

The Universal and the Historical

My wish, in this lecture, is to help my listeners to orient themselves in a debate that important European and American thinkers
are currently engaged in. The two principal foci of this discussion
are, on the one hand, John Rawls's *A Theory of Justice* and the arguments it has led to among jurists, economists, political theorists, and philosophers, especially in the English-speaking world,
and, on the other hand, Karl-Otto Apel and Jürgen Habermas's
"ethics of discussion" and the arguments it has given rise to in the
same settings, but more so in Western Europe. What is at stake
in all these arguments is whether we can formulate on the ethical, juridical, political, and social planes universal principles that
are valid independently of persons, communities, and cultures
which are able to apply them, without any limitation having to do
with the particular circumstances of their application, especially
in light of the novel cases that have appeared in the modern era.
How, it has been objected, can we speak of a formal character of
principles that ignore the variety of contents of their application,
of ahistorical rules alien to the variety of cultural heritages, and
also of the rootedness of such rules for life in common in the
practice of particular communities?

To help clarify this debate, I propose to construct a framework
for the preliminary discussion of these arguments, one in which
the confrontation between the universal and the historical will be
posited differently depending on the level on which we place ourselves. For didactic purposes I shall adopt the same distinction
between the three levels of formulation of the moral problematic
that I set forth in *Oneself as Another*, which have to do not only

with private life but also with rights, the economic and social structures of civil society, and with political institutions.

I

At the first level, for which I reserve the technical term "ethics" owing to its close relation to the customs actually followed in the societies being considered, I will define "morality," in the broadest sense of the term, by the wish to live well, with and for others, in just institutions. The first term of this sequence defines the teleological character of this first approach, that is, the wish for some desirable accomplishment, in our private lives as well as in our life together, popularly known as happiness. One can see, starting already with this first structure, how much the universal and historical dimensions are tangled together. On the one hand, we can say with Aristotle that all action, every practice, is defined by this *telos,* that *all* people want to be happy. But this aim for the good, if it is to merit the name "ethics," has to pass through rational evaluations of what characterizes a good or bad action. Then what we call "virtues" intervene between the root rational desire and the horizon of happiness—temperance, courage, generosity, friendship, justice, and so on. These large-scale structures of moral life reach down deeply into the collective experience of any people, as the different moral theories we have inherited from the Greeks verify. The philosopher here does nothing more than reflect on what Charles Taylor has called the "strong evaluations" (of his own culture). For example, Aristotle begins from the most assured and constant opinions, already brought to language by the poets, such as Homer, Aeschylus, Sophocles, and Euripides, and by orators, historians, and politicians. The philosopher adds a rational project to them that is expressed, for example, by the idea that each of the virtues considered represents a mean, a middle range, but also something like a peak value between two defects (for example, courage is halfway between cowardice and recklessness, friendship between indulgence and severity). The philosopher can then construct the idea of reasoning correctly, of an *orthos logos,* that would constitute the intellectual, rational dimension of what can be summed up in terms of an enlightened moral choice. This is what Socrates, before Plato and Aristotle, designated by the phrase an "examined life." An unexamined life is one that is not worth living. The same concern for rationality is also found in the distinction, familiar to ancient thinkers, between pleasure and utility, or what is practical for life, that is, principally a political, a contemplative, and finally a philosophical life.

The mixture of the communitarian and the universal dimensions becomes more subtle and fragile if we consider the two other components of the definition proposed earlier about ethical desire: living well with and for others. Two relations to others are distinguished here. The first one is a relation of proximity with another who is present through his face. It is implied in the directly dialogical relation of friendship and love. It is perhaps on this side that the ethical intention manifests its greatest universality. Similar praise of friendship can be found in every culture. Yet we ought not to overlook the differences between the aristocratic structure of a city like that of the ancient Greeks and the more popular forms of solidarity characteristic of modern societies. Solicitude, which is supposed to be addressed to concrete individuals, in the most evident form of help being offered to a person in danger, has its limits, if only in the sense of the impossibility of taking up or, as one says, assuming all the suffering in the world. Yet it is with our third basic term that the dialectic of the universal and the historical is most evident. In truth, the conflicts that are the object of communication at this level only really appear at the second level, which we are going to consider in a moment. But the thirst for justice is not reserved for the level of duty and obligation, which we are also going to consider. It is a fundamental component of the wish for a good life. And it expresses itself in terms not only of those near to us but also of those more distant from us, that is, in terms of the institutions of every sort that structure life in society. My other is thus not just the person who appears to me through his face but also everyone defined through his social role. This relation to everyone is constitutive of what Hannah Arendt called "human plurality" in contrast to the relations of proximity found in friendship and love. Human plurality is the place for politics in its root sense, beyond those structures of power and the distinction between rulers and ruled, at the level of what we can call a willingness to live together. We can take this willingness to live together as a universal fact.

But as soon as we qualify it by the wish for just institutions, we place ourselves at a level where the universal is inextricably intermingled with the contextual. The question "What is a just institution?" immediately arises. It is inseparable from the elementary questions about who it is we wish to live with and following what rules.

I continue nevertheless to take the idea of just institutions as a universal idea. We need only to think of our childhood memories, when for the first time we cried, "That's not fair!" The desire for justice arises and is developed out of such indignation. And let us also recall those occasions when we made such exclamations. They were occasions of what we judged to be unequal portions or unkept promises, ones betrayed by adults, or rewards and punishments that we found to be disproportionate or, as I said, unfairly distributed. In these three examples we have in outline so to speak the distinction leading to distributive justice, in charge of such unequal portions, as well as the whole domain of contracts, agreements, and exchanges and, finally, on the occasion of our third sort of recrimination, of the whole realm of the judiciary and of penal law with its cortege of sanctions and punishments. It is at the moment when our indignation seeks to justify itself that we really enter into the problem of justice, for indignation remains caught up in the desire to obtain justice for oneself. It lacks the sense of just distance that only our codes, written laws, courts, and the like can take in hand. But it is then that the differences in cultures, and the history of our juridical institutions, with their inextricable mixture of rationality and prejudices, constrain us to set out to test other criteria than our elementary desire for a good life. But this requires first rooting our desire for just institutions in our desire for a good life. We can say in this regard that the primitive idea of justice is the unfolding of the desire for a good life at the institutional, communitarian, and dialogical level. This connection between a good life and justice found a stable expression, whose emotional and rational strength has not been exhausted, in the idea of a life together.

II

If the universalist and the contextualist theses find arguments of equal force in the ancient Greek reflection on the good life, the universalist version takes the lead when we pass to the second level of morality, which is defined, not by the desire for a good life, but by the notions of obligation, duty, and interdiction. In this regard, I note that the negative form is finally less constraining than is the positive one. There are a thousand ways not to kill, but the obligation to tell the truth in every circumstance sometimes brings us face to face with inextricable situations, as the well-known discussion between Kant and Benjamin Constant bears witness.

Someone may ask why we cannot just stay with the level of the desire for a good life. The reason is that life in society leaves an immense and often frightening space for conflicts of every kind, which affect all the levels of human relationships, in terms of interests, beliefs, and convictions. And these conflicts tend to get expressed in terms of violence, running from betraying one's word to murder. These kinds of violence harm individuals as well as the institutions that are the framework for life in society. And the spirit of vengeance tends to add more violence to this violence in an endless chain, as we see in the Greek tragedy concerning Orestes. From this is born the necessity for a third party, represented in our civilized societies by the existence of a body of written laws, by the establishment of judicial institutions, by the setting apart of a body of judges, and finally by a sequence of sanctions that give a coercive aspect to public morality under the rule of law in the modern state. It is this social necessity for a form of arbitration that poses the question of the nature of the rules capable of delimiting the domain of what is permitted and what forbidden and the allegedly legitimate use of such coercion. The justification of these rules and of the arbitration that they make possible poses the general problem of the justification of any and all rules for life in society.

We owe to Kant the most rigorous formulation of the thesis that the defenders of moral universalism, on the sides of both Rawls and Habermas, have sought to develop. The first presupposition is that there exists a practical reason distinct from theoretical reason but, like it, presenting a fundamental difference in levels between what can be said to be a priori (that is, the conditions of possibility for all the empirical arguments made use of) and what can be said to be a posteriori (where the empirical is constituted by desires, pleasures, interests, prejudices, and other kinds of irrational considerations). The basic hypothesis therefore is that practical reason is structured like theoretical reason, except that the a priori of practical reason is itself "practical." What does this practical a priori consist in? Answer: in a universal obligation, valid for everyone independently of any circumstances of application. Yet, if every practical content finally proceeds from a desire and finally from the desire for happiness, this universal obligation can only be a formal one, that is, one without content.

How then are we to formulate such a formal universal obligation, if not in the form of a rule for universalization to which every maxim of our actions (for example, those of a plan for our life) is to be submitted? At first sight, the rule is only a test meant to verify the claim to universality of my maxim. Nevertheless, it is not difficult to give a more utilitarian version of this test, formulated in the following way: what would happen if the whole world were to act like me? Kant only had in mind a logical contradiction internal to this rule that any alleged exception would destroy. We shall see in a moment how Habermas and others have attempted to remedy the fragility of this distinction between a logical contradiction and one that we can call utilitarian. But we cannot first knock down Kant with the accusation that he offered only a monological criterion of universality: act (you, second-person singular) in such a way that. . . . Kant himself enlarged the field of his universal obligation by giving two other versions of the categorical imperative which permit us to construct a triad on the moral level comparable to that on the ethical one (the desire for a good life, with and for others, in just institutions):

1. Act in such a way that you can take the maxim of your action for a universal law of nature.

2. Act in such a way that you always treat the humanity, in our own person and in that of others, not only as a means but also as an end in itself.

3. Act in such a way that in the kingdom of ends you can behave as both subject and legislator.

This triad defines autonomy in terms of its threefold personal, communitarian, and cosmopolitan figures. The formalism is maintained from one end to the other. In the first formulation, the notion of a moral law is placed in parallel with that of a physical law, which is nothing other than the form of universal determinism. But the second formulation of the categorical imperative is no less formal than this first one, for it is not the person as such, neither myself nor the other person, that is proposed as the object of respect here, but humanity, not in the sense of the overall set of every human being but in the sense of the human character that distinguishes human beings from other living beings and even eventually from other rational beings not endowed with sensibility as we are. As for the rule about the kingdom of ends, it defines, not any known historical community, but only the rational horizon of a law-governed state based on rights that would be immediately universal or, in Kant's words, cosmopolitan. In other words, it is a regulative idea, not a descriptive concept. Its accomplishment depends on the concrete political behavior of historical societies.

Rawls's attempt to give a universal definition for the principles of justice has to be placed against this Kantian backdrop. The formalism of his enterprise is indicated by the fact that the choice of principles of justice is supposed to take place in an imaginary, ahistorical situation said to be "original" in which the participants are placed behind a "veil of ignorance," behind which they can abstract from their real advantages and from the possible disadvantages that will follow from their deliberation. As for this deliberation, it has to do with the rules of distribution by which a society in general is characterized: exchangeable goods (retributions, patrimony, social advantages) and nonexchangeable goods (such as security, health, education, and above all positions of responsibility, authority, and rule across the whole scale of social institutions). This hypothesis of a society conceived of as one vast system of distribution of goods of all kinds allows Rawls to give a peculiar turn to the formalism he inherits from Kant. It is no longer formalism as a universalizing test but rather that of a procedure for dividing things up. It is this procedure that is defined by the two principles of justice:

> First: each person is to have an equal right to the most extensive
> basic liberty compatible with a similar liberty for others.

This first principle governs equality before the law in the exercising of public liberties (freedom of expression, of association, of assembly, of worship, and so forth).

Second: social and economic inequalities are to be arranged also so that they are both (a) reasonably expected to be to everyone's advantage, and (b) attached to positions and offices open to all.

This second principle applies to irreducibly unequal shares in our societies which are productive of added values. But before developing this principle, Rawls insists on the necessity to satisfy the first principle, which indicates that any effort to resolve the social problems of inequality without taking into account the abstract equality of citizens before the law is not justified. Economic and social inequalities cannot serve as pretexts for violating the first principle of justice. As for the second principle, he develops it in the following manner, at least its first part.

> What is just, or at least, less unjust than any other solution, is the distribution in which the gain in advantage to the most favored is compensated for by the diminution of the disadvantage to the least favored; whence the name *maximin* that has been given to this principle.

Later, we shall consider the criticism this principle has drawn from communitarians. Two particular points of this doctrine are, however, already open to criticism. First is the formalism of a procedure of distribution that does not take into account the real heterogeneity of goods to be divided—for example, do problems of remuneration arise from the same rule as do those of the division of authority in one and the same administrative structure? Second, how does the choice of a principle of justice established in an imaginary, ahistorical situation bind a real historical society? More precisely, what kinds of societies, among those that currently exist, are open to such a formula for distributive justice?

But before examining these objections which stem from the third level that I adopt for analyzing morality, that of practical wisdom, let me say a few words about the ethics of discussion. At first sight, it is a wholly different matter. With Rawls, it is a question of a problem of distribution, in the broad sense I have already spoken of; with Apel and Habermas, it is a problem of discussion and more precisely of argumentation. But the two situations considered are not really that far apart: on the one side, the establishment of principles of justice in an original situation and behind a veil of ignorance proceeds in terms of an open discussion capable of falling under the categories of the ethics of discussion; on the other, what will be the preferred topic of discussion, if not those distributions that give rise to conflicts? Habermas, like Rawls, can base his argument on the multiple conceptions of the good in a society like our own characterized by pluralism as a fact. It is therefore outside this conflict that one must look for the rules of a possible agreement. But where are we to look, if not in our very use of language? Every human relationship unavoidably passes through discourse. What is more, the threat of violence, which we have seen justifies the transition from an ethics of happiness to one of obligation, invites us to seek the one human response to violence in the transfer of every conflict to the domain of speech. And the division of speech cannot occur apart from the normative arbitration of rules presiding over any discussion. The whole problem is how to pass from the fact of the mediation of language to the validity of argumentation.

The question, then, is whether there exist universal rules of validity governing any possible discussion and every rational form of argument. Habermas's answer is affirmative. It rests on a use of contradiction that differs from that by which Kant justified his recourse to the rule of universalization. The final justification of the criteria of validity we are going to consider rests, not on a formal logical contradiction, but on a so-called performative one, which we can formulate as follows: if you say that the rules for discussion are not valid, you have begun to make an argument; therefore, you contradict yourself when you say that a rule governing any discussion cannot be universal. You are presupposing this rule as common to both you and your adversary.

As for the rules for validity in communication, they are not numerous and are easy to identify: everyone has an equal right to speak; everyone has the duty to give his best argument to anyone who asks for it; he must be heard with a presumption that he could be correct; finally, and perhaps above all else, the antagonists of a rule-governed argument must share a common horizon which is one of agreement, of consensus. The ethics of discussion thus is to be situated in terms of the horizon of a utopia of shared speech, functioning like a regulative idea for open, unlimited, unrestricted discussion. Without this presupposition of required consensus, there can be no question of truth in the practical order.

In this regard, Habermas insists strongly on the cognitive character of his ethics. There is no difference between practical and theoretical reason when it comes to the requirement for truth in the usage of a shared language.

We can immediately see the strength of this ethics of communication, rightly called an ethics of discourse or of discussion, over against three well-defined adversaries. They are, first of all, the upholders of an ethics of decision, functioning case by case, through abuse, Habermas will say, of the Greek notion of *phronesis* taken as governing unique individual situations. The presupposition is that every singular situation can be placed under the rules of validity for a coherent discussion. The second adversary is constituted by those emotive or emotion-based ethics according to which it is feelings, including noble, higher ones like pity, compassion, respect, and veneration, that are the criteria for the just. Finally, the adversary most often taken as a target is moral or juridical positivism, akin to the conventionalism of the Greek Sophists, for which the rules serving to arbitrate social conflicts are governed by a general principle of utility, made concrete in any given case by the actually existing authorities. As we can see, this ethics courageously takes into account those situations of conflict open to being brought to the level of language, in the best case in terms of an institutional framework comparable to the judicial process. It assumes on the part of the antagonists an equal will to seek agreement, a desire to coordinate their plans of action on some reasonable basis, and finally a concern to make cooperation prevail over conflict in every situation of disagreement.

III

We now have to consider the reasons why it seemed necessary to me to add a third dimension to my moral philosophy, what I have called practical wisdom, thinking partly of what Hegel called *Sittlichkeit* in his *Principles of the Philosophy of Right* and also of the Aristotelian theory of *phronesis*—translated into Latin by the term *prudentia*—as developed in book 6 of his *Nicomachean Ethics*. Why add such a third dimension to ethics and morality? If it is the fact of conflict and more fundamentally the fact of violence that forced us to pass from an ethics of the good life to a morality of obligation and interdiction, it is what we can call the tragic aspect of action that leads us to complete these formal principles of a universal ethics by rules of application concerning historical-cultural contexts. By this tragic aspect of action, let us mean in general those typical situations presenting the following common features. First of all, there is a conflict of duties, as shown in Greek tragedy. In this regard, *Antigone* is a perfect example. Antigone and Creon represent opposed obligations which lead to an irreconcilable conflict. Even if it is true that the absolute duty of fraternal obligation that guides Antigone is perfectly compatible with political service to the city, which guides Creon, human finitude means that each of these antagonists cannot serve the principle he or she identifies with outside the narrow limits of a passionate allegiance, blind to its limits. The tragedy consists precisely in the exclusion of any compromise because of the intransigence of each of these servants of an absolute and sacred duty. Another tragic situation arises when the complexity of social relations multiplies the situations in which the moral or legal rule enters into conflict with concern for the care of individual persons. I have noted how, in the formulation of the second version of the Kantian imperative, the respect for persons is framed by respect for humanity. But it is a question of humanity in the sense, not of every human being, but of the distinctive quality of humanity assumed to be common to every historical culture. Yet medical, as well as juridical, practice always places moral judgment face to face with situations in which the norm and the person cannot be satisfied at the same time. In this regard, let me confine myself to referring to the difficult problems posed for medical ethics by situations affecting the beginning and the end of life. As regards the former, there are good reasons to say that every life merits protection beginning with its conception, given that the embryo has from the beginning a genetic code distinct from its parents. But the thresholds crossed in becoming a "potential person" are multiple, leading to a gradual evaluation of duties and rights. Furthermore, once the threshold of absolute respect for life has been crossed, which prudence recommends to the law, the choice is between bad and worse. We are all aware of those situations of distress where the life of a woman must be preferred to that

of her embryo. It is a problem for public discussion and argument, therefore one of how to take into account the singularity
of such situations, putting off any decision until after an honest
deliberation. We must also refer to those cases where the choice
is not one between right and wrong but, if I can put it this way,
between gray and gray. Should we, for example, submit to the
same penal laws delinquent adolescents and adults, the latter of
whom we take to be more responsible for their actions? What age
should we take then as marking the passage to legal or political
majority? A still more redoubtable problem is when the choice
is not between the good and the bad but between the bad and
the worst. Our laws governing prostitution, and in particular the
question of children, stem from this alternative, which we can say
is truly tragic. There are many moral and judicial decisions where
the stake is not to promote the good but to avoid the bad.

I do not mean to say that the ethics of wisdom knows only
tragic situations like those just referred to. They are extreme cases,
meant only to draw attention to a more general problem, namely,
that the principles of justification of a moral or legal rule leave the
problems of application intact. Therefore, it is the notion of application that has to be considered in its full scope so that we can
set it in parallel with that of validation, which presided over our
earlier discussion. This notion of application comes from another
domain than that of ethics or law, the domain of text interpretation, principally of literary and religious texts. It was in the domains of biblical exegesis and classical philology that the idea of
interpretation as distinct from the ideas of understanding and explanation was formed. By the end of the eighteenth century, particularly with Schleiermacher and later with Wilhelm Dilthey,
hermeneutics reached its full stature, beyond biblical exegesis and
classical philology. It proposed rules of interpretation valid for
every sort of individual text. And it was always recognized that
the application of legal codes called for formulating a third type
of hermeneutics, legal hermeneutics, whose application, we shall
see in a moment, applies to those situations I have referred to in
my discussion of Rawls, concerning distributive justice, as well as
to Habermas's theses concerning public discussion. In both cases,
the problem of the application of universal norms to singular
situations brings into play the historical and cultural dimension

of mediating traditions of the process of application. In opening my discussion, in speaking of the Greek conception of virtue, I referred to the anchorage of ethics in popular wisdom, whence the very name "ethics," which is akin to that of customs and mores. In his treatise on justice in book 5 of his *Nicomachean Ethics*, Aristotle concludes with the distinction between the abstract idea of justice and the concrete one of equity, a distinction he justifies in terms of the inadequacy of the general rule with regard to novel situations. A similar problematic arose, principally among English-speaking theorists, with Rawls's theory of justice and, in Western Europe, with Habermas's ethics of discussion.

Turning back to Rawls, we need to consider the arguments whose formulation I anticipated earlier. As Michael Walzer has argued in his *Spheres of Justice*, a theory of distributive justice, in holding to a purely procedural point of view, must leave aside consideration of the heterogeneous nature of the goods to be distributed. But we cannot discuss commercial and noncommercial goods in the same way, especially ones such as health, education, security, and citizenship. Each of these goods, thinks Walzer, comes from a shared understanding of some given community at a certain time. Thus, the notion of commercial goods is entirely subordinated to the evaluation of what can or cannot be bought and sold. The notion of commercial goods stems from what he calls a "shared symbolism," defined in a certain sociocultural context. And from this shared symbolism results a distinct logic that governs all the entities in the same domain, which Walzer puts under the idea of a "city" or a "world." Where Rawls sees a universal process of distribution, Walzer sees multiple cities, leading to border conflicts that no formal argument can arbitrate. Therefore, fragile compromises express what I earlier called wisdom or prudence. A judicious pluralism thus tends to get substituted for a unitary but strictly procedural conception of justice.

Yet, I would ask, is it really a case of substitution, or rather, is it one of addition? I would be tempted to say that, in the absence of a general and universal project of justice, one cannot really justify an ethics of compromise, which would have as its horizon the constitution or reconstruction of something like a common good. In this sense, the argument arising out of the universalism that Rawls attaches to the idea of justice leads to the complex mixture of universality and historicity that we have recognized at the most elementary level of morality, at the level of an ethics of the good life.

In his essays subsequent to *Theory of Justice,* Rawls himself recognized what we can call the historical limits of his theory. It works only within the framework of those democracies he calls liberal or constitutional democracies, that is, states based on a rule of law, founded on an "overlapping consensus" among several founding traditions that are compatible with one another; in other words, an enlightened version of the Judeo-Christian tradition, along with the culture of the Enlightenment, following the utilitarian and purely strategic reduction of rationality, along with finally the emergence of Romanticism in the form of a desire for spontaneous expression in accord with the underlying sources of a creative nature. In this sense, the universalism of his theory of justice requires as its complement the recognition of the historical conditions of its application.

It seems to me that the ethics of discussion points toward a similar conclusion. One can object that it overestimates the place of discussion in human interactions and even more the place of formalized versions of argumentation. Seeking a reason is an extraordinarily complex and varied social game in which many different passions conceal themselves under the appearance of impartiality. Arguments can be a cunning way of pursuing a struggle. And, in another way, one can object that the mediating role of language, legitimately referred to as the basis for the ethics of discussion, can also point to another conclusion than that of agreement reached through arguments. Reflection on the variety of languages, a fundamental aspect of the diversity of cultures, can lead to an interesting analysis concerning the way problems posed by this massive phenomenon that is language—which nowhere exists in a universal form, but only in terms of the fragmented linguistic universe— get resolved. Yet, even in the absence of a superlanguage, we are not left totally without resources. Translation, which allows for the communication of the message of one language in another one, remains and really ought not to be treated as a secondary phenomenon. With translation, the speaker of one language transfers himself into the linguistic universe of a foreign text. In return, he welcomes into his own linguistic space another person's words.

This phenomenon of linguistic hospitality can serve as a model for all instances of understanding in which the absence of what we might call a third-person overview brings into play the same operations of transference and of welcome whose model can be found in the act of translation.

It is above all in the juridical domain that the necessity of a properly creative application is required. Robert Alexy, it is true, has attempted to derive a theory of legal argumentation from the ethics of discussion. This enterprise is perfectly legitimate in that we cannot conceive of a judge who would believe that the sentence he imposes is not valid. In this way, the validity of any sentence expresses the general idea of validity brought to light by the ethics of discussion. But does this idea of validity still apply in those situations that do not satisfy the most basic presuppositions of the ethics of discussion, those of an open-ended, unlimited discourse situation, stripped of all constraints? The judicial decision is supposed to take place in a legal setting where the exchange of discourse is governed by binding procedural rules thanks to which each party speaks within the limits of a set time frame. Deliberation itself involves a limited number of protagonists whose roles are clearly defined. And the final decision, the sentence properly speaking, has to be made within a limited span of time, since a judge cannot avoid the obligation to make a decision. The very word "decide" indicates the distance between the conditions for discussion within the trial process and the requirement for an open-ended discussion when it is a question of reaching consensus. Even more important than these constraints are the very structures of juridical argument that indicate the place for interpretive processes akin to those used in exegesis and philology. Thus, in what Ronald Dworkin calls "hard cases," appeal is made to a double process of interpretation: a kind of narrative interpretation of the facts in the case and an interpretation of the law that can be invoked to characterize the alleged offense. The argument here cannot really be locked up within the terms of a practical syllogism. It brings together a complicated process of mutual adjustments between the narrative interpretation of the facts and the juridical one regarding the law in question. A phenomenon of "adjustment" leading precisely to the legal qualification of the offense takes place at the intersection of these two processes of interpretation. This quite remarkable mixture of formal argument and concrete interpretation, within the setting of the criminal court, perfectly illustrates the thesis that I want to develop here, namely, that the choice is not one between a universalism of the rule and the singularity of the decision. The very notion of application presupposes a normative background common to the protagonists. To return to Aristotle's terminology, there would not be a problem of equity in unique situations unless there were a general problem of justice capable of universal recognition.

The discussion about Rawls's theory leads to a conclusion of the same order. Would we speak of spheres of justice if we did not have an idea of justice that could preside over the claims of each juridical sphere to overlap the domains of other spheres? And within the framework of the discussion of the formal ethics of discussion, how do we avoid falling back upon violence if we eliminate the horizon of consensus? More basically, how can we take violence out of conflicts unless we have the hope that transferring them to the domain of the spoken word will lead, if not to immediate consensus, at least to the recognition of reasonable disagreements, in other words, to an agreement to disagree? To conclude, let me make the following three proposals.

1. Universalism can be taken as a regulative idea that allows us to recognize heterogeneous attitudes capable of being recognized as cofoundational of the common space unfolded by the will to live together as belonging to the domain of moral obligation.

2. No moral conviction would have any force if it did not make a claim to universality. But we must confine ourselves to giving this presumed universal sense to what first presents itself as claiming universality. Let us understand here by presumed universality the claim to universality offered by public discussion in expectation of being recognized by everyone involved. In this exchange, each protagonist proposes an alleged or inchoative universal seeking recognition. The history of such recognition is itself driven by the idea of a recognition having the value of a concrete universal. The same status of being a regulative idea referred to in my previous point allows us to reconcile two different levels, that of abstract

moral theory and that of practical wisdom, the requirement of universality and the historical condition of any application to a specific context.

3. If it is true that humanity exists only in many different cultures and languages—which is the basis for communitarian critiques of both Rawls and Habermas—the presumed cultural identities of these critics are protected against the return of intolerance and fanaticism only by a mutual labor of understanding for which the translation of one language into another constitutes a noteworthy model.

We can bring these three conclusions together in the following way: universalism and contextualism are not opposed to each other on the same plane but stem from two different levels of morality, that of a presumed universal obligation and that of a practical wisdom that takes into account the diversity of cultural heritages. It would not be off base to say that the transition from the universal plane of obligation to the historical one of application comes down to returning to the resources of the ethics of a good life in order, if not to resolve, at least to pacify the aporias arising from the inordinate demands of a theory of justice or a theory of discussion that bases its formalism only on procedural principles and rigor.

Epilogue

On 19 February 1999, I was called to testify before the Cour de justice de la Républic considering a case arising from HIV-contaminated blood having been allowed to be used for blood transfusions. My testimony was requested by Georgina Dufoix, formerly minister of Social Affairs and National Solidarity, who was accused of having been "one of the leaders in a case of involuntary homicide and involuntary acts against the physical integrity of the victims." The deposition that follows was my answer to a question from her lawyer, Cahen: "You have heard Madame Dufoix's expression from a few years ago: 'Responsible, but not guilty.' I would like you as a philosopher to give your opinion concerning this expression, its applicability, and its truth."[1]

Your honor, I am a witness, not a politician or an expert or a jurist, but let us say a thoughtful citizen who has long been interested in the procedures used to make decisions in situations marked by uncertainty.

I have been interested in this problem as it applies to the domains of medical, judicial, historical, and political judgment. Hence, it is in this respect that I am going to speak to you about how I take and interpret the sentence "responsible, but not guilty" maliciously turned back against Madame Georgina Dufoix, as though it were meant to exonerate her, not only of guilt, but also

---

1. A shorter, uncorrected version of the court reporter's transcript, which had some spelling and syntactical errors, was published in *Le monde des débats* for November 1999. The text presented here represents my corrections to that transcript.

of responsibility. I understand it in the following way: "I am ready to answer for my acts, but I do not recognize any legal fault falling under the criminal code." Thus, I would like to give its full force to this affirmation of responsibility.

I propose a working definition of "responsibility." I see in it three components, all three of which I shall state in the first-person singular in order to indicate that they commit the person who says them.

1. "I hold myself responsible for my acts."

My acts are my own doing and I am their actual author. One can assign them to my account, I accept their being so assigned, and my acts are imputable to me. This is the common root for the two big branches that I will consider later: the political and the legal branches.

2. "I am ready to render an account before a body authorized to demand such an account from me."

The relation to another who demands an account from me and before whom I am ready to appear gets added to the reflexive self-imputation already stated.

3. "I am in charge of the operations of some private or public institution."

This third component comes to the fore when the responsibility in question is that of persons placed by some mandate in a position of authority or power, in particular political authority or power. So I am responsible for the action of my subordinates. I answer for them and their acts before any body that demands such an account from me. A vertical, hierarchical relation gets added to the two earlier so to speak horizontal forms of responsibility.

Now what can be said about these kinds of responsibility in the present case?

I shall not dwell upon the first point. I do not imagine for a moment that Madame Dufoix, any more than Monsieur Fabius or Monsieur Hervé, mean to shirk their responsibility in the sense of something that can be imputed to them. Yet this does not go without saying. Today we are dealing with a serious drift affecting both private and public law, one that tends to substitute risk for any error, an error that may be technical, professional, or whatever, without being a tort or a crime. Because of this, the socialization of risk threatens to leave room only for a notion of insurance, which, I will say, is one that threatens to remove all responsibility. However, it is not only the evolution of the law that runs the risk of obliterating this first sense of responsibility. It is also the whole climate of a press campaign that has pushed public opinion toward two extreme positions, one of demonization and one appealing to a sense of fatality. I would say that responsibility as imputation stands midway between these two extremes, with, on one side, the suspicion that any harm done is deliberate and, on the other, the disappearance of any kind of responsibility at all.

I would rather concentrate on the idea of responsibility before another or before others. It is what is at stake in an argument that has often taken first place among legal theorists, journalists, and politicians, concerning the opposition between political and criminal responsibility.

What is first apparent in this opposition is the difference in penalties. On the political side, in extreme cases, this is discharge from office, a kind of political death, the political equivalent of the death penalty. On the legal side, there is the deprivation of liberty, shame.

But it is necessary to return to the origin of these two procedures; I mean that the legal trial is launched by a complaint, that is, by pain and death. The risk in making "everything criminal" is that politics, once submitted to this kind of intimidation, will be handed over to a rampant process of victimization. This comes about on the political side from what sets such a process in motion; I mean that dysfunction in decision making by a group— and I am going to emphasize this initial lacuna—is more difficult to define than is the starting point for any criminal indictment or civil complaint. In these dysfunctions we find every kind of error, of erroneous but not criminal decisions.

There is a corollary to this duality. On the criminal side, the fault is individual, and therefore the indictment must be precise and stated in advance, as must the scale specifying crimes and their penalties. In politics, it is much more difficult to determine the field of application of what I shall call, if you will allow me, facts of misgovernance, which, rather than being defined in advance, are what is at stake in the investigation that takes place in the process of asking someone to render an account.

Let me add one great perplexity to this. It has to do with the body before which one renders such an account. Things are clear

in cases in criminal court. It is the court, with its precise procedures, its judges, and its great ceremony in language that is the
trial itself. But what about in politics? A single answer seems
available in an elective and representative democracy: parliament,
with its commissions of inquiry, and any other committees that
parliament may choose to invent. This will be my final suggestion.

Here is where my perplexity comes to a head. Why this criminal trial? And before that, why did it require a scandal which only
broke out in 1991 [six years after it was discovered that HIV could
be spread through blood transfusions]? Why were things led by
the press and the media and not by parliament? Was there not an
initial shortcoming on the part of some body capable of opening,
pursuing, and concluding a political investigation?

I have asked myself whether this is a momentary shortcoming or rather one constitutive of an ongoing problem with French
institutions. Hence, my interpretation here is political and stems
from political philosophy. In fact, unlike the British, we have not
included adversarial arguments, drawn from an initial *dissensus*
among the parts of government, as part of our political procedures. We chose Rousseau against Montesquieu, Rousseau and
the general, indivisible will—as our double heritage of revolutionary Jacobinism and the ever-reborn regal sense of government
stemming from the Ancient Regime bear witness.

From this comes a taste for discretionary decisions, with little attention paid to conflicts of interest, to people holding more
than one job, to the accumulation of offices, to a hands-off approach, and to private fiefdoms, to top-down decision making, to
the arrogance of high and low officials. When I say this, I include
myself, for I think that it is part of the political culture of this
country not to have a feel for a debate between contradictory positions as the basis for political relations. Whence, once again, the
institutional silence from 1985 to 1991. Whence scandal rather than
debate, whence treatment in the press in response to a political
void, whence finally—I stop here—criminalization, owing to the
lack of a political way of dealing with any political dysfunctions
that may come about and, worse, the fear, a justified fear on
the part of the public, that unless someone is punished, someone must be hiding something and protecting someone. But the

price to pay is that one leaves the system of misgovernance in place without a remedy or amendment.

From this too comes, if you will allow me to put it with less volume, the uneasiness in reading in parallel the indictment brought by the public prosecutor and the bringing of this case to court, where the former has more to do with the dimension of political responsibility, and the latter pushes the criminalization of politics to a point where one can recognize only personal responsibility and must treat the exercise of responsibility in the third sense of this term—responsibility for what my subordinates do, if I am in a position of power—in terms of the assumption that there is a criminal responsibility for any harm done to anyone, the only category available to criminal law.

My suggestion is that, by not having given a political dimension to the investigation, we have instead a criminalization that prevents us from thinking about the problem politically. I do not mean to say that there is no place for criminalization when it comes to politics, but I think that it ought to be residual and remain at the high level of the great prohibitions of the Decalogue (murder, misappropriation of public funds, perjury, despoliation, and so on). It is at this level, I think, that the argument made by Dean Vedel and Olivier Duhamel is valid that democratic government requires universality and therefore equality before the law, which is applicable to everyone, including government ministers.

On the other hand, the vast domain for errors and mistakes on the plane of misgovernance has not been taken into account in this criminalization of politics. For my part, I would place what has been criminalized as negligence, as a delay in making a decision within the framework of misgovernance. Which is to say that everything that falls under the heading of failing to act should be considered politically rather than in terms of criminality.

More fundamentally, disagreement must not be thought of as something wrong but as lying at the very base of political debate. The requirement here to think politically rather than in terms of crime is no less important, for once the obsession with punishment takes over, errors of misgovernance and the suspicion of such errors are no longer distinguished. What is held to be an error or mistake then is no longer taken as something given but as the objective that also determines the rules of the debate, even though no third party who might pass judgment can be given in advance.

It is this broad domain of governing under the suspicion of misgovernance that is at issue when we come to the exercise of responsibility that I have placed third on my list, in cases of hierarchies of power and authority. It is within this framework that the greatest difficulties in decision making, which I alluded to in beginning, manifest themselves, because of the variety of domains in which one can inquire into the difficulties touching the relationship between judgment and action. And these difficulties are brought to their extreme form when it comes to governmental action.

I want to insist on these difficulties. Not with a view of exonerating anyone of the charge of having responsibility to do something—imputation—but with a view to emphasizing even more than I have so far the shortcoming of our political bodies before which politicians should be called to appear in order to render their accounts. It is this shortcoming, precisely, that opens the door to those dysfunctions which are a threat to decision making and which require hierarchical responsibility. In this regard, everything that leads to complexity and—I think I can add—opacity in the process of decision making in such hierarchical structures of power has to lead to reflection on the necessity to reinforce, even to create, bodies before which politicians are called to render account, to explain, to justify their action.

The public, in my opinion, knows little of the problems connected to the relationship between a minister and his agency or about the role of political advisers or technical advisers (experts who themselves stand at the head of a technostructure). In the present case, the whole medical world is implicated, its scientists, agencies, administrators, clients, finances, rivalries, internal hierarchies, and also risks. A few specialists have helped us penetrate the arcana of government ministries: delegations, interagency commissions, studies, the circulation of information, ministers' dependence on their advisers when it comes to technical issues.[2] I simply want to underscore the peril that lies in resolving things

2. See, for example, Beaud and Blanquer, *La responsabilité des gouvernants*; Beaud, *Le sang contaminé*.

after the fact, not only by believing that we know what was known, for someone did know something, but also by defining what was the actual range of political options open at that moment. Knowledge that has become certain could only have been one option among others at the time. I am wary here of entering into facts concerning which I have no special competence. I will confine myself to emphasizing the difficulty in trying to orient oneself with regard to the pyramid of advisers and experts, as well as with regard to the conditions pertaining at the time decisions were made. I am more prepared to insist on two or three other points, with which I will conclude.

1. The confrontation among heterogeneous logics between politics, administration, and science, not to mention the administration of the rules governing blood donations in our prisons, technology, industry, and so on.

2. The confrontation between discordant temporal rhythms, between the urgency of a danger to health and the tempo with which information circulates, by which things get verified, of administrative procedures, of testing, of ratification. In this regard, we oversimplify things by ridiculing the proverbial slowness of any administration.

3. The discordance of different times is perhaps not the greatest difficulty. There is also, more hidden, the discordance regarding what might be at stake symbolically. Think of the value we give in France to the free gift of blood donations, with its residual aura of sacrifice and redemption. Or of the refusal during a certain period of time to distinguish so-called at-risk groups out of fear of making quasi-racist discriminations. Or of our quasi-patriotic fantasy of preference for French-made products, with no suspicion that financial interests may play a part. These are all quite respectable symbolic allegiances.

All these remarks about conflicts of competency, logic, the use of time, and symbolic reference only serve to sharpen the question that torments me regarding our political culture: what political body is capable of taking up and demanding a political accounting?

I will leave this question open by returning, with my friend Antoine Garapon,[3] to the example of debates over contradictory

---

3. Garapon, "Pour une responsabilité civique."

positions aimed at preventing as much as correcting the dysfunctions that come from misgovernance. Something like a civic space or court open to civil society, implementing the values inherited from the Age of Enlightenment: publicity versus opacity, promptness versus procrastination, but maybe especially an openness to the future versus a stalemate over a past that will not pass.

This Cour de justice de la République, Your Honor, ladies and gentlemen, might it not be the beginning of such an institution? If so, it would be not only exceptional but inaugural, civic, that is to say, beyond the bifurcation of the political and the criminal.

Allow me to end by referring to the victims, those who have suffered, for justice must have passion and, as I said in beginning, it is under the cloud of death that we are gathered to reflect on the eventual shortcomings of our political thought, of our political system.

Why must we listen to the victims? Because when they come to the tribunal, it is not a naked cry that is heard. It is already a cry of indignation—not fair, unjust! And this cry includes several demands. First, that we understand, accept an intelligible, acceptable narration of what happened. Second, the victims ask that acts be qualified in a way that sets in place a just distance between all the protagonists. And perhaps we need also to hear, in our recognition of their suffering, a demand for an apology addressed to our politicians by those who suffer. Their request for indemnification comes only in the last place.

But, above all, it would be wise to recall that, in our investigations, there will always be something inextricable about decisions that were made in groups and something irreparable about misfortune.

WORKS CITED

Arendt, Hannah. *Between Past and Future: Eight Exercises in Political Thought*. New York: Viking Press, 1968.
———. *The Human Condition*. Chicago: University of Chicago Press, 1958.
Aristotle. *Nicomachean Ethics*. Translated by Terence Irwin. Indianapolis: Hackett, 1985.
Askani, Hans-Christoph. *Das Problem der Übersetzung—dargestellt an Franz Rosenzweig*. Tübingen: J. C. B. Mohr, 1997.
Beaud, Olivier. *Le sang contaminé*. Paris: Presses universitaires de France, 1999.
Beaud, Olivier, and Jean Michel Blanquer. *La responsabilité des gouvernants*. Paris: Descartes et cie, 1999.
Benjamin, Walter. *Illuminations*. Translated by Harry Zohn. Edited by Hannah Arendt. New York: Schocken, 1977.
Berman, Antoine. *The Experience of the Foreign: Culture and Translation in Romantic Germany*. Translated by S. Heyvaert. Albany: State University of New York Press, 1992.
Boltanski, Luc, and Laurent Thévenot. *De la justification: les économies de la grandeur*. Paris: Presses universitaires de France, 1987.
———. *Les économies de la grandeur*. Paris: Gallimard, 1991.
Bouretz, Pierre. *Les promesses du monde: Philosophie de Max Weber*. Paris: Gallimard, 1995.
Canguilhem, Georges. *La connaissance de la vie*. Paris: Vrin, 1992.
———. *The Normal and the Pathological*. Translated by Carolyn R. Fawcett in collaboration with Robert S. Cohen. New York: Zone Books, 1989.
Changeux, Jean-Pierre, and Paul Ricoeur. *What Makes Us Think?* Translated by M. B. DeBevoise. Princeton: Princeton University Press, 2000.
Chouraqui, André, trans. *La Bible*. Paris: Desclee de Brouwer, 2003.

Eco, Umberto. *The Search for the Perfect Language.* Translated by James
Fentress. Malden, MA: Blackwell, 1994.

Ferry, Jean-Marc. *Les puissances de l'expérience: Essai sur l'identité con-
temporaine.* 2 vols. Paris: Cerf, 1991.

Garapon, Antoine. *Le gardien des promesses: Le juge et la démocratie.*
Paris: Odile Jacob, 1996.

———. "Pour une responsabilité civique." *Esprit* (March–April 1999):
237–49.

Gauchet, Marcel. *The Disenchantment of the World.* Translated by Oscar
Burge. Princeton: Princeton University Press, 1997.

Ginzburg, Carlo. *The Cheese and the Worms: The Cosmos of a Sixteenth-
Century Miller.* Translated by John Tedeschi and Anne Tedeschi.
Baltimore: Johns Hopkins University Press, 1990.

Hegel, G. W. F. *Philosophy of Right.* Translated by T. M. Knox. New
York: Oxford University Press, 1967.

Höffe, Otfried. *L'état et la justice: Les problèmes éthiques et politiques dans
la philosophie anglo-saxon John Rawls et Robert Nozick.* Translated by
B. Schwagler. Paris: Vrin, 1988.

———. *Introduction à la philosophie pratique de Kant.* Translated by
François Rüegg and Stephane Gillioz. Abbeuve: Castella, 1985.

———. *La justice politique.* Translated by Jean-Christophe Merle.
Paris: Presses universitaires de France, 1991.

———. *Principes du droit.* Translated by Jean-Christophe Merle. Paris:
Cerf, 1993. Translated by Mark Migotti as *Categorical Principles of
Law: A Counterpoint to Modernity* (University Park: Pennsylvania
State University Press, 2002).

Homans, Peter. *The Ability to Mourn: Disillusionment and the Social Origins of Psychoanalysis.* Chicago: University of Chicago Press, 1989.

Humboldt, Wilhelm von. *On Language: On the Diversity of Human
Language Construction and Its Influence on the Mental Development of
the Human Species.* Edited by Michael Losonsky. Translated by Peter
Heath. New York: Cambridge University Press, 1999.

Husserl, Edmund. *Cartesian Meditations: An Introduction to Phenomenology.* Translated by Dorion Cairns. The Hague: Martinus Nijhoff,
1960.

Kant, Immanuel. *Critique of Practical Reason.* Translated by Lewis
White Beck. Indianapolis: Bobbs-Merrill, 1956.

———. *Grounding for the Metaphysics of Morals.* Translated by
James W. Ellington. Indianapolis: Hackett, 1981.

———. *Practical Philosophy.* Translated and edited by Mary J. Gregor.
New York: Cambridge University Press, 1996.

———. *Religion within the Boundaries of Mere Reason and Other
Writings.* Translated and edited by Alan Wood and George Di
Giovanni. New York: Cambridge University Press, 1998.

Ladrière, Jean. "Herméneutique et épistémologie." In *Métamorphoses de la raison herméneutique*, edited by Jean Greisch and Richard Kearney, 107–25. Paris: Cerf, 1991.

Leclerc, Gérard. *Histoire de l'autorité: L'assignation des énoncés culturels et la généalogie de la croyance.* Paris: Presses universitaires de France, 1986.

Lenin, Vladimir Illich. *The State and Revolution.* New York: International Publishers, 1943.

Le Roy Ladurie, Emmanuel. "Sur l'histoire de l'état moderne: de l'Ancien régime à la démocratie; Libres réflexions inspirées de la pensée de Guglielmo Ferrero." *Commentaire* 75 (1996): 619–29.

Levi, Giovanni. *Le pourvoir au village: Histoire d'un exorciste dans le Piémont du XVIIᵉ siècle.* Translated by Monique Aymard. Paris: Gallimard, 1989.

Nagel, Thomas. *Equality and Partiality.* New York: Oxford University Press, 1991.

———. *The View from Nowhere.* New York: Oxford University Press, 1986.

Olender, Maurice. *Les langues du Paradis: Aryens et Sémites; Un couple providential.* Paris: Seuil, 1989. Translated by Arthur Goldhammer as *The Languages of Paradise: Race, Religion, and Philology in the Nineteenth Century* (Cambridge, MA: Harvard University Press, 1992).

Rawls, John. *A Theory of Justice.* Cambridge, MA: Harvard University Press, 1971.

René, Louis. *Code français de déontologie médicale.* Paris: Seuil, 1996.

Ricoeur, Paul. *The Course of Recognition.* Translated by David Pellauer. Cambridge, MA: Harvard University Press, 2005.

———. *Être, essence et substance chez Platon et Aristote.* Paris: Société d'édition d'enseignement supérieur, 1982.

———. "From Metaphysics to Moral Philosophy." Translated by David Pellauer. *Philosophy Today* 40 (1996): 443–58.

———. "Ideology and Ideology Critique." In *Phenomenology and Marxism*, edited by B. Waldenfels et al., 134–64. London: Routledge & Kegan Paul, 1984.

———. "Ideology and Utopia as Cultural Imagination." *Philosophic Exchange* 2 (1976): 17–28. Also in D. M. Borchert and D. Stewart, eds., *Being Human in a Technological Age* (Athens: Ohio University Press, 1979), 107–25.

———. "Imagination in Discourse and in Action." In *The Human Being in Action*, edited by A.-T. Tyminenica, 3–22. Dordrecht: D. Reidel, 1978.

———. *The Just.* Translated by David Pellauer. Chicago: University of Chicago Press, 2000.

————. *Lectures on Ideology and Utopia.* Edited by George Taylor. New York: Columbia University Press, 1986.

————. *Memory, History, Forgetting.* Translated by Kathleen Blamey and David Pellauer. Chicago: University of Chicago Press, 2004.

————. "Multiple étrangeté." In *Fremdheit und Vertrauheit: Hermeneutik im europäischen Kontext,* edited by R. Enshat, 11–13. Louvain: Peters, 2000.

————. *Oneself as Another.* Translated by Kathleen Blamey. Chicago: University of Chicago Press, 1992.

————. *Time and Narrative.* Translated by Kathleen Blamey and David Pellauer. 3 vols. Chicago: University of Chicago Press, 1984–88.

Scheler, Max. *Formalism in Ethics and Non-formal Ethics of Values: A New Attempt toward the Foundation of an Ethical Personalism.* Translated by Manfred S. Frings and Roger L. Funk. Evanston, IL: Northwestern University Press, 1973.

Steiner, George. *After Babel: Aspects of Language and Translation.* 3d ed. New York: Oxford University Press, 1998.

Taylor, Charles. *Sources of the Self: The Making of the Modern Identity.* Cambridge, MA: Harvard University Press, 1994.

Walzer, Michael. *The Revolution of the Saints: A Study in the Origins of Radical Politics.* Cambridge, MA: Harvard University Press, 1965.

————. *Spheres of Justice.* New York: Basic Books, 1983.

Weber, Max. *Economy and Society: An Outline of Interpretive Sociology.* Edited by Günther Roth and Claus Wittich. Berkeley and Los Angeles: University of California Press, 1978.

————. *Essais sur la théorie de la science.* Edited by Julien Freund. Paris: Presses pocket, 1965.

————. *The Vocation Lectures.* Translated by Rodney Livingstone. Indianapolis: Hackett, 2004.

————. *Wirtschaft und Gesellschaft: Grundriss der verstehenden Soziologie.* 5th ed. Rev. and arranged by Johannes Winckelmann. 2 vols. Tübingen: J. C. B. Mohr, 1976.

Weil, Eric. *Logique de la philosophie.* Paris: Vrin, 1950.

————. *Philosophie politique.* Paris: Vrin, 1956.

INDEX

action, 13, 65, 67, 77, 82, 86, 111,
134, 150, 155, 170, 173, 196, 203,
233; moral, 86; social, 135, 149;
tragic dimension of, 41
Aeschylus, 233
agape, 171, 175, 177
Alexy, Robert, 37, 88, 246
alterity, 80–81; moral, 84
Althusser, Louis, 143
Apel, Karl-Otto, 6, 7, 10, 37, 40,
85, 129, 130, 131, 132, 232, 239
approbation, 83, 166, 170, 196
Arendt, Hannah, 21, 25, 74, 77,
85, 94–95, 97, 98–99, 103, 111,
138, 155, 164, 234
Aristotle, 2, 3, 4, 5, 8, 18, 46, 49,
50, 51, 52, 53–54, 58n1, 60, 63,
68, 69, 74, 96, 98, 126, 168,
209, 224, 233, 234, 243, 247
Aron, Raymond, 35, 152
Askani, Hans-Christoph, 115
attestation, 11, 18, 66, 75, 79, 81;
truth of, 69
Augustine, 175, 179, 209
authority, 18, 19–22, 36, 84–88,
91–105, 143–44, 146, 157, 158,
162–63, 164, 165, 167, 172,
176, 250, 254; discursive, 101;
enunciative, 94–97, 101, 137;
institutional, 94, 96, 97, 100;

political, 20, 97–98, 250; pragmatic, 104; and tradition, 99
autonomy, 2, 5, 10, 16–17, 32, 40,
48, 62, 64–66, 72–74, 80, 103,
124, 180, 209, 237; capacity for,
192; paradox of, 19; project of,
73–74

Bacon, Francis, 110, 179, 210
Beauchamp, Paul, 111
Benjamin, Walter, 31, 110, 111, 113,
114, 150, 155, 182
Benveniste, Émile, 117
Berman, Antoine, 26, 28, 106, 113
biolaw, 206
Boltanski, Luc, 5, 23, 147
Bourdieu, Pierre, 81, 145
Bouretz, Pierre, 133, 149
Bossuet, Jacques Bénigne, 101
Breton, Stanislas, 10, 58

Canguilhem, Georges, 32,
186–90
capable human being, 2, 39, 47,
65, 74, 77, 82
casuistry, 209
categorical imperative, 6, 7, 47,
52–53, 62, 67–68, 88, 124–28,
203, 237–38, 242; juridical,
127, 130